**Achievement
and
Women**

Achievement and Women: Challenging the Assumptions

Debra R. Kaufman
Barbara L. Richardson

THE FREE PRESS
A Division of Macmillan Publishing Co., Inc.
NEW YORK

Collier Macmillan Publishers
LONDON

The Free Press
A Division of Macmillan Publishing Co., Inc.
866 Third Avenue, New York, N. Y. 10022

Collier Macmillan Canada, Inc.

Library of Congress Catalog Card Number: 81-68324

Printed in the United States of America

printing number
1 2 3 4 5 6 7 8 9 10

Library of Congress Cataloging in Publication Data

Kaufman, Debra R.
 Achievement and women.

 Includes bibliographical references and index.
 1. Women--United States--Social conditions.
2. Success. I. Richardson, Barbara L. II. Title.
HQ1426.K38   305.4'2   81-68324
ISBN 0-02-916780-9   AACR2

For each generation who achieves in its own way

for children
Alana and Marc Kaufman,

for sisters
Sondra Grunberger, Genie Kraig,
Ginny Richardson, Janice Richardson

for mothers
Ida Horwitz, Pauline Kaufman,
Marjorie Richardson, Grandma Myrtle Smith

Contents

Preface *ix*

Acknowledgments *xv*

1. In the Beginning: Achievement Motivation *1*

2. Adolescence and the High Achiever *30*

3. Adult Roles: Links between the Private Script and Public Achievements *60*

4. Adult Roles: The Public Script *84*

5. The Mature Woman: Calculating Her Worth *111*

6. Achievement, Moral Commitment and Life Choices *136*

References *145*

Index *179*

Preface

Despite the recent outpouring of popular and academic works explaining women and their achievements, or perhaps because of this literature, we may now be in a situation similar to that of Gertrude Stein on her deathbed—finally feeling we know the answer but having forgotten the question. In this book we turn to the academic, political, and historic contexts within which theoretical questions about women and their achievements (what motivates them, their goals, what influences their performance, and their feelings about achievement) have been formulated over the past few decades. Only in this way can we understand and appreciate the answers that have been offered.

Some decades ago M. Carey Thomas, the first president of Bryn Mawr College, wrote an essay entitled "Our Failures Only Marry." Thomas struck the essential dilemma facing women in our society: they are not men. Nevertheless, Thomas's belief in individual assertion and social class superiority mitigated her analysis of woman's predicament, echoing long-standing academic, if not popular, assumptions about achievement. For she expected Bryn Mawr women because of their innate superiority and class privilege to transcend the political, social, and economic barriers they faced as members of a subordinate sex (Schneider, 1974).

For generations of writers on achievement, personal attributes, not gender, have been paramount. Today it is commonly agreed that "women are able to successfully compete in the masculine occupational world to the extent that they can bring 'masculine' personality qualities to the role" (Bardwick, 1971:163). However, to stress individual will or "masculine personality qualities" misses the important interplay between socially created gender roles and individual behavior.[1] A fundamental premise of this book is that women are forced to relate to the educational and occupational world (the arenas of public achievement) first as members of a subordinate sex and only secondarily as individuals. Some have even used the word "class" to describe woman's position in society. The nineteenth-century suffragist Elizabeth Cady Stanton attributed the decline in young girls' "aim" and "ambition" to their awakening ". . . to the fact that they belong to a subject, degraded, ostracized class; that to fulfill their man-appointed sphere they can have no individual character, no life purpose, personal freedom, aim or ambition. They are simply to revolve around some man" (Papachristou, 1976:112). Twentieth-century "revelations" that as girls age their occupational aspirations decline resonate with the same truth Stanton proclaimed roughly a century ago.

The stress on individual ambition and personal attributes has historic roots that cannot be neglected if we are to understand female achievement. Our twentieth-century focus on the individual can be linked in some measure to the nineteenth-century split between the public and private spheres of life (Zaretsky, 1973). In America prior to the nineteenth century nearly "all community functions—production, socialization, civil government, religious life—presumed the family as the basic unit of social organization. The whole range of social roles drew on familial roles" (DuBois, 1975:64). But by the nineteenth century a "new creature," the individual, had come to rival the family in importance: "In the nineteenth century, we can distinguish two forms of social organization—one based on this new creature, the individual, the other based on the family. These overlapping but distinct structures became identified respectively as the public sphere and the private sphere" (DuBois, 1975:64). But whereas the emergence of social roles not based on family affected both men and women, women remained confined and defined primarily by their familial roles in the private sphere. Indeed, the suffragists believed that because the vote rested on individual citizenship it would represent a new kind of power and social connectedness for women. In this book we emphasize how the interplay between public and private roles operates differently for men and women. Variations in the public and private spheres of life, and the changing relationships between them, create unique structural conditions and consequently place different limitations and demands upon individuals. Thus, historic and individual timing affects the achievement process.

The impact on women's achievements of this unequal system operating in both the public and the private sphere has long been part of feminist consciousness. Stanton, and Mary Wollstonecraft before her, clearly linked the negative attributes ascribed to her sex to problems facing women in the public arenas of work and education (their achieved roles) and to feelings of lowered self-esteem. Such leaders as Charlotte Perkins Gilman, Catherine Beecher, and Women's Christian Temperance Union reformers were able to associate their private grievances with larger public issues.

Attempts of domestic reformers (see especially chapter 3) either to reintegrate the female into the public sphere or to "upgrade" the private arena have emphasized women's unique power disadvantage. The early reformers understood that as members of a subordinate sex women relate to the public sphere (the educational and occupational worlds of achievement) differently from men, but not necessarily with less ability or talent. However, the realities of women's lives generally have not been reflected in twentieth-century academic theories and measures of achievement. Most contemporary social science models—the set of concepts that help the social scientist select problems, organize information, and pursue inquiries—are based on the lives that men lead. Only recently has the female experience become part of the academic consciousness. Fortunately this awakening has spurred critiques that go well beyond gender-role issues (Duberman, 1975; Hartman & Banner, 1974; Hochschild, 1973a; Kaplan & Bean, 1976; Mednick, Tangri & Hoffman, 1975; Parlee, 1975; Unger & Denmark, 1975). One such issue is the long-term impact of early socialization.

The first generation of scholars interested in female achievement inherited theories stressing achievement needs, motives, aspirations, and expectations rooted in social and gender-role learning during the early years (McClelland, Rindlisbacher, deCharms, 1955; McClelland, Baldwin, Bronfenbrenner & Strodtbeck, 1958; McClelland & Winter, 1969). The key ingredients for adult success, according to these theories, were found in early childrearing experiences (McClelland & Friedman, 1952; McClelland, Atkinson, Clark & Lowell, 1953). Furthermore, the presence or absence of these key ingredients within an adult population was often described as a permanent, or irremediable, feature of an entire generation (McClelland, 1955; 1958(a); 1958(b); 1961). McClelland, a man often called the father of achievement motivation, exemplified this perspective when he commented on the effectiveness of Third World management training programs:

> Perhaps the difficulty with all these studies is that the educational influences which might produce higher n-Achievement . . . need-achievement or motivation occur too late in life after character has already been formed.[2] Both psychological theory and research . . . strongly suggest that the crucial period for acquiring n-Achievement probably lies somewhere between the ages of 5 and 10. Perhaps exposure to high standards of excellence and the like will have a lasting effect on n-Achievement only if it occurs early in life. (1961:415)

The theory guiding achievement research stressed that motivation was acquired early in life and, more important, was carried within the individual in some stable and predictable fashion over the life course. Thus, the continual and dynamic interplay between changing external reality and internal motive, itself often fluctuating, was neglected.

According to McClelland even so major an event as war scarcely disturbs the high achiever:

> After all, from the theoretical viewpoint . . . external events, whether for good or for ill, are turned to one account or another depending on the motives of the people involved. In a sense history is *what happened*, not what *might* have happened if there hadn't been a war, depression, or an invasion. If we take the hypothesis in its strongest sense, it says that people with high n-Achievement will tend to focus on economic matters to the exclusion of other interests like fighting wars, so that in the end they will be better off economically. This is exactly what our data show and a strong case can be made for not giving extra credit to those countries which spent their time and resources doing other things. (1961:96)

The individual's place in history or in the social structure remains external, for in this model social location can be "turned to one account or another depending on the motives of the people involved." The pure case of a high achiever is none other than the lonely, heroic entrepreneur. Against such a theoretical backdrop the questions asked about females' achievements were answered by describing young girls as sadly lacking in achievement motivation (given their early gender-role socialization) and therefore not sufficiently developed for adult accomplishments.

While we agree that the process of weighing and evaluating adult roles begins in early childhood, we do not see such a process as developmentally possible at only one stage of life. Personal investments in and commitments to life scripts and schedules are made by actors who are rational and sentient—capable of negotiating and renegotiating their roles over the life course. The achievement process is related to all the rules of social change, especially those concerning power differentials. In examining female achievement and the achievement process, we must always keep in mind that culture influences our values; history, our reference points; and social structure, our options and boundaries.

We have organized our analysis of achievement so that each chapter moves us not only over the life course but outward in analysis as well, from the intrapsychic process of acquiring and maintaining the motive to achieve (chapter 1) to the sociohistorical forces conditioning and defining achievement (in subsequent chapters). In each chapter we show how achievement derives its meaning as much from academic models of achievement as from real life. One of the book's purposes is to make explicit the intellectual landscape wherein the definition of achievement has been created. Therefore, we pay close attention to the early work on gender roles and to the impact female oriented questions have had (or not had) on academic theories and measures of achievement. Specifically, we examine how academic models of achievement have contributed to the popular interpretation of women's capabilities and how in general social science models of human behavior have focused on rather narrow and male-specific criteria regarding the relationship of ability, ambition, personality, achievement, and worldly success. Because historic time and individual timing have been largely ignored in the theories and measures connected with such models, we recognize through our interdisciplinary analysis an individual continually acting and reacting to varying social contexts, both public and private, over the life course.

In chapter 2 we evaluate the socialization literature that emphasizes the primacy of the early years and present our understanding of the content of early gender learning and its relationship to achievement. In this chapter we note that the first wave of research on female achievement, while making important methodological refinements, proved inadequate because it failed to break with models of achievement that focused on internal forces and the individual. Two areas of research in particular, the motive to avoid success and attribution research, neatly illustrate the need for new models.

Chapter 3 reviews the economic impact of industrialization, the split between the public and private arenas of life, and what this development has meant in assessing the value of women's achievements in the twentieth century (Zaretsky, 1973). In a sketch of women's entrances and exits into the educational and labor markets we note how women's achievements have always been circumscribed by cultural understandings of female ascriptive roles (wife, mother, daughter) and by economic forces.

In chapter 4 we focus on the occupational sphere, showing how an individual's motive to achieve is often a by-product of her/his location in the labor market. We end this chapter with an analysis of professional women.

Chapter 5 brings together the psychological and sociological perspectives as we analyze women in their later years. Achievement, like development—emotional or intellectual—is a lifelong process. Since the public and private arenas of women's lives are never divorced, we end by noting that women are presently renegotiating their worth in both spheres.

By organizing this book around four main life stages (childhood, adolescence, young adulthood, and maturity) we trace the meaning and measurement of achievement not only over the individual life course but also in both the private and the public realm. In keeping with a sense of time and timing, we do not begin with any one social science definition of achievement. The meaning of achievement is relative to the state of knowledge and the predominant models in the field at a particular point in time. Accordingly, in each chapter we present a historical sketch of the achievement literature so that the intellectual landscape wherein we work may be better understood. We pay special tribute to the first generation of scholars investigating gender role and its impact on female achievement, for their intellectual legacy prompted us to write this book.

Notes

1. Throughout this book we use the term "gender role" instead of "sex role," basing the decision on the following distinction:

   Classification by "sex" refers to the dichotomous distinction between male and female based on physiological characteristics; classification by "gender" refers to the psychological and cultural definitions of the dimensions "masculine" and "feminine," and only tends to a strictly dichotomous distinction between groups. When speaking of learned roles, the proper term is "gender role." . . . Despite the wealth of literature, assuming that "sex" and "gender" are interchangeable, the primatologists persist in using the term "sex role" correctly to describe positions in intercourse. Thus there is every reason to regard most sociological uses of male-female differences as involving gender role. (Tresemer, 1975:308–309)

2. The terms "n-ach" and "achievement motivation" are often used interchangeably, referring sometimes to measurement, sometimes to observed behavior, and sometimes to inferred aspects of behavior. Since the early 1950s McClelland, Atkinson, and their colleagues have been key figures in achievement motivation research and theory (as the bibliography amply indicates). Tresemer has summarized the complicated interplay between and among variables in Atkinson's tradition of research and theory. He wrote: ". . . motivation or a tendency to act toward a certain goal is based on a multiplicative relationship between Motive (latent, stable predisposition to action learned early in life), Expectation (cognitive judgement of the probability of succeeding at the task), and Incentive . . . , the 'discrepancy between what is and what should be' . . . is assumed to vary inversely in relation to Expectation . . . Furthermore, Incentives combine with Motives to give the Value of the goal. . . ; hence the name 'Expectancy X Value' theory of motivation. With all the variables known, one could determine the tendency to act in a certain way. . . " (1977:28) Both McClelland and Atkinson frequently use the term "need-achievement" (n-ach) when referring to the operational definition and measurement of a relatively stable, socially acquired trait or motivational disposition (achievement motivation) (Korman, 1974).

Acknowledgments

We cannot hope to acknowledge all the women and men who commented, lamented, criticized, praised, read and reread different drafts of this book. Their influence is imprinted on every page. The support we received from the Sociology/Anthropology department at Northeastern University is gratefully acknowledged. The long and sometimes difficult process of producing a book was eased by the constant assurance of three departmental chairs, Patricia Golden, Ron McAllister, and Carol Owen that the unexpected is the most expected aspect of writing a book. The typing assistance we received from Dennis Chin should not go unacknowledged. Dennis often typed the manuscript, on his own time, even after he thought the book had been published. Augusto Diana was a model of patience and thoroughness as he tirelessly helped with bibliographic references. One other person deserves acknowledgment for his tireless effort, careful thinking, gentle criticism, constant support and good humor. Thank you, Michael Kaufman.

This book developed in a climate in which women's rights were in a continuing struggle both in the academic community and beyond. Groups like "The Friends of the Cornell Eleven," organizing in defense of the rights of academic feminists and feminist scholarship, have provided ongoing moral and political support throughout the duration of our labors.

CHAPTER 1

In the Beginning: Achievement Motivation

Despite the outpouring of research on achievement-related behavior since McClelland, Atkinson, Clark and Lowell's landmark publication, "The Achievement Motive" (1953) Horner noted that "the data related to achievement motivation[1] in women have been very scarce" (1978:41). She wryly observed that "female achievement motivation occupies less than a page, in fact only a footnote, in Atkinson's . . . more than 800-page compilation of available theory, data, and method concerning achievement motivation" (1978:41-42). Although McClelland and his colleagues were puzzled by sex differences in the early achievement studies (1953), Horner pointed out that in "The Achieving Society" (McClelland, 1961), women were still neglected. In fact she observed that "every other possible source of evidence for the motive, e.g., Indians, Quakers, Ancient Greeks, vases, flags, doodles, children's books . . ." (1978:42) were investigated.

Because they did not conform to the accepted pattern of achievement arousal, women in achievement motivation experiments were commonly described as anomolies. Frequently, the motive to achieve is assessed by a score taken from imagery in a Thematic Apperception-type projective test. A subject's response to ambiguous pictures is scored to assess the frequency and kind of achievement imagery present. From the very first studies of achievement motivation, sex differences were noted (Field, 1951; Veroff,

1

Wilcox and Atkinson, 1953; McClelland, Atkinson, Clark and Lowell, 1953; Veroff, 1958). Females seemed less affected by cues that reliably aroused achievement imagery in male subjects. High school girls and college women, for instance, did not increase their achievement imagery as did males when exposed to arousal cues stressing intelligence and leadership ability. Yet "under neutral conditions," Horner observed, "the scores of the high-school-aged girls and college women were as high as and sometimes higher than those of young men under arousal conditions" (1978:42).

Although such early results should have questioned the validity of achievement motivation measures, researchers either ignored, or, at best, puzzled over female achievement motivation findings, while they continued to investigate the determinants of achievement-related behavior based on the interpretation of findings from only one sex. It wasn't until the development of a generation of researchers expressly interested in women's achievement patterns that the androcentric biases of achievement behavior were seriously questioned. The questions soon extended beyond biases, striking even more fundamental issues within achievement research and theory. Did early studies reflect a "stable," "enduring," "situation-free," and "general" personal motive, or did the data simply corroborate stereotypical notions both sexes shared about masculinity and femininity? Did these tests merely reveal deeper truths about who was allowed to achieve in our society?

The First Generation's Legacy

The first question posed by those interested in female achievement centered on the issue of cues. While some interpreted "lack of arousal" by achievement-oriented cues as evidence of generally low need-achievement among females, others were not content with these assessments, and focused back upon the experimental cues themselves. Since theoretically there was no simple equation between the motive and a specific experimental condition, Field (1951) and Veroff and colleagues (1953) experimented with a broader range of cues. Field, for instance, tested arousal cues centered around social acceptability. This manipulation did not increase male achievement scores from an initially very low level, but did raise females' achievement imagery. Without a gender-role theory, however, it was difficult to explain the link between cues and behavior.[2]

Now, some three decades after the original research began, we can reexamine these studies with new knowledge based on gender-role theory. For instance, the authors of an excellent compendium on sex differences, have admirably summarized the once problematic interpretation of cues and women's responses. Maccoby and Jacklin perceptively suggested that when girls respond with fewer achievement related themes to pictures showing females than to pictures showing males, their responses may reflect not their own low achievement motivation but their assessments that girls and women as a social group are not generally achievers in our society (1974). Such scores, the authors noted, may parallel stereotypical concepts culturally shared with men: "It would be unwise . . . to equate the projective measure with the subject's own real life achievement motivation. Subjects may differ in how thoroughly they project themselves into the storied characters; furthermore, the stimulus-pictures must necessarily constitute a very limited representation of real-life situations" (p. 150).

Maccoby and Jacklin came to their conclusions with at least a decade of research on gender roles behind them. A major contribution of the early work on gender was the recognition that children, as well as adults, are highly sensitive to cultural stereotypes and values attached to masculinity and femininity. Even before the age of three children are capable of expressing their preferences regarding gender related roles and activities. Interestingly, although a majority of children state a preference for their own sex, girls are more likely to express a desire to be boys than vice versa (Goslin, 1971; Kagan, 1964; Maccoby, 1966). Also, while children of both sexes prefer interacting with same-sex peers, girls are more likely to report relationships with boys than boys with girls (Kohlberg & Zigler, 1967).

When children's preferences are assessed, little girls prefer their feminine roles much less strongly than boys prefer their masculine roles (Hartup & Zook, 1960; Kohlberg & Zigler, 1967; Rabban, 1950). A variety of methodological factors have been suggested to account for these findings, but the evidence overwhelmingly suggests that children are displaying a knowledge of which set of gender roles—and consequently which sex—is more valued and therefore destined to achieve in this society. In short, stereotypes and perceptions of power, competence, prestige, strength, and size are attached to children's earliest understandings of their gender roles (Mischel, 1971; Parsons & Bales, 1955). The evidence suggests that from middle childhood, both males and females can predict and evaluate the achievement roles ascribed to adult men and women.[3] In our review of models of identification and socialization, we will again stress the critical importance of perceptions of power in children's development, particularly females' acquisition of an achievement motive and of personal attributions and expectations for success and failure in the achievement arena.

With gender-role theory it is easy to explain females' responses to the achievement cues in the early studies. The arousal cues were sex biased. Why should we expect being a leader or an effective organizer to arouse females' achievement motives since the cues refer to achievements commonly linked to males? In fact, female subjects in a variety of experimental situations had *higher* achievement related responses than did males. (Frieze, Johnson, Parsons, Ruble & Zellman, 1978, Maccoby & Jacklin, 1974; Mednick, Tangri & Hoffman, 1975; Tresemer, 1977; Unger & Denmark, 1975).

Maccoby and Jacklin concluded after reviewing the early work on achievement motivation that females show a high level of achievement imagery whether exposed to "arousal" conditions or not; men show a high level of achievement *only* when aroused by reference to their intelligence and leadership ability (1974).

During the 1950s boys typically were asked to write stories about pictures of males. However, when Veroff and colleagues studied both females' and males' responses to pictures of the opposite, as well as the same sex, some complications arose (1953). When viewing pictures of males, *both* male and female subjects had higher achievement scores than they did when viewing pictures of females. This finding was replicated in later work (Lesser, Kravitz & Packard, 1963; Veroff, Wilcox & Atkinson, 1953). Given the low and similar responses from *both* sexes toward female figures, one might have anticipated that the researchers would have preferred female, not male, figures for the cue cards. We suggest that this possibility apparently was not seriously considered because without the theoretical backdrop of a gender-role analysis sex differences were not anticipated.

In the early studies experimenters labeled tasks feminine or masculine or sex-appropriate or sex-inappropriate not on the basis of children's responses or empirical pretests but rather on the basis of labels borrowed from a theoretical understanding (usually psychoanalytic) of gender-appropriate behavior (Hoffman & Hoffman, 1964). This labeling problem has stayed with us. As late as 1976 Constantinople called masculinity and femininity the "muddiest concepts in the psychologist's vocabulary" (p. 29):

> *   A search for definitions related to some theoretical position leads almost nowhere except to Freud [and] Jung. . . . The most generalized definitions of terms used by those developing tests of M-F would seem to be that they are relatively enduring traits which are more or less rooted in anatomy, physiology, and early experience, and which generally serve to distinguish males from females in appearance, attitudes, and behavior. (P. 29)

Achievement data collected through the 1960s were commonly interpreted within the psychoanalytic framework Constantinople described. Researchers constructing measures of subjects' masculinity or femininity were vulnerable to such a priori assumptions about gender based traits. Their measures often accentuated the differences rather than the similarities between the sexes. For instance, in the achievement literature even similar behaviors by both sexes were labeled and consequently interpreted differently: masculine behaviors associated with competitive striving were associated with healthy responses in the male but often were seen as pathological or neurotic in the female. (In chapter 2 we see that preoccupation with self among adolescent males is often interpreted as generally leading to autonomous achievement striving but as potentially leading to narcissism among females.)

Latent in much of the early literature on female achievement was an even more subtle yet equally misleading set of assumptions about the sexes. The theoretical assertions within this model suggested that males and females actually respond—emotionally, cognitively, and behaviorally—to the same stimulus in a different fashion. Such assumptions were predicated on the belief that there is a distinctly asymmetrical or qualitatively different process of personality development in males and females.

Embracing the asymmetrical view of gender development, theorists anticipated greater problems for females than males in the establishment of a strong motive to achieve. The source of conflict was rooted in the presumed clash between affiliative and achievement based needs. This explanation for women's achievement behavior is part of what we call the *asymmetry* tradition. In this tradition the female, throughout the life course, is constantly faced with a potential conflict between achievement and affiliation; the masculine personality is less vulnerable to tensions generated by affiliative motives. This conceptualization laid the groundwork for contemporary explanations for female underachievement—particularly those associated with the "fear of success." By way of illustration we turn next to an issue that stood out in the expectancy-value tradition of achievement motivation —need affiliation (Atkinson, Heyns & Veroff, 1954; Bardwick, 1971; Hoffman, 1972, 1975; Shipley & Veroff, 1952).[4]

The Asymmetry Tradition: Affiliation versus Achievement

Bardwick summarized much of the work in the mid-1960s as following the asymmetry tradition (1971). Despite early findings, that children in the first to third grades showed *no* sex differences in achievement, competition, or play activities—in fact, girls valued intellectual accomplishment over other areas more than did boys (Crandall, Katovsky & Preston, 1960)— girls' motives were suspect. The early work by Crandall and Rabson (1960),[5] Sears (1962), and Tyler, Rafferty, and Tyler (1962) popularized the supposition that young girls use achievement behaviors as a primary means of securing love and approval. The Sears study reported that for females affiliation needs rather than achievement needs correlate with academic success (1962). Tyler and colleagues reported that girls in nursery school who tried to get recognition for achievement also made more attempts to get love and affection (1962).

Stein and Bailey summarized Crandall's (1963) more complicated explanation:

> Achievement behavior for *both* boys and girls is initially directed toward obtaining social approval. With development . . . boys *internalize* standards of

excellence and come to rely on their own satisfaction in meeting these standards rather than on reinforcement from others. Girls' achievement efforts
were thought to remain more dependent on *external* social rewards. (1976:243)

Implicit in such an argument were notions of appropriate gender identification. At issue for Crandall were two propositions: there are age developmental changes beginning with striving for extrinsic and then moving
toward intrinsic rewards; and instrumental activity is more often under-
taken for affiliative reasons by females than by males.

During this period, Veroff suggested that a child of four or five is not
yet able clearly to distinguish which behaviors lead to praise and affection
and why (1969). Thus, many general types of behavior might be seen as
leading to rewards. The need to achieve as conceived by Veroff is a general
tendency for highly motivated persons to extend their effort in many areas.
In young children, the motive to achieve results from a combination of
social responses from parents and the children's own awareness of their
growing capabilities. However, Veroff then hypothesized that while interpersonal rewards remain salient for girls, internalized efforts, criteria of
achievement, and personal satisfaction become more important for boys.
The reasons for this divergence are perhaps best explained by theories of
identification, explored later in this chapter. Here it is important to remember that boys' motives appeared more independent or autonomous than
girls'.

Veroff's early analysis provides a fine example of asymmetry by suggesting not only that the two sexes differ in *styles* of learning but also that
boys' motives are more independent than girls' (1969). The sequence proposed by Veroff, in contrast to Crandall, begins with a stage in which the
child learns to evaluate his/her own performance against internalized standards. Then some time after entering school, children are expected to set
standards in relation to the performance of peers. In addition to altering the
sources of a child's standards, this second stage also implies a change in the
nature of the rewards, from internal to external. To explain gender differences Veroff used the distinction between an autonomous motive associated
with internalized rewards and a socially dependent (interpersonally oriented) motive associated with extrinsic rewards: if girls are motivated more
by affiliative than by achievement needs, they will depend more on extrinsic
or social rewards. As was so often the case in the early work on female
achievement motivation, the theory was more complex than the data war-
ranted. For instance, contrary to his theoretical expectations, Veroff found
in reviewing his data that children did not differ by sex on any of the social-
dependency scores (1969). He has since explored achievement in other populations (Veroff & Feld, 1970; Veroff & Veroff, 1971; Veroff, McClelland,
Ruhland, 1975).

Building on this work of the late 1960s, Hoffman began a critical article on female achievement research with the assertion that the failure of women to fulfill their intellectual potential had been adequately documented. She saw the roots of adult women's underachievement in early developmental patterns and she located the source of the problem clearly within the asymmetry tradition:

> Even at preschool age girls have different orientations toward intellectual tasks than boys. Little girls want to please; they work for love and approval; if bright, they underestimate their competence. Little boys show more task involvement, more confidence, and are more likely to show I.Q. increments. . . .
>
> Boys and girls enter the world with different constitutional make-ups and recent studies show that parents treat boys and girls differently, even from birth. Social roles are first—and most impressively—communicated through parent–child relations and events in early childhood may have an impact that later cannot be duplicated in effectiveness. (1975:130)[6]

According to this model, then, adult female achievement evolves from early childhood needs for love rather than for mastery. Therefore, poorer achievement on the part of women can be attributed to the establishment of an incorrect or inappropriate motive.

Interestingly, achievement was seen in very specific terms. Hoffman was clearly *not* referring to early academic performance, for the data showed that girls on the average received better grades than boys throughout elementary and high school (Clark, 1959; Coleman, 1960; Maccoby, 1966; Northby, 1958). In fact, the Northby study reported twice as many boys in the bottom 10 percent of their class and twice as many girls in the top 10 percent. Studies going back as far as 1929 have shown better grades for females from elementary school through early college (Terman & Tyler, 1954; Tyler, 1965). Maccoby and Jacklin concluded that girls' "better grades must reflect some combination of greater effort, greater interest, and better work habits. Evidently, their school-related motivations are not what is meant when assertions are made about girls' lower achievement motivation" (1974:135).

Hoffman, however, expected good academic performance from girls "since it is often compatible with affiliative motives" (1975:135). Ironically, then, at the childhood stage the only real achievement problem for a female might be posed this way: is she doing well for the wrong reasons?

Challenges to Need Achievement

Throughout the 1960s technical experimental concerns were raised to explain sex differences in achievement motivation. Such concerns included sex of experimenter and sex bias in the achievement goal. Considerable empirical attention was given to variations in the experimental situation, yet few challenges were made of the assumptions underlying the model—not, at least, until researchers familiar with the newly burgeoning literature on gender-role development entered the debate. No longer were females referred to as a puzzle. Instead, they were described as having a sex-typed hierarchy of motives; a sensitivity to social cues; a differing set of goals and skills; or an incorrect, underdeveloped, inappropriate, or socially conforming set of needs. However, despite these gender adjustments, other suppositions lingered, for instance, the invidious distinction between intrinsic and extrinsic standards.

Only an intrinsic motive based on internalized standards of excellence (i.e., stressing mastery rather than love or praise) could motivate one to life-long achievement. Once internalized, such a motive was relatively situation-free. The correct time for the establishment of such a motive was still childhood. We document the arguments that reinforced affiliative needs for females and achievement needs for males later in this chapter and in chapter 2 when we review theories of identification and socialization. Next, however, we turn to issues equally damaging to the need-achievement model, which, if not directly spurred by the gender debate, paralleled it.

Three debates are of particular interest to us. Since need-achievement theory relied heavily on the assumption that what had been measured in the empirical work was indeed intrinsic, debates about measures of extrinsic and intrinsic motivation created controversy. Another issue that plagued the theory was its predictive value. Virtually none of the projective measures of achievement motivation correlated with commonsense understandings of achievement behavior. And, finally, suppositions about harmful personality traits—harmful, that is, to achievement striving—presumably formed and irrevocably situated in childhood did not stand up to testing.

Intrinsic versus Extrinsic Motivation

Although theoretical distinctions between intrinsic and extrinsic motivation seemed relatively straightforward, various authors warned that two measures were not (at least operationally) mutually exclusive (Smith, 1968). In an essay on the origins of competence motivation, Smith recognized that the intrinsic rewards of a child's self-initiated activities are often parallel to or fused with gratifications from social acceptance or social approval. He also noted that the source of gratification may change over time. Emphasizing distinctions first stressed by Allport in 1961, Smith observed:

> Something that is not initially rewarding for its own sake becomes intrinsically rewarding as one achieves skill . . . conversely, something that is rewarding

may cease to be so once mastered, especially if it is not highly valued by others. (P. 305).

His critique shattered some of the basic assumptions of the achievement model. One of his most damaging arguments was that the motive being measured in the need-achievement theory had more to do with "competitive striving in a context of social comparison" than with "intrinsic effort towards excellence" (p. 308). Smith, in short, was questioning McClelland's frequent assertion that the motive to achieve existed in a pure state within the personality of the individual, uncontaminated by invidious social comparisons. He questioned the validity of the measurements of achievement in the expectancy-value model:

> There are questions about its generality, its applicability to women, its openness to influences that contaminate its values as a measure of motivation. The findings in regard to its relationships to achievement oriented behavior have been ambiguous, except as a predictor of entrepreneurial strivings in businessmen. Given this less than encouraging record, one suspects that there has been *slippage between the theoretical definition of the motive and what has actually been captured in the measurement.*

> The technique of arousal that was employed in developing the scoring system did not directly arouse "standards of excellence." Rather, subjects were led to be concerned about their competitive standing in a quality that was important to them: intelligence. Perhaps after all the motive thus imperfectly tapped has more to do *with competitive striving in a context of social comparison than with intrinsic effort towards excellence.* (P. 308; emphasis added)

By the mid-1960s, Atkinson and Feather entertained the possibility that the theory of achievement motivation might need considerable refinement: "Under some conditions in thematic apperception N-ach scores may reflect extrinsic motivation instead of, or in addition to, achievement motivation. The possibility is sufficiently important to make this one of the most significant problems for future study" (1966:350). In his introduction to a 1978 book containing a revised model of achievement, Atkinson again expressed the hope that future research would sharpen and extend our conceptual analysis to embrace those other motivational factors that now are merely lumped in the category "extrinsic motivation" (Atkinson & Raynor, 1978:38). He also noted that extrinsic motivation, particularly social approval, "has already gained the special status of the most neglected variable in research on achievement oriented activity" (p. 38).

Several decades after the theory was formulated, scholars are still plagued by questions about internal and external motives and intrinsic and extrinsic rewards. Even the strongest proponents of the original theory of need achievement find it difficult to differentiate between internal and external motives, social and autonomous rewards, and ultimately, as we see in later chapters, social-role behavior and personality.

The Predictive Value of the Model

As Murstein pointed out in 1963, the need-achievement model is not a powerful one. How well does this theory predict achievement effort and academic or intellectual performance? There appears to be a great gap between the experimental world of the laboratory and real life. Studies attempting to establish a link between the *need* for achievement and behavioral and social indicators of achievement have not been very impressive (Korman, 1974; Weinstein, 1969). And, while the projective measures of achievement motivation have not been correlated with achievement effort or with academic or intellectual performance for females (Entwisle, 1972), such correlations have likewise been poor for males.

Ironically, the distinctions that have served to separate the sexes in the classical expectancy-value model have done so in the direction of underestimating the female's potential and capacity for expressing achievement behavior. Theoretical fears about girls' lower achievement motivation usually are not based on empirical indicators (Stein & Bailey, 1976). As we pointed out earlier, girls value intellectual accomplishment over other areas more than do boys (Crandall, Katovsky & Preston, 1962), they receive better grades than do boys throughout school (Anastasi, 1958; Maccoby, 1966; Terman & Tyler, 1954), and they do not differ from males on social comparison scores (Veroff, 1969). Why, in the face of these data, have researchers continued to question girls' achievement motivation?

The answers seem to rest with the concern for females' "ultimate" adult achievements. Implicit in the need-achievement model are normative timetables for the development of the motive. Psychology characteristically locates the roots of adult motivation in the experiences of early childhood. Thus, fears about poor timing or improper focus at this critical stage generate worries about a qualitatively less complex and/or complete development of the motive. In short, researchers wondered whether females' high need for affiliation would compete or conflict with their progression toward an autonomous stage of development.

Hoffman summed up the possible dangers of predicating achievement behavior on an affiliative rather than an achievement motive, on extrinsic rather than intrinsic sources of reward:

> In elementary schools, excellence is rewarded with love and approval by parents, teachers and peers. Even in the lower socio-economic class, sociometric studies show that academic excellence in girls is rewarded with popularity. . . .
> In college, however, and professional pursuits, love is less frequently the reward for top performance. Driving a point home, winning an argument, beating others in competition, and attending to the task at hand without being sidetracked by concern with rapport, require the subordination of affiliative needs. (1975:135)

The developmental timetables offered by Crandall (1963) and Veroff (1969) suggested that females, given their different gender development (remaining at the external rather than progressing to the internal stage) in the early years, will *not* subordinate their affiliative needs. This approach foreclosed change later in life. Such views underlay models that described females as underdeveloped in their adult abilities and sadly lacking in achievement motivation. But once again, despite the determinism of the model, the data, particularly with regard to feminine personality attributes, have presented some annoying complications.

Dependence: A Lifelong Trait?

The concept of affiliation is commonly linked to a trait or characteristic —sometimes called dependence—thought to be lodged in the female personality, obstructing achievement growth (Hoffman, 1972; Shipley & Veroff, 1952). In the achievement literature the two elements deemed critical to the establishment of adult achievement were "correct motive" and "intellectual ability." Optimal intellectual development and performance, particularly in research of the 1960s, seemed to depend upon the correct personality makeup developed in childhood; passive-dependency in females and impulsiveness in males were the major stumbling blocks to optimal intellectual functioning (Maccoby, 1966). Thus, much of the research on female achievement in this period focused on the "problem" of feminine passive-dependence.

Maccoby, in an influential review, argued that dependency interfered with intellectual functioning for females (1966). Although she was careful to point to other aspects of development that dependency might facilitate— need affiliation and the desire for social approval—she generally described feminine passivity as a problem.[7] The "problem," however, has not turned out to be consistently present. Almost a decade later, reflecting on the role of personality differences and intellectual functioning, Maccoby apologized to her readers:

> The earlier argument began by assuming the existence of certain sex differences in intellectual performance that have not turned out to be consistently present; it then attempted to explain these on the basis of personality differences that have also proved to be more myth than reality. In view of this, the senior author can do little more than beg the reader's indulgence for previous sins. However, the studies on personality correlates of intellectual performance have continued to suggest that intellectual development in girls is fostered by their being assertive and active, and having a sense that they can control, by their own actions, the events that affect their lives. (Maccoby & Jacklin, 1974:133)

Sex differences once thought to be stable and possibly innate were no longer apparent. Maccoby reconsidered her own analysis:

> The 1966 Maccoby paper attempted to explain some portion of the sex differ-
> ences in intellectual performance in terms of sex differences in personality
> structure. . . . These arguments have not stood up well under the impact of new
> evidence appearing in the intervening years. . . . there is now good reason to
> doubt that girls are more "dependent" in almost any sense of the word than
> boys. . . . There is no evidence . . . that the sexes differ on tasks calling for
> serial internal processing; furthermore, girls are not more oriented toward in-
> terpersonal cues. (P. 132)

She also reminded us that "it is still a reliable generalization that the sexes
do not differ consistently in tests of total (or composite) abilities . . . girls do
appear to have a slight advantage on tests given under the age of 7" (p. 65).

By the 1970s the exact composition of sex-linked personality traits had
been modified somewhat by research. Although claims that girls were more
social and more suggestible than boys, have less self-esteem and achievement motivation were dismissed in the 1970s, doubts lingered about females
as achievers in adolescence and adulthood. For instance, Maccoby and
Jacklin suggested that sex differences in fear, timidity, anxiety, and competitiveness among young children remained open to debate because
evidence was insufficient or ambiguous (1974:353).

In summary, then, the classical expectancy-value formulation of
achievement was an academic theory with a narrow conceptual purview, a
highly specific frame of reference, and inadequate empirical support. Most
of the intuitive correlates associated with success and achievement in American culture were only remotely, if at all, related to the formal concept of
need achievement. Intelligence, school grades, achievement tests, even self-
descriptions by subjects were not considered reliable evidence of that highly
regarded motive associated with need achievement (Heckhausen, 1967).

Most of the literature reviewed so far documented the experimental
psychological perspective in early work on the achievement motive. Where
variables beyond personality were introduced, such as the socialization
process, they, too, had poor explanatory power because of their limited
conceptualization. Heavy responsibility for the individual's acquisition of
the achievement motive was placed on the family through the socialization
process. Researchers were particularly concerned with aspects of female socialization thought to undermine achievement motivation in academic and
career pursuits. In the next section we see how close analysis of female
achievement raised theoretical and methodological questions about the socialization process in general, thereby promoting the theoretical development of the field as a whole.

Achievement Orientation

The achievement motivation equation calls for a goal directed young
actor filled with intrinsic motivation, free from sentiments of invidious so-

cial comparison, autonomously controlled, aroused but not overanxious, realistic in aspirations (see note 7), and independent in judgment. While motives and goals are basic, achievement striving in the classical fashion really boils down to a matter of style. Overt displays of fear, social timidity, gross competition, or undue displays of appreciation for audience response are definitely bad form.

The 1970s represented a fertile period for scholars interested in analyzing and understanding the aspects of female socialization that were thought to jeopardize achievement motivation in academic and career pursuits (Bardwick, 1974; Barnett, 1975; Hoffman, 1974(a), 1975, 1977, 1979; Tyler, Rafferty & Tyler, 1962). This literature stayed away from notions of biological predispositions in the human organism, emphasizing socially acquired motives, interests, aspirations, expectations, anxieties, and defense mechanisms (Bar-Tal & Frieze, 1977; Baruch, 1967, 1974, 1975; Campbell, 1973; Deaux & Emswiller, 1974; Deaux & Farris, 1974; Stein & Bailey, 1976; Hochschild, 1973a). Hoffman, for instance, continued her interdisciplinary analysis by raising social psychological issues. Focusing new attention on sex differences in the *social* experiences of infancy and early childhood, she argued that female children are given inadequate parental encouragement in early independence striving. She also suggested that the separation of the self from the mother is slower and less complete for girl children both because they are the same sex and face the same gender-role expectations and because girls have fewer conflicts with parents. As a result, the young female does not develop confidence in her ability to cope independently with the environment.

Psychologists then urged closer attention to the behaviors of socializing agents in early childhood, to the sex-typing of tasks among children, and to attributes of parents and variations among subgroups in the population. Women's apparently lower performance expectations in competitive situations were linked to a variety of early learning experiences: direct training by parents, consistently negative cultural messages, and the narrow and stereotypical range of adult role models.

In the following section we focus on just a few of the key identification and socialization issues, showing where gender related issues once again have spurred major critiques. As we move outward in our analysis of female achievement, we are leaving behind the laboratory setting and experimental studies of the need to achieve for the broader context in which the motive is nourished. As before, however, we are faced with some major theoretical and methodological problems. For instance, the literature on gender identification lacks clarity with regard to what aspects of the gender role a child is supposed to learn and how closely behavior will actually mirror norms. Even more disturbing is the apparent ease with which females are to adopt the generally less prestigious and less powerful roles of mother and wife. Moreover, the characteristics attributed to both parents are based on middle-class role patterns. Lastly, and most evident in the socialization literature, there appears to be little distinction between the social role and the actual person. Consequently, the complex process whereby we learn and enact our roles is oversimplified. The ongoing process of negotiation and the many different sources of evaluation (e.g., those outside the family) are underestimated. The literature on independence training and the working mother highlights how inadequate socialization theories have been and in some ways continue to be.

Gender Identity

In the 1960s most theories of child development assumed that it was mentally healthy for boys to be masculine and for girls to be feminine (Brown, 1965; Goslin, 1971; Hoffman & Hoffman, 1964; Mischel, 1971). One of the more popular mechanisms used to explain the gender-role learning process was the psychoanalytically based process of identification. In learning-theory terms, successful resolution of the Oedipal crisis increases the child's motivation to observe and imitate the attributes, attitudes, and behaviors of the same-sex parent (Brim, 1958; Hartley, 1964; Hartley & Hardesty, 1962; Hartup & Zook, 1960; Rabban, 1950; Sears, Rau & Alpert, 1965). Characteristically, most of the empirical research up through the 1970s, like the experimental literature on achievement motivation, focused on male children.

Most discussions of identification followed the psychoanalytic tradition of concentrating on the problems facing young males in transferring allegiance from mother to father. Kohlberg, in his 1966 analysis of gender-role development, summed up the then current consensus on female identification in one sentence: "All theories have assumed that the girl identifies primarily with the mother throughout childhood, and available research data seem to support this assumption" (p. 143). Beginning a line of questioning (continuing to the present), he went on to address a related paradox in the gender-role literature that challenged the process and importance of same-sex identification. Citing longitudinal studies of boys' development in father-absent homes (McCord, McCord & Thurber, 1962:158), Kohlberg argued that the physical presence of the father is *not* critical in the formation of a basic gender-role identification (1966, 1969, 1971, 1973a, b).

Heretofore the masculine identification process had turned on the presence of the father and the power and prestige attached to the masculine role (M. Hoffman, 1963). Freudian theory, status-envy theory, learning theory, and role theory all suggested that for a boy to develop an adequate gender identity, he must perceive his father as very powerful (Bowerman & Elder, 1964; Caplow, 1968; Hess & Torney, 1962; Hetherington, 1965; Straus, 1964; Whiting, 1960). Freud hypothesized that the father is viewed as an aggressive competitor with the power to castrate the child (1938). Whiting's status-envy theory postulated that the male child identifies with the father and the male role because he perceives the father as the consumer of valued resources (1960).

Bandura noted that while a child's personal attraction to a model can facilitate emulation, other qualities like power and status are also important (Bandura & Huston, 1965; Bandura, Ross & Ross, 1963; Bandura & Walters, 1963; Hess & Torney, 1962). In fact, Bandura, Ross, and Ross demonstrated that the mere recognition of a role as powerful, prestigious, or competent is likely to lead to modeling (1963). What of the female? Is she subject to the same gender identification process as the male? If so, we have problems explaining her same-sex identification with a less powerful role. The alternative is that these models are describing patterns valid only for males, a possibility raised infrequently in the review literature of the time (Mischel, 1968, 1971; Mischel & Liebert, 1967). In the remainder of this section we examine two leading theorists' work. We do not find satisfactory answers to the aforementioned questions, but we do find implicit contradictions in the theories explaining females' same-sex identification.

Utilizing concepts from a variety of traditions, Parsons's theory of gender-role development advanced two notions of particular interest to us (1955). First, he proposed that children's perceptions of parental roles and gender roles change in a predictable fashion as children pass through specific stages of physical, cognitive, and social development. Second, he emphasized the child's use of a "power-prestige axis" in differentiating among roles. Parsons suggested that the child's attribution of superior power or competence to particular roles (e.g., parent vis-à-vis child; mother vis-à-vis father) also will vary with age. Moreover, a child's perception of a role as rewarding and powerful can act as motivation for internalizing a gender-role preference (Sears, Whiting, Nowlis & Sears, 1953; Sears, Rau & Albert, 1965).

Parsons's theory of identification was built around the idea of the nuclear family as an interacting system of social relationships. The fundamental notion was that the child passes through a series of identifications. The nature of these successive identifications is determined by the reciprocal roles being taken by parents and children at successive stages of development (Zelditch, 1955). During the pre-oedipal period (about thirty months to five years) the child is assumed to be in some senses sexless. As in Kohlberg's 1966 model, early gender roles were closely linked to physical differences between males and females. Biological differentiation was said to provide the first and firmest gender identity. The irreversibility of one's sex was for Kohlberg the bedrock of later sexual and gender-role attitudes. While both Parsons and Kohlberg stressed the biological base for early gender identity, they also emphasized that children develop a sensitivity to the social order, especially to the power hierarchy. We will note again and again that the place of power in the identification process often has been neglected in discussions of adult gender-role behavior.

Basic to Parsons's theory of child development was the proposition that the structure of the nuclear family is a consequence of differentiation along two axes: that of hierarchy and power and that of instrumental and expressive function. For example, there must be an instrumental superior, expressive superior, instrumental inferior, and expressive inferior set of roles. Children of both sexes need parents of both sexes: "Neither boy nor girl . . . can be adequately socialized without a parent—or some substitute—of the opposite sex whose role pattern he can never assume" (1955; p. 108). What is not clear is why the young female, given her growing sensitivity to the power structure, apparently is eager to overlook the prestigious, instrumental superior role of the father. Parsons was typical of most early analysts concerned with sex-role identification. He was preoccupied with the place of power in the father-son relationship and relatively neglectful of the motivational dynamics of females. However, both Parsons and Kohlberg did expand the array of motives open to the young female. As we discuss in chapter 2, such expanded conceptualizations are necessary for an authentic accounting of the female experience.

Kohlberg observed an increase by young children in the awarding of power and competence to the male role (1966). He attributed this development to a growing understanding of the occupational order. Looking at evidence that girls' preferential evaluations of females *decrease* with age, he concluded that for girls this decline coincides with a growing awareness of the *superior prestige* of the male role. Kohlberg's explanation for same-sex identification by the young female was rather weak. He postulated that her motivation for choosing the appropriate sex is that her mother is still more powerful and competent than she is—"nicer" and "prettier." The power comparison is not mother to father but rather parent to child.

Kohlberg summarized the importance of instrumental-expressive role differentiation in gender-role learning in similar fashion to Parsons. However, Kohlberg was far more explicit about the vital components of the father's role—for him, power and prestige:

A boy's desire for power and instrumental competence promotes his desire to be masculine, but his identity-maintaining desire to play masculine roles crystallizes competence motivation into a striving for power and achievement values. . . .

In the case of girls, feminine roles award an ample, if somewhat less, scope for power and competence motivation but much of this motivation is channeled into values that are not competence or achievement values in the usual sense. . . . However, the pursuit of attractiveness, goodness, and social approval is ultimately based on the same needs for control of the environment for self-esteem, and for successful achievement, as are the more obvious masculine competence values. (1966:122)

As defined by Kohlberg, the gender-identity process for females includes an implicit conflict. That is, the female child (like the male) recognizes the superior prestige of the male role but then identifies with the devalued role of her own sex.

Parsons recognized a developmental pattern similar to Kohlberg's when he suggested that children make judgments about gender roles based on realistic social evaluations of worth and performance (1955). He argued that in relations outside the family the child encounters a whole system of superiority-inferiority relationships that are not institutionally ascribed (e.g., peers). As the child begins to differentiate between *ascription* and *achievement* and can see distinctions between who one is and what one can *do*, she or he acquires a new understanding of the superior-inferior relationship: "There comes to be an internalized attitude of 'admiration' or 'respect' for the person who 'can do things' regardless of who he is" (p. 118).

What, then, is the young female's understanding of her mother's role in the social order or her mother's motives for conformity or her sentiments about women's lot in life? What is the young female actually internalizing? After all, both Parsons's and Kohlberg's theories of identification stressed identification with a powerful and prestigious role.

Psychoanalytic models of development have been far more conflict oriented than those presented by Kohlberg and Parsons (Miller & Dollard, 1941; Dollard and Miller, 1950; Sears, Whiting, Nowlis & Sears, 1953). In such models the female's response to social impotence is not an immediate and conflict-free identification with mother but, instead, an envious hankering after masculine instrumentality (Mischel & Liebert, 1967). Aware of this theoretical dilemma, Parsons weakly held out the promise of influence for females through the expressive socioemotional functions of family life. We would argue that when the female child in the Parsonian model comes to internalize an attitude of admiration and respect for persons who appear powerful, she may also have profoundly ambivalent feelings about being ascribed to the instrumentally inferior role of female.

Both gender roles and achievement orientation are clearly influenced by early childhood relationships in the family. Problematic, however, are attempts to label just what it is the child learns from such observations (Kagan, 1956; 1964; Kagan & Lemkin, 1960; Johnson, 1963). Even more questionable are models that attempt to translate the child's objective realities into personal motivations and sentiments. The early literature on gender-role identification and gender-role learning remarkably constricted the range and depth of an actor's (person's) responses. Despite the potential for conflict in the most prominent models of identification, females' socialization into gender roles has been described as a relatively *conflict-free* choice process. Despite clear indications that powerful, prestigious roles enhance identification and preference, theorists have generally failed to consider why this might present problems, if not conflict, for girls.

The Sentient Actor

Feminist scholars in particular have been calling for a reexamination of the motives, feelings, and emotions that have been attributed to social actors of both sexes. In the area of achievement, as we have noted, the spotlight has focused on motives based on internal rewards. In the literature on gender identification, females find themselves filled with awe and respect as they learn to envy male roles and to acquiesce in their own. Allowed to love their fathers, girls are entitled to win his approval only through conformity —not through competition.

Theories of identification suggest that although females may recognize their relatively powerless and devalued roles in life, they are expected to approve of their place in the social order. It follows that they will experience self-doubt, fear, conflict, and anxiety over challenging the male role. To boot, most of this process is assumed to occur unconsciously during childhood, to become enduringly rooted in the self, and therefore to last a lifetime. Somewhat facetiously Hochschild has suggested that the organism or subject in such a model is "guided by unconscious motivations, and does or thinks things whose meanings are better understood by the social scientist than by the actor" (1975:282). The actor in this typology is thought to be driven by a limited number of instincts, impulses, or needs—for instance, the need to achieve, affiliate, or "do any number of things that merely surface as ends or means" (Hochschild, 1975:282).

In her analysis Hochschild has differentiated between the "having of the goal (not the doubt or triumph attached to it) and the use of the means (not the guilt, apprehension, or glee attached to its use)" (p. 282). As Hochschild summed up this view, "Those who posit a model of a rational actor generally do not deny that actors feel. However, they imply that little is lost when feelings are ignored or tidily bunched under the terms " 'ends and means,' " (p. 282). Whether the focus is on conscious thinking or on unconscious promptings, Hochschild feared that conscious feeling seems to "fall into a no-man's-land in between," (p. 283). She preferred the image of the *sentient actor*, both conscious *and* feeling.

This clearly expands the vocabulary available to us. We cannot assume that withdrawal in competitive situations is motivated by fear alone. It may be motivated by a high degree of calculation, desire for conformity, boredom, sexual attraction, or all of the above factors simultaneously. The sentient actor can examine her feelings, reidentify the sources of old conflicts, and rationally and consciously displace them from the self to others and to the social setting. In reexamining the role of mechanisms like internalization and socialization, we wish to leave the actor more room for emotional and conscious negotiation.

The documented awareness of cultural stereotypes and gender attributes is often presumed to lead irrevocably to gender identification, conformist behavior, and ignorance of alternatives. Even recent feminist authors have slipped into equating socialization into gender roles with internalization:

> Most children learn their gender roles primarily by role-taking. . . . They learn the "proper" attitudes, values, behaviors, and goals associated with the sex status. They learn the rights, obligations, and prestige accompanying their sex status. Gradually and irrevocably, the children internalize their gender roles until the attributes come to seem like the only possible way to behave and feel.

> Jerome Kagan has demonstrated that cultural definitions of masculinity and femininity are *internalized* by children as young as three years old. Children of this age can tell us that daddies should be aggressive, big, and strong; mommies should be little, pretty, and cuddly. They understand that little girls are expected to be more conforming and dependent than little boys, and they are likely to become very upset if their peers violate these normative prohibitions. (Duberman, 1975:26–27)

Duberman used "internalize" to mean "accepting the norms of the group as part of one's self-image" so that the attitudes and behaviors approved by society appear to have no alternatives. This view of development leaves little room for negotiation between parents and children. Peterson and Enarson have reminded us that:

> there is a fine distinction to be made between recognizing the environmental source of "feminine" characteristics and accepting these characteristics as given, as properties of women regrettably "socialized into her" but hers nonetheless; between acknowledging the impact of situation upon character and presuming the characteristics implied by the situation have been duly incorporated into the personality. (1974:7)

Must we assume that the human organism, born with a wide range of potentialities, undergoes a narrowing down into customary and acceptable behavior and attitudes? For those who envision society as a steady state, internalization may be comfortably described as the means of insuring social and cultural continuity. But implicit in the definiton of socialization is coercion. Furthermore, conformity and commitment are not maintained in a social vacuum. Recent feminist analysis has suggested that observers have overemphasized the importance of public, socially recognized scripts embedded in traditional institutions. These writers argue that social arrangements that survive over time and become standard also become reified, the nuclear family being a case in point. In turn, our theories reflect contemporary "formulas for routine action, scripts for the actors, backed up by ideology which stresses their *rightness* as much as their efficiency" (Laws, 1977:5). The gender-role literature gives the young female no choice but to embrace her ascribed role. She is expected to incorporate her gender role as a major organizational force in her social identity on stage and off. In both her cognitive conscious and her autonomously monitored conscience she is expected to remain faithful and morally committed to the female gender role.

But Hochschild (1975) and Skolnick (1973) have suggested that we cannot be sure just what the child is internalizing. As we have seen there are methodological and theoretical problems in understanding the identification and internalization processes. We also see problems in analyzing the familial process whereby females come to learn the customary gender script.

In the following section we note two interrelated problems in the socialization literature: first, the tendency to neglect some kinds of interpersonal dynamics by focusing on the *expected* behaviors and attitudes of persons playing out traditional social roles within the family setting; and second, the failure to see role making, role playing, and role taking as a dynamic series of exchanges between parents and children. For instance, although the children in models offered by Parsons (1955) and Kohlberg (1966) generally appear to "choose correctly" and "internalize appropriately," the mechanisms for bargaining and negotiating are at least present in their theories—a dynamic process frequently missing in the early socialization literature.

Achievement Socialization

From the sociological perspective, socialization is critical in establishing children's reference groups and standards of evaluation. In these models achievement is credibly indexed by worldly success in work and education rather than by personal, self-relevant standards, as described by Atkinson, McClelland, and others. Both focuses, sociological and psychological, have adopted a sequential model of development whose seeds, according to Featherman, "are sown within families of orientation, nurtured and developed within the schools, and harvested within the domestic and market economies in adulthood. Such a view has been termed the 'socioeconomic life cycle'. . ." (1978:2–3). The questions commonly addressed in this literature have revolved around efforts to understand the typical "trajectories" of achievement experienced by men and women from early childhood through to retirement from economically productive work roles.

The models of socialization used in the more sociological analyses of achievement have emphasized direct training and parental role modeling. Both expectancy-value research in psychology and the status-attainment literature in sociology have based their descriptions of socialization on a limited number of studies. In the sections that follow, we review in some detail the socialization process so critical to these theories.

Independence and autonomy are personal qualities commonly thought to foster adult success (White, 1959; Rosen, 1964). Research on the origins of the achievement motive set out to observe the parents of boys with high and low need achievement scores. Socialization models suggested that early "mastery training" appeared to promote high need achievement provided that parents' behavior did not reflect generalized restrictiveness, authoritarianism, or "rejection" (Bronfenbrenner, 1958; 1960). Several investigators attempted to describe and contrast the child-rearing practices of families more or less successful in their achievement training.

Rosen used some of the most innovative methods (1964; 1969). He wanted to differentiate between observed behaviors and reported values and attitudes. His study was also unusual in that he observed parents of both sexes, a relatively rare methodological approach in the 1960s, a decade that produced a child development literature characteristically concerned with mothers and sons.[8] Despite the dominance of models emphasizing the unique roles of mothers and fathers in the socialization process, few data were available on sex differences in parenting. When fathers were observed, they appeared to differ from mothers in their behavior; furthermore, fathers' behaviors were perceived differently by children (Strodtbeck, 1954; Straus, 1964).

Investigators increasingly suggested that mothers and fathers played distinct roles as socializing agents (Strodtbeck 1954, 1955, 1958). Although gender-typing was not a central concern in these early reports, sex became more problematic as an intervening variable. Even when they engaged in apparently identical behaviors of rewarding and punishing, mothers and fathers seemed to evoke different emotional states in their children.

Children benefited from the achievement training of both parents, but the effects of independence training and sanctions—in particular, autonomy and rejection—were different depending upon their source. In order for high need achievement to develop, the boy seemed to need more autonomy from his father than from his mother:

> The father who gives the boy a relatively high degree of autonomy provides him with an opportunity to compete on his own ground, to test his skill, and to gain a sense of confidence in his own competence. The dominating father may crush his son (and in so doing destroy the boy's achievement motive), perhaps because he views the boy as a competitor and is viewed as such by his son. On the other hand, the mother who dominates the decision-making process does not seem to have the same effect on the boy, possibly because she is perceived as imposing her standards on the boy, while a dominating father is perceived as imposing himself on the son. (Rosen, 1969:83)

Rearing a successful son and transmitting socioeconomic inheritance from one generation to the next represented complex processes in this model: father must be powerful but judicious in his displays of authority; mother can be pushy, enthusiastic, and emotionally involved in her son's achievements provided that she knows her place in the overall family structure. The mother handles the emotional motivational sphere while the father acts as instrumental role model or neutral translator of the arrangement of sanctions in the economic opportunity structure. Unfortunately, although socialization was seen as a familial process, the literature on socialization focused primarily on dyadic relationships.

Although psychologists would be quick to admit that most parent-child interaction takes place in the family, the family as a dynamic unit is rarely studied (Bandura & Huston, 1965). In his call for an "ecologically valid model for the socialization process," Bronfenbrenner urged the profession to expand its models from two-person to at least three-person systems and thus to include the nuclear family. He warned that this step alone could seriously complicate analysis and assumptions:

> To take the classical example of a three-person system—the nuclear family— we have within it the possibility of differential allocation of parental roles between father and mother, and, now, instead of only one dyadic relationship, a total of three—mother with child, father with child, and mother and father. In each of these, patterns of reciprocal socialization take place which may duplicate, complement, or even contradict each other, with profound consequences not only for the behavior and development of the child but also of the two adults in their roles as parents, and of the nuclear family as a total system. (1976:115)

Both in sociology and psychology the family is often viewed as a mediator or transmitter of culture (Bronfenbrenner, 1958, 1960). As a result, descriptions of the socialization process and the actors involved often lack the vitality of conflict and bargaining, which are virtual constants between generations.

Female Independence Training and the Working Mother

Absent also from our discussion so far is the role of parental achievement training in the development of young females. Again, this lack parallels the historical development of the research in the field.

In describing the socialization process for female achievement, researchers have devoted more attention to the presumed conflicts between gender roles and achievement than to the actual achievement behaviors of women. Both psychologists and sociologists have been accused of describing the socialization process overdeterministically (Clausen, 1968; Homans, 1967; Wrong, 1961). As we have seen, the literature on gender roles and achievement presents the family more as a neutral transmitting station than as an arena for evaluation and negotiation. Knowledge is transferred from high-power to low-power persons; the content of the knowledge appears to be unambiguously transmitted and unambiguously understood. In this section we illustrate the criticisms we have just offered by looking at families with employed mothers. By bringing employed mothers and their daughters into the socialization analysis, we expose the androcentric orientation of in-

quiry in the field and the slow appreciation of the complexity of the socialization process for both sexes.

Questions about the employed mother as a socializing agent, how her
role is perceived, and the social motives inferred from her behavior brought
new variables into the analysis, revealing the socialization process to be, if
not more predictable, certainly more dynamic than previously acknowledged (Stolz, 1960). One of the earliest and most straightforward sets of hypotheses linking maternal employment to female achievement emerged
from the literature on independence training. The problem revolved around
the *motives* underlying parental *independence* training. Examining for motives made the socialization process appear more complex, especially regarding what message the parent was sending and what message the child
was learning. Was the parent attempting to reward or punish the child in
pressing early responsibilities upon her/him? What was the content of these
duties? How did the employed mother's demands upon her children compare to those of mothers at home full-time? Furthermore, did the children
perceive the parental demands as warm or hostile, loving or rejecting? In
approaching the question of the working mother, researchers became increasingly interested in motive and intent (McCord & McCord 1963).

The Fels Research Institute's longitudinal studies led to the generalization that high-achieving females had mothers who were less affectionate,
more hostile, and less positive in their responses to dependency (Kagan &
Moss, 1962). The problem in the literature, however, was to create a frame
of reference for assessing the absolute value of specific parental behaviors
on the instrumental-expressive continuum (Siegel & Haas, 1963). Was the
relationship negative and linear or curvilinear? Were there critical periods
that differed for girls and boys?

Independence is commonly operationalized as taking a greater share of
household responsibilities (the reader may note the problem, then, in con-
ceptualizing dependence as not helping mother out). Women employed outside the home were thought to expect earlier and greater assistance from
their children in family chores. A study by Yarrow, Scott, De Leeuw, and
Heinig, on employed and nonemployed mothers suggested that the age of
the child and the social class or education of the mothers made a difference
in interpreting the data (1962). In their sample, the employed mothers who
had not gone to college were likely to indicate more stress on independence
training and to assign their children a greater share of household responsibilities; on the other hand, the employed, college-educated mothers showed
the opposite pattern. To appreciate the feelings underlying the working
mother's practices, this study went on to explore the mother's motivation
and satisfaction with her current status as either full-time housewife or paid
worker. The mother's feelings about the organization of her domestic roles
appeared to be more salient than the fact of holding a job or not. The
mother's motivation and her satisfaction with her work status were a crucial
intervening variable. Yarrow concluded, ''If mothers are in their preferred

work or nonwork roles, working or not makes little difference in their child-rearing" (p. 226).

In a related series of studies on adolescents, Douvan reported substantial interaction effects among maternal employment, socioeconomic status, sex of children, and independence training (1963). Daughters of middle-class, full-time employed mothers were relatively active, self-reliant girls who did not appear to be unusually dependent upon their families. The parents expected them to be self-reliant, gave them a share in the rule making, and apparently permitted discussion and open arguments. On the other hand, daughters of employed working-class mothers were labeled "task-dependent" and described as exhibiting strong emotional dependence upon the family.

By bringing employed mothers into the analysis, these studies, at first only implicitly, demanded that we expand our notions of the socialization process itself. They brought into the socialization model a thinking, feeling, and sometimes ambivalent parent. The first generation studying female achievement and mother's employment provided some important insights (Douvan, 1963; Hartley, 1961; Hoffman, 1963; Siegal & Haas, 1963; Baruch, 1967). Maternal employment was cast in a positive light: it could provide the opportunity for ego development and self-respect through meaningful task involvement with other adults (Bardwick, 1971). The same qualities and experiences that make one a good worker could operate to make one a good mother as well. That is, employment and motherhood were not necessarily incompatible; they might even be mutually enhancing. The recognition that the mother's feelings and attitudes about roles *other* than being a parent could affect her interaction with her children was a breakthrough, as was the notion that women in fact have extrafamilial role commitments and that these may be important elements in the socialization process (Hoffman, 1963a, b; Yarrow, Scott, De Leeuw and Heinig, 1962).

What is the impact of the employed mother on her children's achievements? The methodological and theoretical problems we have described in the socialization literature have plagued studies on maternal employment, distorting if not confusing the answers offered over the past few decades. In a seminal work, Hoffman & Nye anticipated many of the methodological and theoretical difficulties we have highlighted (1975). The complex interplay among mother's feelings toward her roles (familial and occupational), her socioeconomic status, the nature of her employment, the age and sex of the child, and child care arrangements was seen as critical in analyzing the effect of maternal employment. The typical study of maternal employment seldom dealt with the many variables in the complicated familial interaction process. Hoffman particularly noted that the distance between an antecedent condition like maternal employment and a child characteristic (e.g., academic achievement) is "too great to be covered in a single leap" (1975:128). Particularly problematic were the studies pertaining to academic achievement. In fact, Hoffman looked at the data on maternal employment and children's academic achievement separately from other working-mother issues "because most of these data are from simple, two-level studies where it was impossible to say what process was involved" (Hoffman & Nye, 1975:165).

In reviewing the literature Hoffman cautiously concluded: "There is evidence . . . that college-educated daughters of working mothers have higher career aspirations and achievements than do college educated daughters of nonworking mothers. In one study daughters of working mothers obtained higher intelligence test scores at six and fifteen years of age" (Hoffman & Nye, 1975:162–163). Hoffman insisted however, that although we might predict higher achievements for the daughters of working mothers, the reasons for such attainments are not always clear (Hoffman & Nye, 1975). We do not know, for instance, whether daughters are modeling themselves after their mothers or if, by working, the mothers have provided more money for the daughters to pursue college and/or career. In addition, Hoffman warned, the kind of work the mother does, particularly in relation to her education, is seldom controlled for. For instance, in reexamining Banducci's 1967 study of children's college aspirations and maternal employment, Hoffman discovered a "peculiar" problem. Banducci's sample consisted of Iowa high school seniors living with both parents. Three occupational levels were considered—laborer, skilled worker, and professional. Here is Hoffman's analysis:

> For most subjects, males and females, maternal employment was positively associated with desires and plans for college. But for the group classified as professional the opposite relationship prevailed; the daughters of working mothers were significantly less likely to expect to go to college, and the sons were less likely to expect or to aspire to go, the latter relationships being significant. How can we interpret this curious pattern of findings? Did the presence of a working mother indicate the lower socioeconomic end of the professional group? Were the working mothers employed in a family business, and thus the family less education-oriented? (Hoffman & Nye, 1975:159)

We can only agree with Hoffman's warnings and echo her concern that social class is a more complex variable than father's occupation and education (see also Hoffman, 1977, 1979). Mother's occupation and its relationship to her education not only may reflect on her feelings toward employment but also may have an important impact on the family's style of living (this point is pursued in chapter 4).

We cannot resist recounting an additional example of the complications in analyzing maternal employment, for these twists express many of the wrinkles explicit in academic research. Often, however, when such findings are popularized the wrinkles remain behind. Frankel's 1964 study of intellectually gifted high school boys indicated that low achievers were more likely to have non-professionally employed mothers and that high achievers were more likely to have employed professional mothers. Hoffman puzzled over this pattern:

> Although the socioeconomic status as conventionally measured did not differentiate the groups, education of the mothers (and possibly both parents) did. While the higher achievement of the children of professional mothers is easily interpreted, it is not clear why the low achievers tended to have nonprofessional working mothers. Frankel describes these women impressionistically as dissatisfied and hostile. This judgment may or may not be valid. . . . it would be worthwhile to compare . . . the effects of mother's employment on the mother's psychological state. (Hoffman & Nye, 1975:161)

In one of the few studies that addressed achievement motivation, Powell, using the projective techniques developed by McClelland and Atkinson, measured achievement motivation in relation to maternal employment (1963). Using longitudinal data for subjects at nine, ten, eleven, and twelve years of age, he found that while children of employed mothers showed higher achievement motivation, this finding was significant for the nine year olds only. Jones, Lundsteen, and Michael carried out a similar study with sixth-graders and found once again a non-significant but positive relationship (1967). Hoffman perceptively noted that in neither study were the findings examined separately by sex. She implied that had this been done the researchers might have found significant relationships for girls between achievement motivation and working mothers.

Although we might tentatively conclude from the data that daughters of working mothers compared to those of nonworking mothers are more likely to want to work, to see themselves engaged in a broader range of work activities, to see women as competent and effective and men as warm and expressive, to name their mothers as the person they most admire, and to be role innovative (Hoffman and Nye, 1975), such findings are only correlations. We know little about the dynamics behind these correlations. Moreover, in almost all of the studies that uncovered these correlations, important qualifiers were offered. For example, Baruch noted that almost all the positive relationships between employed mothers and their daughters' career commitments, aspirations, belief in female competence, and role innovativeness were positive *only* if the mother were viewed by the daughter as having successfully integrated her work and family roles (1972).

The maternal employment literature brings us back full circle to the problems involved in measuring and interpreting family dynamics and understanding the identification and socialization processes that are seen as critical to developing and nourishing the achievement motive. These gender-linked issues have brought into focus variables heretofore understated or simply missed. They help us focus on a broader range of feelings, motives, sentiments, and behaviors available to both parents and children in the socialization and identification experience. Although gender-related research may not provide the answers, it has at least awakened us to some key questions that we must ask before we can conclude very much about the personality make up of the young child or the setting in which achievement potential may be reached.

Conclusion

The acquisition and maintenance of a gender role and achievement orientation take place in a social context. Cooley's famous concept of the "looking-glass self" emphasized the importance of learning to see the self as seen by others. The socialization literature recognizes the importance of the parents in shaping the mirror image, but the process has often been described as one-way (from high-to-low authority figures) and, as we have seen with the working-mother literature, the variables have been too limited in scope. In order for the female child to see her image from a parent's point of view, she needs to acquire an interpretive framework for identifying the feelings and actions imputed to her and others. Herein we have the helpful concept of the sentient actor, who has a self, an identity, or a personality that is brought to any role played and that, in turn, is conditioned by all the roles played throughout the life course.

Actors, then, are persons playing roles for a variety of reasons. Their interest and involvement in a particular role at a moment in time may be marginal or impassioned. Once this role is played, the actor may easily and comfortably move on to others. We do not assume that because a part has been played, it has been internalized in such a way that it will guide later behavior in either a conscious or an unconscious, predetermined fashion. We presume that merger between actor and role, or person and actor, occurs only under a highly specific pattern of circumstances and requires a complex set of maintenance mechanisms.

Armed with this concept of the actor, we explore adolescence in the next chapter. We once again look at the contributions of scholars interested in female achievement and the ways in which they have highlighted the general problems in the achievement literature.

Notes

1. The motive to achieve has been described as a relatively stable disposition to strive for success in any situation wherein standards of excellence are applicable. Despite many revisions, as recently as 1978 the motive was called "general," not situational, and "stable" and "enduring," not dynamic (Atkinson & Raynor,

1978). The enduring and stable nature of the motive necessarily limits change over the life course.

2. Overlooking for the moment the question of what in fact is or is not being aroused, we can give the data several interpretations. While female subjects do not increase their scores under aroused conditions, they continue to tell stories containing achievement themes in comparable proportion to those found among men. It is misleading, then, to suggest that even under these carefully defined experimental conditions women exhibit less achievement motivation than men. As we continue our review of the literature on female achievement, we regularly emphasize the importance of reexamining the methods and concepts applied to women in the absence of an adequate gender-role theory.

3. For a good review of research on sex-typing from the early 1950s through the early 1960s see Kagan (1964:137–168); measures included toy choices, role playing, and gender descriptions of purportedly neutral, or genderless, pictures. As with the cues on the TAT, cited earlier, the children's responses commonly were treated as "projections." Only in the 1970s were these explanations scrutinized more critically (Maccoby & Jacklin, 1974).

4. The theoretical tradition of expectancy-value stressed that the direction, magnitude, and persistence of achievement efforts depend upon an individual's incentives and expectancies concerning success and failure (Hull, 1943; Lewin, 1935, 1951; Tolman, 1932). The motive to achieve is one of three components in the expectancy-value model; the two situational components are expectancy or probability of success and the incentive value associated with that success.

5. The search for different motives for seemingly similar behavior was prompted by early findings that the sexes differed on all variables *except* achievement efforts (Crandall & Rabson, 1960). That achievement should be a gender exception led researchers to explore other possiblilities, that is, other motives (Bardwick, 1971:173).

6. Space does not permit a detailed discussion of internalization and its long-term impact. Nevertheless, sociologists, like social psychologists, have relied upon internalization of norms to account for the actor's personality structure in role theory. Thus, Parsons argued for long-term impact:

It may be concluded that it is the internalization of the value-orientation patterns embodied in the role-expectations for ego of the significant socializing agents which constitutes the strategic elements of his basic personality structure. And it is because these patterns can only be acquired through the mechanisms of identification, and because the basic identification patterns are developed in childhood, that the childhood structure of personality in this respect is so stable and unchangeable. (1951:228)

Parson's work strongly influenced theoretical formulations about socialization, most particularly the relative stability of value-orientation patterns internalized early in life. Since the internalization process is mostly unconscious and since it usually occurs under conditions of high power and affect within the familial setting, the childhood structure of personality appears stable and relatively unchangeable. Moreover, since the components of this personality system are derived largely from interaction with significant others, internalization suggests that the actor voluntarily, or consensually, *becomes* the role. Brim and Wheeler, after arguing that "socialization occurring during childhood correctly receives primary emphasis in research and theory" (1966:21), stressed the same point Parsons made. In this schema we cannot distinguish analytically between internalization and posturing.

7. So-called impulsiveness is a problem for males as much as passive-dependency is for females. We suggest that early research indicating that little girls are more likely than little boys to choose easier tasks or puzzles pointed up a problem found in both sexes. Their "impulsiveness" might make boys less cautious, shown by the choice of difficult tasks and overestimation of their abilities; little girls might be "overcautious" choosing easier tasks and underestimating their abilities (Stein & Bailey, 1976:258). In this sense both sexes have unrealistic expectations.

8. One of the benefits of experimental designs that omitted fathers from analysis was that there were fewer variables to observe or control. Most of the child development literature discussed parents as mothers. Fathers, rather than being viewed as unknowns, were more commonly "controlled" in the analysis on the basis of their occupations. Mothers were assumed to be known quantities in their occupational status of housewives although variable in their childrearing practices.

CHAPTER 2

Adolescence and the High Achiever

As we noted in chapter 1, the achievement motive embodies the desire to do something independent of others, and according to internal criteria of excellence. Therefore, an independent sense of self, not dependent on others for standards and values, is necessary to the high achiever. Two interrelated variables pertaining to the self are important in understanding why an individual will tend to approach or avoid achievement situations: expectations about success or failure and self-esteem. If, as Erikson noted, the quest for identity is the central developmental task of adolescence, then those years become a critical period for the development of expectations and esteem (1950, 1976).

The gender-role literature, certainly through the early 1970s, described the dominant source of self-esteem and related identity issues for the female as dependent upon her heterosexual affiliations (Bardwick, Douvan, Horner & Gutman, 1970; Mischel, 1971). Bardwick and Douvan, in an often quoted essay, identified the important change for females from childhood to adolescence: "While girls characteristically achieved in grade school because of rewards for their 'good' behavior from others (rather than for achievement's own sake), in adolescence the establishment of successful interpersonal relationships becomes the self-defining, most rewarding, achievement task'' (1972:54). In a sophisticated rendering of both psychoanalytic and gender-role interpretations, Bardwick and Douvan called attention to the ambivalence in adolescent females' socialization experiences. Until adolescence the ideal of equal capacity, opportunity, and lifestyle is held out to girls. The authors then cautioned: ''But sometime in adolescence the message becomes clear that one had better not do too well, that competition is aggressive and unfeminine, and that deviation threatens the heterosexual relationship'' (p. 55). The authors noted that while young girls are not ''prohibited from going to college, seeking school office, or achieving honors,'' their concerns (prodded by the ''ferment'' of such biological changes as menstruation and a revived eroticism) turn increasingly to the culturally prescribed goals and roles associated with marriage and maternity (1972:55). The domestic script demands skills different from those associated with competitive achievement. According to Bardwick and Douvan, young women respond to this adolescent turn of events by withdrawing:

> . . . from what is clearly masculine. In high school and increasingly in college, girls cease clearly masculine pursuits and perceive the establishment of interpersonal goals as the most salient route to identity. This results in a maximization of interpersonal skills, an interpersonal view of the world, a withdrawal from the development of independence, activity, ability, and competition, and the absence of a professional work commitment. (P. 55)

The male's identity challenge is quite different: his goals (and the future roles associated with them) are clearly defined and earned through individual, competitive excellence.

We argue that while the so-called interpersonal route to identity for the female does seem at odds with strong achievement motivation, we should not overlook the possibility of other developmental paths and outcomes. Competence, as much as social sensitivity, may be the by-product of a developmental process that emphasizes heterosexual and interpersonal relationships. Indeed, the expectancy-value models of achievement occasionally make reference to ''sizing up'' ability, or ''dispositional expectancy'' (the ability of an actor to evaluate the skills necessary to play a particular role and the rewards associated with successful performance), as an important motivator in achievement related situations (Atkinson & Raynor, 1978). The ability realistically to assess the interpersonal strategies and skills necessary for success in a particular setting is an important component of successful achievement. This estimating ability may be described as a form of competence especially necessary for people typically low in social power. Therefore, while we recognize the powerful gender-role constraints imposed upon young females, we also recognize the potential achievement strengths they may be developing in their adolescent years.

Social Sensitivity: Female Strength or Weakness?

Drawing heavily from nineteenth-century psychoanalytic models of the self, some writers have described the female as suffering from diminished self-esteem (Horney, 1937, 1950, 1973).[1] In this view the deterioration of self stems from a "paralysis" of "adequate aggressiveness," "capacities for work," "taking initiative," "making efforts," "carrying things through to completion," "attaining success," "insisting upon one's rights," "recognizing one's goals," and being able "to plan one's life according to them" (Horney, 1979:67). The female in Horney's view usually manifests widespread inhibitions, even "helplessness in the life struggle," along with a "tendency to recoil from competition of any kind." (1979:67). Such an individual hardly seems capable of achieving anything.

The nineteenth-century psychoanalytic model of the mature female as passive, masochistic, and compliant is not very different from the current psychological image of her. Today the mature adult women is commonly stereotyped as dependent, compliant, and submissive (Broverman, Vogel, Broverman, Clarkson & Rosencrantz, 1972). The roots of this weak self are attributed not to nature, as they often were in the nineteenth century, but rather to the developmental tasks of adolescence. The young girl's investment of psychological energy in others—particularly males—is seen as her central developmental task given the adolescent gender-role script. While heterosexual skills preoccupy the adolescent male as well, his success presumably is derived from displays of independence and initiative.

In the social sciences, the earliest and most elaborate efforts to explore the growth of an autonomous self in female personality (critical for the achieving personality, described in chapter 1) were made by Douvan (Douvan, 1960; Douvan & Adelson, 1966; Douvan & Kaye, 1956), relying on the work of Erikson (1950) and on social learning theory in general (Bandura & Walters, 1963). The independent person was thought to be motivated by a high need for achievement and to possess a well-internalized set of values and standards. The dependent person, on the other hand, was portrayed as motivated by high needs for affiliation, social approval, and love. The well-adjusted female, according to the Eriksonian and Parsonian models then in vogue, fell in the dependent category. For the young female, personal identity and adjustment (ego strength) came with the development of interpersonal skills. Bardwick summarized the rationale behind this reasoning:

> While boys rebel, girls remain compliant, continue dependency relationships with their parents, and do not express an intense internal need to break the old familial bonds. . . . While the boy's preoccupation and development of internal standards allows one to predict his ego strength, only the girl's interpersonal relationships are related to her ego strength.

> In social relations girls are very much more mature than boys. The girl's identity is critically dependent upon the man she marries and the children she has. She perceives her major task as assuring her acceptability as a person who will be loved, a person someone will marry. (1971:148-149)

The psychoanalytic overtones of Bardwick's argument are clear. For girls, identity formation is delayed until they marry. Similarly, according to Douvan, young females do best by remaining "fluid and malleable in personal identity in order to adapt to the needs of the men they marry. Too clear a self-definition during adolescence may be maladaptive" (1972:45)—maladaptive, of course, if the only acceptable goals for the female are marriage and maternity. Therefore, while the adolescent script for the female stresses interpersonal skills, the positive value of such skills is related to her future and private achievements as wife and mother:

> Many of the skills and sensitivities encouraged by this constant orientation to an audience are probably useful to her later in performing her adult roles of wife and mother. Moreover, her attention to charm and the winning of affection serves an important defensive function in that it forestalls anxiety about whether she will in fact be chosen in marriage. (Douvan, 1972:41)

Douvan thus recognized the multiple functions these feminine skills could serve over the entire life course and the potential strengths derived from an interpersonal orientation.

Such skills do not, however, lead to the development of the enduring, autonomous sense of self that presumably is necessary for public achievements:

> for most women, popularity and social charm will not sustain self-esteem for a lifetime and it seems to me that we miss an important opportunity to help the girl enlarge her self-concept when we fail to capture and turn the ferment of adolescence to this purpose. (Douvan, 1972:41)

The sharp contrast between male and female development was caught in Bardwick's fine summary of Douvan and Adelson's 1966 landmark work on adolescence:

> During the ages of 14 through 16 boys consistently view their relations with their families as combative, with the major battles over independence, behavior control, and an individual sense of autonomy. In terms of the actual development of internal controls and values, the boys have developed much further than the girls. Boys think of their future in an instrumental way. . . . A boy's hopes for adult status reflect his faith in himself, and the goal he chooses is realistic in terms of his talents and opportunities. He is highly motivated to be independent, and his identity and capacity for erotic ties depend upon autonomy and separation from the parents. . . . His vocational identity and his sexual identity are separate. (1971:148)

It is clear from such descriptions that the past and the future come together in very important ways. The identification process that helps determine the personality makeup of the male child (described in chapter1), combined with the growing recognition of appropriate gender goals and roles in adolescence, turn him toward the development of a self ripe for socially recognized achievement (Elder, 1968). In this "same-sex similarity" scenario, the typical young male would reject his mother's occupation as a goal on two grounds. If she is a full-time homemaker, her job would appear to be gender-inappropriate for him. If she is employed, we would most likely find her in the female occupational ghetto. Her employment as typist, bookkeeper, receptionist, teacher, librarian, or nurse would render her occupational status an inappropriate goal for him as well. Finally, in their search for status mobility males are expected to move up and away from parental status (Elder, 1973). Elder summed up this view:

> Boys become oriented toward sex-appropriate images that have vocational significance, such as power, competition, and strength, while girls select the feminine qualities of attractiveness, interpersonal skills, goodness, and social approval. Attachment to like-sex parents reinforces sex-appropriate learning and structures attitudes towards tasks in the home and community. (1971:106)

On the other hand, the female's experience is relatively continuous. "The only change from childhood," noted Bardwick and Douvan, "is that the most important source of esteem is no longer the parents but the heterosexual partner" (1972:54). The developmental literature of the 1960s and the early 1970s suggested that the ferment of adolescence and the search for identity did not lead to a strong, autonomous self for females, as it apparently did for males (Bardwick, 1971, 1974; Baruch, 1967, 1975; Lesser, 1973). Bardwick explained:

> For the adolescent girl, the interpersonal sphere is pivotal. Her sensitivity and skill in interpersonal relations express her developing eroticism, and her efforts to gain popularity express her erotic needs and her skills in winning and maintaining love. . . . What the boy achieves through separation and autonomy, the girl achieves . . . through her attachments to others. Douvan and Adelson found that the girl's vocational identity and her sexual identity were interlaced, her vocational ideas were infused with sexual and sex-role themes, and her goals were closely tied to the objects she identified with. This served to continue her tendency to be dependent, compliant, and conformist. An independent sense of self is not accomplished without severance of old interpersonal ties, without the establishment of internal, individual criteria for achievement, without a sense of identity that is relatively independent of other people. (1971:149)

A young female's dependence upon others is perhaps best illustrated in the dating relationship. The adolescent dating relationship, as analyzed by Douvan and Adelson, demands that a young woman develop and concentrate on the most external, superficial aspects of the self at a time when the inner demand for self-definition is considered equally pressing (1966). They described a "good female date" accordingly:

> [She] is cheerful, easy in conversation, a good listener, neither too aggressive nor too passive, and never grouchy, moody or too sexual. The dating personality is a codified system known to girls in early and middle adolescence by the teen columns and magazines. (P. 38)

Douvan and Adelson suggested that the sense of continuity that Erikson put at the center of the adolescent's identity task—that is, the connection between what one is and what one seems to be—is specifically obstructed by involvement in the dating ritual (1950).[2]

A 1978 survey by *Seventeen* magazine suggested that the qualities of a good date have not changed much over the past few decades. When asked what initially attracted them for a first date, nearly half the boys questioned mentioned the girl's figure and a third mentioned her face. *Seventeen* learned that in order for a girl to be asked out again she needed a good sense of humor. The major reason given for not calling a girl again was boredom or lack of attractiveness. When the boys were asked to name the most important quality a girl could have, personality and beauty came first and warmth was second. Opinions and ambitions trailed the list (Gaylin, 1978).

Beauty and personality have had universal appeal to men, and it should not be surprising that women are both fashion-conscious and quick to laugh at men's jokes and to show interest in and empathy toward their concerns (warmth). In the achievement literature this kind of socially oriented behavior is often attributed to dependency or affiliative needs deeply rooted in the self. However, the same skills and qualities in another theoretical framework might well be interpreted as valuable interpersonal techniques used by members of any social group who have low power and influence (Hochschild, 1975).

In general, since women have fewer sources of concrete power than do men in our society, they are often forced, as were the women in Aristophanes' *Lysistrata*, to use indirect sources of power. The giving and withholding of sex, for instance, has been a major resource for women and continues to be so even today (Johnson, 1976). The use of indirect or manipulative power, however, often serves to reinforce the user's powerless position. As Johnson explained, "Since the source of the power is concealed, use of indirect power could easily keep its user in a subordinate position" (p. 101). The use of direct power, on the other hand, could bring the epithet of "pushy, overbearing, unfeminine, and/or castrating" (Johnson, 1976:101). In 1973 Zellman and Connor suggested that women are viewed less favorably when they transmit information directly than when they use a soft voice, smile, and/or hesitate (Frieze, Johnson, Parsons, Ruble,

Zellman, 1978:316). Stein argued that women are explicitly trained to use such indirect power (1971). Her description of the "doctor-nurse game" is as entertaining as it is revealing. In order not to challenge the doctor's authority directly, the nurse is often forced to use an indirect, manipulative approach when she wishes to make a recommendation. Frieze and colleagues quoted from Stein's description of one doctor-nurse scenario:

> The medical resident on hospital call is awakened by telephone at 1:00 A.M. because a patient on a ward, not his own, has not been able to fall asleep. Dr. Jones answers the telephone and the dialogue goes like this:

> "This is Dr. Jones," (an open and direct communication)

> "Dr. Jones, this is Miss Smith on 2W. Mrs. Brown, who learned today of her father's death, is unable to fall asleep." (This message has two levels. Openly, it describes a set of circumstances, a woman who is unable to sleep and who that morning received word of her father's death. Less openly, but just as directly, it is a diagnostic and recommendation statement; i.e., Mrs. Brown is unable to sleep because of her grief and she should be given a sedative. Dr. Jones, accepting the diagnostic statement and replying to the recommendation statement, answers:)

> "What sleeping medication has been helpful to Mrs. Brown in the past?" Dr. Jones, not knowing the patient, is asking for a recommendation from the nurse, who does know the patient, about what sleeping medication should be prescribed. Note, however, his question does not appear to be asking her for a recommendation. (Miss Smith replies:)

> "Pentobarbital mg 100 was quite effective night before last." (A disguised recommendation statement. Dr. Jones replies with a note of authority in his voice:)

> "Pentobarbital mg 100 before bedtime as needed for sleep; got it?" (Miss Smith ends the conversation with the tone of grateful supplicant:)

> "Yes, I have, and thank you very much doctor." (1978:315)

Hochschild labeled the use of such tactics the "art of appeasement" (1975). Citing a 1971 study by Bugental, Love, and Gianetto, she noted that women are more likely to smile, even when angered or frustrated, than are men: "Those who experience themselves at the bottom of social hierarchies (women, for example) may be more concerned about looking, smiling, or talking right than are those at the top, whose presentation of self rests peacefully upon reputation and title" (p. 282).

As Frieze and colleagues observed, women generally are better at interpreting the nonverbal messages of others (1978). The same authors added: "Informal observations support the data that women are more responsive to cues than [are] men in social situations" (p. 334). Finally, the authors noted that these findings were similar to other studies that uncovered the greatest interpersonal sensitivity among those in low-status groups, whose

members needed to be aware of the feelings and attitudes of high-status individuals (Goffman, 1967).

Persons on the bottom of power hierarchies are more likely not only to
be sensitive to others' cues but also to feel their anger:

> Women, for example, receive not only their husband's frustration displaced
> from the office to home, but also the anger of other women who are similarly
> displaced upon. If a woman takes her anger down (to children) and occasional-
> ly across (to other women), she, by the same token, becomes the less powerful
> target of both men's and women's anger. The least powerful become the target
> of a wide variety of hostility. In a sense they become the complaint clerks of
> society and make a similar art of appeasement. (Hochschild, 1975:296)

What, then, of the adolescent female? Where does she direct her
anger? It may be safely directed toward people who can do little psychic
harm:

> Their aggression is largely directed toward people whose return anger will not
> be catastrophic to self-esteem—that is, other females. In their relationships
> with their fathers and later with their boyfriends or husbands, girls do not
> threaten the important and frequently precarious heterosexual sources of love.
> Instead, aggression is more safely directed toward other women with whom
> they covertly compete for love. (Bardwick & Douvan, 1972:55)

We can now place female dating behavior in a slightly different framework.
Rather than solely a reflection of a dependent, compliant, other-oriented
self, such behavior might be seen as a composite of interpersonal techniques
developed in response to a particular role situation. A central developmental task for young women is the conscious and comfortable exercise of
strategies and tactics for manipulating heterosexual relationships. At stake
is the control of an unequal bargaining situation. The balance of power has
always been unequal in the American dating situation. Even today, the male
occupies the public and legitimately sanctioned role of initiator. It might
therefore be important for a female to conceal or disguise her real motives,
especially in the dating situation, beneath socially approved or gender-
appropriate role behavior. The search for social approval or love and praise
may lead to the development of important forms of interpersonal influence
and sensitivities that have been both theoretically and empirically underestimated in the locus-of-control and self-esteem literature (Goslin, 1971).

We are offering a different interpretation of the style and complexity
of the learning that takes place during female adolescence. Practice in
gender-role bargaining and negotiation, say, in adolescent dating, may
enhance the growth of a strong and assertive ego. These skills potentially expand the resources a woman brings to her adult achievement roles. Learning
the distinction between social definitions and self-definitions may equip
females to size up the multiple dimensions of a situation better than do
males. Realistic assessments of her unequal influence need not mean that

the woman accepts such inequality as legitimate. Nor does it necessarily cause her to believe that she has no control over her destiny. Instead, she may be acquiring a sharper awareness of the techniques necessary (even if not immediately available) for playing certain roles.

Self-esteem and Fear of Failure

The data on the degree to which women's self-concepts may lead them to underestimate their own abilities and potential are rather weak; namely, there appears to be some slippage between the culture's assessment of the female role and the woman's own assessment of her personal worth as both are now measured by psychologists.[3] The critical question is how can women have a very high regard for themselves when, according to research, both sexes assign greater value to stereotypically masculine traits such as independence and assertiveness than to stereotypically feminine ones such as dependence and passivity? Empirical studies have shown that both sexes agree not only as to what traits define masculinity and femininity but also that feminine traits are less valued (Broverman, Broverman, Clarkson, Rosenkrantz & Vogel, 1970; Broverman, Vogel, Broverman, Clarkson & Rosenkrantz, 1972; Rosenkrantz, Vogel, Bee, Broverman & Broverman, 1968). Interestingly, however, three of the most comprehensive research reviews of the psychology of sex differences found little evidence that females score lower than males on general measures of self-esteem (Frieze, Johnson, Parsons, Ruble & Zellman, 1978; Maccoby & Jacklin, 1974; O'Leary, 1977). We repeat, women do not appear higher or lower in self-esteem than men. Although the explanations for this seeming contradiction between social and personal estimates of the self are many, we wish to focus on two.

First, there is no necessary correlation between acknowledging a social stereotype about one's sex and internalizing that stereotype as one's own personal belief (Brookover & Erikson, 1969). Researchers concerned with an accurate description of changing race and sex differences in self-esteem and self-concept currently are developing far more refined measures than were used in the 1960s and the early 1970s (Banks & Grambs, 1972; Safilios-Rothschild, 1979). Some studies on the black community help to make this point. For instance, McAdoo found that black children of both sexes were able to maintain a positive self-concept while acknowledging that in the culture at large theirs was not the more valued race (1974). Ladner noted that recognition of stereotypes does not necessarily affect personal belief or identification (1972). In her extensive study of the attitudes of lower-class, urban, adolescent black females, she found no evidence that her subjects had any desire to be white. Furthermore, these adolescents identified with the positive qualities of their own mothers (strength, resourcefulness, self-reliance). Ninety-four percent of the black women Myers interviewed reported identifying either with black women they knew or with black women in general (1975). Therefore, although we might expect black women to devalue themselves because they are both female and black, recent empirical evidence does not support this assumption. In addition, Wright found that whereas white women focus on heterosexual relationships and physical standards of beauty as the primary basis for their feelings of self-worth, black women stress independence and individual action (1975). Each set of criteria may well reflect the different realities white and black women experience. For example, working-class black women have had to assume major breadwinning responsibilities; independence and individual action are part of their reality.

The second point we wish to stress in explaining the apparent contradiction between social and personal estimates of the self has to do with the operationalization of academic constructs. Masculinity and femininity, for instance, are academic constructs based upon some untested assumptions about reality (Bem & Bem, 1970, 1972). Constantinople noted that a typical masculinity-femininity measure rests on "sex differences in item responses . . . a single bipolar dimension ranging from extreme masculinity at one end to extreme femininity at the other . . . unidimensional in nature and . . . adequately measured by a single score" (1976:28). Constantinople concluded that measures based on such assumptions are largely inadequate because masculinity and femininity are not necessarily mutually exclusive. By ridding ourselves of bipolar gender-role constructs, we can envision a female, for instance, who views herself as both concerned for others (a stereotypically female trait) and independent (a stereotypically male trait). In this light the self-concept, insofar as gender role plays a part, may not be harmed by a feminine role identification. As Stein and Bailey found: "Women who manifest achievement effort in areas that are usually considered masculine have relatively high masculine role identification, but not necessarily low identification with the feminine role" (1976:248).

However, although the sexes do not differ on general measures of self-esteem, data indicate that women appear less confident about themselves than do men on achievement-related issues. In their review, Frieze and colleagues concluded that women are more likely than men to evaluate their abilities, performances, and the likelihood of future success negatively (1978). We note, however, that these measures of self-concept have not always been carefully differentiated from the theoretically related concepts of fear of failure and fear of success.

Some of this confusion arose from Atkinson and Feather's 1966 research and from Atkinson's even earlier formulations about the motive to avoid failure (1957). In 1966, Atkinson and Feather wrote of two motives, hope of success and fear of failure, as important in determining the strength of the individual's achievement striving. Hope of success corresponded to the early formulations of the motive to achieve, as described in Atkinson's early work with McClelland (1953). Therefore, like the motive to achieve, the motive to avoid failure was formulated by males and about males in the expectancy-value tradition and posed many of the same theoretical and operational problems. Does behavior in achievement-related research represent a subject's responses to the motives under investigation or does it reflect gender-role strategies and/or stereotypes? The fear of failure was part of a model that presupposed that there is great shame in not attaining an achievement-oriented goal. This model assumed that concern over the negative consequences of failing leads to anxiety. Therefore, the motive to avoid failure was based not on the Thematic Apperception Test but on paper-and-pencil measures of test anxiety. The Mandler-Sarason Test Anxiety Questionnaire, a common measure, is an objective, self-report instrument that includes such items as "While taking an intelligence test, to what extent do you worry?" "Before taking a course examination, to what extent do you perspire?" Mandler and Sarason reasoned that individuals high in anxiety, as measured on this test, tend to make task-irrelevant responses, thereby avoiding the task at hand (1952).

The data generated up through the late 1960s did not clearly support the predicted relationships among fear of failure, anxiety, and achievement striving. Korman presented a table summarizing nine studies conducted by Atkinson and his colleagues and concluded that the various instruments used to measure need achievement and fear of failure did not show the intercorrelations to be expected if they were indeed measuring what they claimed to measure: "We frankly along . . . with others are puzzled. It seems clear that something is being studied that is of behavioral significance, but is it what Atkinson claims it to be?" (1974:199)

Weiner noted other inconsistencies in the work of Atkinson (1974). For instance, he cited findings that suggested that for highly anxious subjects performance decreases as a function of the degree of prior failure. Conversely, however, for subjects low in anxiety, performance increases as a function of the number of past failures. Weiner cited a personal communication to the effect that Atkinson's theory also failed to explain why individuals high in anxiety perform *better* than those low in anxiety on an easy task (1972:227).

In yet another critique, Maddi suggested that although most behaviorist models would expect highly anxious persons to be beset by self-doubt (low self-esteem) and therefore concerned with pleasing others and avoiding negative evaluations, such does not seem to be the case (1972). He reported that many anxiety questionnaires have been found to correlate *negatively* with measures of the tendency to respond to personality test items in a socially desirable direction (pleasing others). The interpretation of this particular finding holds implications for our review of sex differences: it is the person who is low in anxiety, not high, who appears to be especially concerned with pleasing others. Maddi speculated, "Perhaps a high score on anxiety scales reflects a willingness to be particularly frank and open, or a special sensitivity to one's own reactions. . . . If this were so, then the construct validity of anxiety scales would be seriously questioned" (p. 168).

To sum up, the links among anxiety, fear of failure, and achievement motivation are not simple. The research on sex differences among and between these variables serves only to increase rather than to reduce the theoretical and operational problems we have just recounted. Are girls more anxious and fearful about failure than are boys? In their review of the literature Stein and Bailey concluded that "females are more anxious about failure in academic situations than males and . . . their anxiety levels increase during the elementary years more than males. Females score higher than males on questionnaire measures of test anxiety" (1976:251). O'Leary, in her review of sex differences, reached the same conclusion (1977). Maccoby and Jacklin stated that teacher ratings and self-reports show young girls to be more timid and anxious (1974). However, the same authors also noted:

> Since boys are less willing to admit to fears or anxious feelings (have higher scores on lie and defensiveness scales), the sex differences on anxiety scales may be due to this factor. . . . Physiological measures of fear states have not so far clarified differences on psychological measures within and between the sexes. (P. 189)

In short, the findings are anything but clear-cut: are girls more fearful of failure or are they simply more willing than boys to admit such fears? As Maddi suggested, perhaps a high score on anxiety tests reflects "willingness to be . . . frank and open," an attitude not typically associated with males in our culture (1972).

Crandall, Katovsky and Crandall (1965) studied adolescents between the ages of eleven and seventeen. In their sample males tended to attribute their failure to external causes. Females of the same age were more likely to assume responsibility for their lack of success. This study was one of the first to suggest that females become more anxious and concerned about failure as they progress through school and more likely to blame themselves rather than others for failure. More recent achievement research has confirmed the same pattern, suggesting that males commonly attribute success to a stable internal factor (ability) and failure to an external unstable factor (e.g., bad luck), whereas females appear to be less likely to credit themselves if they succeed (Deaux & Emswiller 1974; Deaux, 1976; Frieze, 1975; O'Leary, 1977). These findings have been used as evidence that women are less likely than men to view themselves as skilled or competent, showing reluctance to accept personal responsiblity for achievements.

Do women actually feel less pride in their accomplishments or are they simply more modest than men? For instance, Bem and Bem contended that males are expected to show self-assurance while females are taught to present themselves in a self-effacing fashion (1970). Mead suggested that males may receive more thorough training in defending themselves against social humiliation because of their more publicly demanding gender role. In the public arena, males are socialized to compete to win and to rise to a challenge despite the consequences (1935). The greater public humiliation would be to withdraw and avoid the competition; defeat is far preferable to staying outside the game. The very act of assuming the role of competitor is thought to be intrinsically motivating; to reject this behavior is to violate a central aspect of the gender role. Once in the role, males appear to feel more comfortable in attributing responsibility for failure in performance to external causes. (For a nice overview of the explanations for such behavior, including biosocial ones, see Williams, 1977).

O'Leary summarized the explanations for failure-related anxieties and attributions of failure among females:

> To the extent that women internalize (incorporate into their self-image) the stereotypic assumptions that competence and stability are incompatible with femininity, their tendency to attribute the outcome of their performance to external and/or unstable causes may indeed reflect the belief that women are less able and more unpredictable than men. However, the demonstrated tendency of females to attribute their performance to unstable factors such as effort and luck may also represent a defensive strategy used to avoid being held personally responsible for success and/or failure. (1977:97)[4]

The criticisms are by now familiar. Are we measuring internalized traits, motives, and fears or are we measuring role-appropriate strategies and tactics? Furthermore, even if we were actually measuring greater fear of failure among girls than boys, the links to achievement striving in response to failure are not different for the two sexes:

> Thus, despite the fact that females are more anxious about failure and are less likely to select tasks that threaten failure when given a choice, they apparently can function at least as efficiently and with at least as much persistence as males when they must cope with failure. (Stein & Bailey, 1976:252)

As in our review of the connections between dependency and achievement, we have difficulty uncovering consistent sex differences in fear of failure, anxiety, and self-esteem. The narrow experimental definitions of these concepts reported in the expectancy-value achievement literature offered theoretically predictable results for a very small group of subjects. When data on females did not conform to those on white college males, the women, rather than the theory, were regarded as the source of error. Females were singled out as being different from males because they did not fit a model that was already proving inadequate for expanded samples of male subjects.

Late Adolescence: Female Achievement and Fear of Success

Related to the fear of failure and directly derived from the expectancy-value model of achievement is the fear of success or, more accurately, the motive to avoid success. Soon after Horner's research was summarized in a *Psychology Today* article in 1969, fear of success entered the public lexicon: national newspapers and magazines proclaimed the message that the reason for women's unequal status in work and education was that they could not deal with their anxieties about making it to the top:

> CAN YOU COPE WITH THE FEAR OF SUCCESS?
> The professional barriers are tumbling down. You have the opportunities you've never had before. Yet few women advance beyond the ranks of middle management. . . . Pyschologists say it's because of fear of success. (Walsh, 1977:8)

In psychological terms, the motive to avoid success was an "inhibitory tendency against achievement-directed behavior stemming from the negative consequences anticipated for success" (Tresemer, 1976:217).

Like the motive to approach success, the motive to avoid success was measured through projective techniques. In Horner's 1968 research undergraduates were asked to write stories in response to the following cue, the women writing about Anne and the men writing about John. The projective cue read: "After first-term finals, Anne/John finds herself/himself at the top of her/his medical-school class." Horner found that women more than men responded with anxiety and negative imagery to the cue. Bardwick cited an extreme but thematically typical anxiety response about Anne's success. "She starts proclaiming her surprise and joy. Her fellow classmates are so disgusted with her behavior that they jump on her in a body and beat her. She is maimed for life" (1971:182). In another part of her study Horner tested the arousal of the motive under competitive conditions, "women, especially those high in the motive to avoid success, will explore their intellectual potential to full measure only when they are in a noncompetitive setting and least of all when competing against men" (1978:65).

Horner pitted the motive to avoid success against the motive to approach success (to achieve). She anticipated negative consequences for women as a result of succeeding. The costs included feeling a loss of femininity and social rejection if they competed and won against males. Although the fear of success theoretically incorporated gender-role appropriate and inappropriate expectations, it also remained firmly in a tradition that emphasized "latent, stable personality dispositions acquired early in life" (Horner: 1968:67). Horner was explicit about the source and kind of anxiety women faced:

Our data argue that unfortunately femininity and competitive achievement continue in American society, even today, to be viewed as two desirable but mutually exclusive ends. As a result, *the recent emphasis on the new freedom for women* has not been effective in removing the *psychological barrier* in many otherwise achievement-motivated and able young women that prevents them from actively seeking success or making obvious their abilities and interests. (1975:217; emphasis added)

Bardwick, Horner's contemporary at the University of Michigan, affirmed much of Horner's argument:

While men may develop a motive to achieve that remains consistent over their life spans, women experience both a desire to achieve and an anxiety related to achievement, the desire and anxiety occurring in different amounts at different times during their lives. Although opportunity is there for the grasping, the outstandingly successful or relatively professionally committed woman is still an exception. (1971:167–168)

Assuredly, both Bardwick and Horner expanded in different ways the motivation theory concepts. Horner focused on gender-role expectancies and feelings, suggesting that "in order to feel or appear more feminine when faced with competition women disguise their ability" (1975b:217). In effect, we have an actively engaged actor capable of subterfuge if necessary.[5] Bardwick, while positing a stable motive, suggested that the intensity of the motive may vary over the life course (1971). But, several assumptions in the model remained unchallenged: the motive is acquired early in life and remains with the actor over the life course; and that the motive rather than the larger social, political, and economic structure accounts best for achievements throughout the life course. Thus, for all the refinements, the fear-of-success theory still located the problem within the woman.

The impact of these theories on female achievement was swiftly felt outside the academy. The popular implication was that women's lack of achievement could be interpreted as self-imposed. Even Bardwick noted that "opportunity is there for the grasping" and Horner cited "new freedoms" for women. In this sense the personal uneasiness of individuals was not linked to structural or public sources of such uneasiness, but to the self. In the following chapters we systematically explore the structural realities of the occupational and educational institutions confronting women, recognizing that motivational constructs can be understood only within a broad sociopolitical context.

Subsequent research has not confirmed some of the early formulations about the motive to avoid success (Hoffman, 1974b, c; Safilios-Rothschild, 1979). Two propositions critical to Horner's original formulation of the concept generally have not been clearly and repeatedly supported: that the motive to avoid success was inextricably tied to a woman's feelings of femininity, and that it was the motive to avoid success (a stable characteristic of the personality) that was being tapped in the fear-of-success research. Horner's original formulations were restated as late as 1978 when she wrote that the:

> Motive to avoid success is a stable characteristic of the personality acquired early in life in conjunction with sex role standards. It can be conceived as a disposition a) to feel uncomfortable when successful in competitive (aggressive) achievement situations because such behavior is inconsistent with one's femininity, an internal standard, and b) to expect or become concerned about negative consequences such as social rejection following success in such situations (Horner, 1978:49)

Combining the results of over 150 studies of the fear of success in order to assess the current state of knowledge about the topic, Tresemer concluded that ". . . the hypothesis that there is a gender difference in FOS is not supported" (1977:119). Puzzled, he wrote:

> The social psychological approach to Horner's work has construed FOS as a perception of what is and is not culturally appropriate gender-role behavior. Thus FOS responses to the "medical school" cue would be expected to be greater for females writing about Anne than for males writing about John. . . The lack of gender differences in FOS responses in studies using the "medical school" cue appears to suggest that FOS means something other than a response to gender-role inappropriate achievement. (P. 118)

Furthermore, Tresemer notes that the proportions of fear of success imagery elicited by men and women in response to verbal cues has seen an erratic and weak but slight decrease over the last decade (1977:172).

While major sex differences were not consistently supported over time, the motive to avoid success spurred some important questions which went beyond personality. For instance, while some psychologists and social psychologists had doubts about the kind of motive being tapped, others looked for environmental (macro) sources of success-avoidant behavior. This research has not determined whether fear of success represents a motive, a stereotype, an attitude, or a gender-scripted strategy. It does, however, emphasize how unclearly and ambiguously most measures of success-avoidant behavior or fear of success (as a personal motive) are.

As with achievement motivation, some of the first critiques focused on the cue itself. When the presumably negative impact or deviant aspect of the arousal cue was changed—Alper used nursing rather than medical school and Lockheed put Anne in a medical school class with an equal number of men and women—a decrease in FOS imagery among subjects was found (Alper, 1974; Lockheed, 1975). Lockheed interpreted the motive to avoid success as a normative response to social deviancy (1975). She used two cues: one made it clear that Anne's medical class was all-male; the other, that it was half female. There were no sex differences in FOS imagery to the latter cue.

When subjects responded to the former cue, a higher percentage of men than of women reported negative consequences for female success. Monahan, Kuhn, & Shaver (1974) suggested that the sex of the actor *in the cue* is important in understanding FOS imagery: both sexes in their sample gave negative responses to the female cue, thereby lending some force to the argument that respondents might be reflecting cultural stereotypes about appropriate gender-role behavior rather than a motive to avoid success (1974).

During the past few years of research the motive to avoid success has become increasingly suspect as a useful explanatory variable. Even if one concentrated only on motivational dynamics, it is hard to determine whether it is success that is being avoided. Note how similar are the methodological questions about the motive to achieve and the motive to avoid success.

Horner asserted that the motive to avoid success should be "conceived as a disposition . . . to feel uncomfortable when successful in competitive (aggressive) achievement situations" (1978:49). She originally found that high-FOS females did better working alone than with or against others. Did competition per se account for this finding or specifically competition against males? At issue for some researchers was the context within which competition took place. Was the presence of any male troublesome or did the men have to be significant in the lives of the females? Did the nature of the task (gender-appropriate or inappropriate) make a difference? In Horner's work were all high-FOS females equally affected or only those with a strongly (traditional) gender-role orientation? We shall see that although researchers set out to answer these questions, their conclusions more often raised new questions.

Groszko and Morgenstern found that although high-FOS women did more poorly (in terms of grades) in mixed competition in intimate classroom settings, this was not true in anonymous lecture halls (1972).

Directly questioning the fear-of-success motive as a causal explanation, Makosky concluded that the gender appropriateness of the situation was more important in understanding achievement-avoidant behavior than the motive to avoid success.

> Fear of success alone, as measured here, was not an accurate predictor of performance, as indicated by the fact that there was no significant main effect for fear of success imagery in the analysis of performance. All of these women performed competitively when the conditions were appropriate. In addition, there was no apparent relationship between motive to avoid success and reported attitudes toward striving, importance of personal excellence, or competition. (Makosky, 1976:246–247)

Makosky summarized her data by suggesting that women perform best on tasks and against competitors whom they perceive as compatible with their personal gender-role orientations.

Peplau suggested that high fear-of-success women could *not* be treated as a unitary group (see also Alper, 1974). Peplau argued that high-FOS women and low-FOS women could be subdivided into those who had a high or low traditionalism score on sex-role attitudes (as measured by a question-naire containing several measures of sex-role attitudes). Peplau reported that when working alone on an intellectual task, women who combined high FOS with a strong female role orientation (traditional attitudes) were the highest-scoring group; in contrast, when competing with their boyfriends on an intellectual task, these same women scored lowest of the groups (1976:257). Reviewing her empirical findings, she concluded: "Researchers interested in FOS may do well to assess sex-role attitudes as well as mo-tives" (1976:257).

Depner and O'Leary came to a similar conclusion when their data did not support Horner's original formulations (1976). In addition, these authors suggested that women's psychological barriers to entry into male-dominated occupational roles need not be limited "to the realms of achieve-ment motivation or motivation alone" (p. 267). They claimed that the issue of achievement among women is broader than the question of why women fail to strive for success: "Individuals often fail to aspire to roles which they view as attractive. There are probably many reasons for this, some of them motivational or otherwise intrapsychic, others better understood at a macro level" (p. 267). These researchers pointed to the wide range of variables that help determine achievement expectancies. Their thrust was clearly outward to a psychology that looks beyond the individual to experiences, situations, opportunities, and expectations—in short, a social psychology of motiva-tion.

In a revised and second edition of their 1974 book Atkinson and Raynor attempted to deal with many of the points we have raised. Introduc-ing the notion of cumulative achievement, for example, they cautioned:

> To predict cumulative achievement, we need to put all the pieces together: dif-ferences in *true* ability, differences in motivational dispositions (motives, knowledge, beliefs, conceptions), nature of the task, incentives, and op-portunities in the immediate environment. (1978:227–228)

In summarizing new directions for expectancy-value theory, Atkinson expressed the wish to investigate the "richness of the environment" more closely.

After several decades of research it appears that those most active in the psychology of achievement motivation are coming closer to social psy-chology.[6] In retrospect, the turn to social psychology seems a natural devel-opment. The causal link between motive and achievement behavior was problematic from the very beginning (McClelland, 1955; 1958b; 1961). The motive to avoid success, a theoretical construct introduced to explain gender-role related inhibitors to achievement, fared no better than the ap-proach motive in the early need-achievement models. Similarly, the fear motives (whether of success or of failure) were left ambiguously linked to achievement-avoidant behavior. In the fear-of-success research the gender-role stereotype of the cue and the gender-role orientation of the subject seemed to explain success-avoidant behavior (as measured in the experimental setting) better than did FOS. Finally, but not unexpectedly, women proved *not* to have a monopoly on the fear of success.

Expectancy: Social Structural and Personal Dimensions

Tangri cited Ginzburg, Ginsburg, Axelrod & Herman's (1951) early work in her critique of the achievement motivation literature and employed a straightforward sociological approach (1975). Borrowing from the poverty research literature, she asserted that expectancy is affected by membership in a group that is systematically denied success. Arguments in the poverty literature (such as the 1964 contention by Keller and Zavarolli that aspirational level will vary with perceived opportunities) were useful in the early feminist critiques of the achievement model. Tangri reflected, for instance, on occupational choice among members of the lower class and women: "The prospect of realizing a future goal is one of crucial importance in determining present action because only the exceptional person will continue to put forth a major effort in the face of a very small chance of accomplishment" (p. 241). Tangri concluded that two factors limit expectations, namely, an awareness of gender-role stereotypes and a realistic assessment of the reward structure.

Laws, reviewing the occupational aspirations, or "choice," literature, added yet another objection (1976). She suggested that male and female life experiences are different not only in the options and rewards available but in the timing of events as well. Early measures of occupational aspiration may predict well for men, who realistically expect fewer disruptions in their career paths, but are clearly dependent on life stage for females: "Work aspiration (or occupational choice or career commitment—rarely are these concepts distinguished) is usually treated as a discreet event, like the menarche, which occurs at some time in adolescence and never again" (Laws, 1976:34).

Perhaps the occupational choice research best illustrates how static the models of achievement really are. To measure choice as though attitudes at any one point in time can reliably predict future behavior is to neglect the series of events that might determine behavior and/or change attitudes. As Ireson noted in her review of the occupational choice literature:

> In a longitudinal study of teenagers and their parents from seventh through twelfth grades . . . when the daughters reach the ninth and tenth grades, many

parents begin to value the development of homemaking qualities and a domestic orientation in their daughters. By the late high school years, these parental values are reflected in their daughters' newly adopted occupational values: helping others and working with people. By the time these girls are seniors, their occupational aspirations are lower than boys' aspirations for the first time. (1978:185)

Realistic assessments of their occupational futures affect women's expectations. Ireson further observed that the higher a girl's class origins, the higher her school achievement and the higher the level of occupation she chooses. Realistically, a working-class girl has a narrower range of occupations to choose from than a middle-class girl: "As a result, more working-class girls want to be office workers, and fewer want to be teachers or professionals" (Ireson, 1978:183).

Marriage, family, and work are very much part of the demographic picture for a female. These options grow more obvious as she matures. For example, comparing the future plans of junior high, high school, and college women to their expectations at age twelve, studies have found a marked drop in popularity over time for both the most traditional life course plan (i.e., marriage only) and the most nontraditional (i.e., career only) (Rand & Miller, 1972):

> Longitudinal studies (e.g., Schwenn, 1970) confirm the interpretation that women actually lower their occupational aspiration as they proceed toward adulthood. Moreover, this drop is not a "realistic" adjustment of aspiration following failure: rather, a number of studies (Schwenn, 1970; Baird, 1973) show this behavior in women of outstanding academic performance. (Laws, 1978:295)

Contingency planning based on a realistic assessment of the future becomes clearer as one ages. As Ireson reported: "Of the 7,000 ninth-grade girls first studied by Astin in 1960, 16 percent planned to have careers in the natural sciences or the professions (excluding teaching); except for nursing, these are male-dominated fields. When these same girls were studied four years later, only 5 percent of them planned to have natural science or professional careers" (1978:182). Realistic adjustments are even more apparent in working-class girls, most of whom "see obstacles to the achievement of even their modest aspirations: only one-fourth expect to enter the occupation of their choice, while most of the rest expect to be housewives" (Ireson, 1978:183). Rubin contrasted the hopes of middle-class and blue-collar young women, suggesting that while they share similar childhood dreams of glamour occupations and Cinderella rescues, the working-class girl, with little expectation for high occupational attainment, pins her hopes on marriage. For most young working-class girls, getting married was—and probably still is—"the singularly acceptable way out of an oppressive family situation and into a respected social status—the only way to move from girl to woman" (Rubin, 1976:10). According to Rubin, even fantasies about marriage are tinged with reality for the working-class girl:

> Indeed, traditionally among girls of this class, being grown up *means* being married. Thus, despite the fact that the models of marriage they see before them don't look like their cherished myths, their alternatives often are so slim and so terrible—a job they hate, more years under the oppressive parental roof—that working-class girls tend to blind themselves to the realities and cling to the fantasies with extraordinary tenacity. For in those fantasies there remains some hope. (P. 41)

Realistic options, then, are a part of adolescent expectancies. These options differ not only by social class but by generation as well. Assessments of "personal costs," based on the "ends," or "goals," upon which expectancy and incentive estimates are being made, change across the life course. For instance, Monahan, Kuhn, and Shaver found that negative responses to female achievement seemed to decline with age (1974). They suggested that the older girls in their sample had grown up with the women's liberation movement and were aware of the social issues surrounding female achievement. Lockheed identified a similar process in comparing her female population to the generation of females in Horner's study (1975). Her subjects expressed little fear-of-success imagery. Tresemer, too, suggested that there might be generational differences reflecting the realities of the time:

> One interesting coincidence emerges: Just at the time the proportion of women dips . . . to start its steady increase in admissions to medical school, there is the sudden drop in FOS imagery. . . . This was the end of 1969 through 1970, significant years in anyone's memory. Perhaps the proportion of women entering medical school and the proportion of college women writing FOS to the 'medical school' cue were both subject to the same large-scale social changes. (1976:124)

We finally see a deflection from latent, stable, personality dispositions acquired early in life to a recognition of the way macro factors and economic changes may be reflected in women's achievement behavior, imagery, and aspirations. Condry and Dyer sum up their review of the fear of success literature this way: ". . . some of what has been called fear of success may simply reflect realistic expectancies about the negative consequences of deviancy from a set of cultural norms for sex-inappropriate behavior" (1976:72). Most importantly, the authors note that there is little support throughout the FOS literature for the notion that fear of success is common in women with high achievement motivation or capability or that the presence of the "fear" serves to dampen achievement strivings in women. Citing Zuckerman and Wheeler (1975) the authors note that "fear of success is not related in any consistent way to direct and indirect measures of achievement motivation" (1976:68–69).

Social Expectations and the Self: Attribution Theory

Attribution theory suggests that acceptance of personal responsibility is important for successful academic and problem-solving performance. Weiner argued that the causal attributions individuals make for success and failure in achievement-related situations influence the degree and quality of affect they experience and consequently their expectations for future achievements (1972; 1974). Four such attributions are usually cited: luck, task difficulty, ability, and effort. It is generally thought that the person who attributes success in a task to a stable internal factor, such as ability, is more likely to expect success of her/his own making than one who attributes success to an unstable factor, such as luck, and thus tends to approach new achievement situations with less confidence. The ties between self-esteem and control of outcome are most obvious in this theoretical model.

Although the research shows some inconsistencies, the consensus is that men generally attribute success to a stable internal factor and failure to an unstable external factor. Women "generally rely on external and/or unstable explanations for performance regardless of whether they succeed or fail" (O'Leary, 1977; see also Bar-Tal & Frieze, 1973; Feldman-Summers & Kiesler, 1974; Deaux & Emswiller, 1974; Frieze, 1975; Deaux, 1976). By and large, researchers' attempts to explain women's attributional patterns have returned to gender-related stereotypes. Bem suggested that women's tendencies not to attribute their success to stable internal causes may result in part from perceiving themselves through *others'* perceptions of them (1972). Thus, if it is widely believed that females are less predictable (stable) and less competent (able) than males, women's attributions of failure or of success may reflect these general societal expectations.

This view touched off a spate of research. O'Leary, in a fine and thorough review of this literature (1977), noted that Feldman-Summers and Kiesler failed in their 1974 study to find a single occupation in which women were expected to outperform males, even in elementary school teaching and nursing. Touhey argued that the anticipation of greater participation by women in high-status occupations has resulted in a decline in the prestige and desirability of these occupations by both males and females (1974a). The converse was found in previously female occupations, recently entered by males (Touhey, 1974b). Goldberg's research has long been taken as support that women show prejudice against other women in assessing females' intellectual and professional competence (1968). When Goldberg asked female college students to evaluate journal articles, the articles attributed to female authors received lower evaluation than the same articles attributed to male authors. In a later and similarly designed study, Pheterson, Kiesler, and Goldberg found that both men and women evaluated women's paint-

ings less favorably than the same paintings ascribed to male artists identified as entry-level contestants (1971). Only when subjects believed that the
paintings had been judged superior by a panel of experts did female and
male artists receive equally favorable evaluations from the subjects. Aspiring women were judged less favorably than those assumed to have achieved.
In this study the evaluation of women in achievement related situations by
both males and females seems to be equal to or better than the evaluation of
men *only* when the women's achievements presumably have received prior
approval. Attribution theory has stimulated new research on the role of bias
in evaluations of male and female ability (Deaux & Taynor, 1973).

As noted earlier, women's apparent reluctance to accept personal
responsibility for their success often has been attributed to the socialization
process. Such explanations are rooted in the gender-role literature, which
suggests that males are socialized to show self-assurance while females are
taught to present themselves in a self-effacing fashion either because of
modesty (Vaughter, Gubernick, Matassin & Haslett, 1974; Frieze, Johnson,
Parsons, Ruble & Zellman, 1978) or because of fear of being labeled con-
ceited (O'Leary, 1974). Those concerned with changing female achievement
patterns have suggested that the solution is to teach women to raise their
aspirations, to perceive themselves as more competent, and to stop
underestimating their own abilities. These recommendations were summarized by Parsons, Ruble, Hodges & Small:

> Divesting the female stereotype of its implied incompetence would reduce the
> likelihood of young girls' concluding that they must be incompetent solely by
> virtue of being female. However, the tendency to stereotype and to incorporate
> these stereotypes into one's self-image is very strong; therefore, it appears that
> initial changes in this area must occur at the family level. . . .

> Particularly, parents and teachers could encourage girls to attribute their suc-
> cesses internally and stably, i.e., to ability, rather than encouraging them to
> "modestly" deny responsibility for or underrate the magnitude of their suc-
> cesses. Likewise, they could encourage girls to attribute their failures to
> unstable yet controllable causes like lack of effort rather than to lack of ability
> or task difficulty. (1976:58–59)

While we note that attribution theory takes into account a feeling, conscious actor (one who makes attributions) as opposed to a passive subject,
this model still focuses on early childhood socialization and assumes a one-
to-one relationship between others' opinions and expectations and those of
the individual actor. For instance, we began our discussion of the attribution literature by citing findings that women appeared to take less personal
credit or responsibility for their achievements than men did. At issue are
several questions. Are women responding to attributions about gender role
acquired in early socialization or to present assessments? Are they feeling
the same way they are responding? To what are they responding—a cue, a

stereotype, an experimenter, an achievement-specific context? Are their responses merely socially approved tactics as opposed to real devaluation of self? How much carry-over exists between the experimental context and the objective reality women face? In addition, even if we were convinced that we had adequately and neutrally measured prevailing gender-role attributes, not social stereotypes, it is important to remember that our methods and samples still minimize variation, conflict, and ambiguity. What consensus we have achieved may be an outcome of having focused on a limited range of age, class, and ethnic groups (mostly white, middle-class, college students). Finally, besides the more general problems noted in summarizing the empirical literature on fear of failure, fear of success, and attribution, there is the problem that the referent in most studies is never made explicit. For instance, in the Goldberg study were women or their work being devalued? Do women merely say they have lower intellectual levels or do they believe it? What costs and what conditions do women take into consideration when they make their expectancy estimates? What place do perceived and real bargaining inequities have in estimating the costs of achievement?

In the next section we attempt to integrate the notion of interpersonal orientation (assumed to be the female adolescent's primary orientation) with the broader social science understanding of bargaining and negotiation. In this way, we can stress several interrelated theses of this book. Achievement motivation and behavior are better understood as processes than as internalized predispositions (expressed as either needs or personality). As processes they are not irrevocably located at some developmental stage but may vary over the life course. As processes they are subject to all the rules of social change, especially those related to power differentials.

Bargaining and Interpersonal Orientation

Earlier in this chapter we emphasized that adolescence is a time when females are gaining important sources of control through their interpersonal orientation. We argued that this learning might represent an achievement strength. The female's sensitivity to situations may be useful in accomplishing achievement goals. Dispositional expectancy is a term for the kind of expectancy in the expectancy model that calls for these types of subtle skills. Unfortunately dispositional expectancy has received the least attention by researchers. V.C. Crandall's seminal research on sex differences in each sex's expectations about intellectual and academic reinforcements led the way toward the reconceptualization of this variable in the expectancy-value equation. In a key review article she described dispositional expectancy as the ability to identify or evaluate the kinds of reinforcements available in a situation (Crandall, 1964; 1969; 1975; Crandall, Katovsky &

Crandall, 1965; Crandall & Battle, 1970). We include in our concept of expectancy the actor's ability to size up a situation. As noted earlier, females seem particularly competent at these estimating tasks. Unfortunately, however, the empirical links among dispositional expectancy, interpersonal competence and achievement are seldom explored together.

Weinstein described interpersonal competence as dependent upon three variables (1971). First, the individual must be able to take the role of the other accurately; s/he must be able correctly to predict the impact that various lines of action will have on the other's definition of the situation. Weinstein called this skill "empathy stripped of its affective overtones." Second, the individual must possess a large and varied repertoire of lines of action. Third, s/he must be capable of employing effective and appropriate tactics (p. 758).

The capacities underlying empathy are intelligence and cue sensitivity. The skills that Douvan and Adelson found necessary in the dating situation are similar to those necessary for empathy (1966). Projective and positional role taking is a prerequisite to interpersonal competence. Not only must one learn the tactics of bargaining and negotiation; one must also learn to identify and work within normatively given boundaries. Dispositional expectancy, which relates to the ability to identify and maneuver within socially prescribed boundaries, must play an important part in achievement. We would expect low-power groups to be especially familiar with this kind of expectancy. We would also expect them to be very good at social bargaining and negotiation.

Much of the work on children's achievement orientation has focused on concepts linked to personality, with limited analysis of social psychological factors (Goslin, 1971). In contrast, research on bargaining and negotiation has placed much greater emphasis on process rather than on the motivation of the actor.

After an extensive review of the research literature, Rubin and Brown posited the existence of a bargaining world "comprised of two fundamentally different types of people" (1975:158). The bargainer high in interpersonal orientation (IO) is first and foremost "responsive to the interpersonal aspects of his relationship with the other. He is both interested in, and reactive to, variations in the other's behavior" (p. 158). In contrast, the bargainer low in IO exhibits "nonresponsiveness to interpersonal aspects of his relationship with the other. His interest is neither in cooperating nor competing with the other, but rather in maximizing his own gain—pretty much regardless of how the other fares" (p.159). When changes occur in the bargaining situation, a low IO attributes variations in the other's behavior to situational factors rather than to the other's personality. As explained by Rubin and Brown, the low IO's behavior, regardless of the other's behavior or disposition, is designed to *achieve* as much tangible or intangible gain for the self as possible.[7]

Who is it who carefully studies every move of her/his competitor? Among persons high in need affiliation but low in authoritarianism and risk taking we find high interpersonal orientation. Blacks and women lead the list of groups in this category. Who can afford a calculated disdain for all sentiment but self-interest? Characteristically, people who are high in need achievement, authoritarianism, and risk taking. White males head this category. Even though we are describing behaviors in an experimental setting, the patterns resonate in the larger social structure. Power and social status are good indicators of the available bargaining techniques. Rubin and Brown suggested that out of necessity low-power or low-status individuals learn to pay close attention to interpersonal cues (1975). For them, sensitivity to interpersonal cues may be a way to shift the balance of power. Conversely, individuals in high-status positions may attempt to maintain or at least to justify their advantaged status by selectively tuning out interpersonal cues that might argue for changing the status quo.

Rubin and Brown's work reflects an old historical truth:

> To be charming was, in Roman eyes, an admission both of weakness and of ambition. *Unless a woman wanted something she ought not to have, she had no need of charm*; and if she stooped to its use, it must be because she had not the force of brains and character to reach her end by *more manly* means. Why did an honest woman wish to be attractive? (Putnam, 1970:65; emphasis added).

In this quote the Roman moralist glimpsed an important truth taught early to girls across the generations. A female is free to employ "manly means"—that is, to be direct and forthright in her achievement strivings— only when there is a socially approved goal and her motives are not suspect. She needs charm, artifice, and all the qualities that students of bargaining and negotiation link with an interpersonal orientation when she is attempting to achieve ends "she ought not to have" (or when she wishes to shift the balance of power). Early socialization involves learning not only what one should desire but also, perhaps, how to obtain things one should not desire. The publicly defined achievement script has been off limits to women; to date, the manly ways of competition are still not open to them. The positive aspects of women's achievement potential are now being explored (Howe, 1975; Deaux, 1976; Miller, 1976; Denmark, Tangri & McCandles, 1978).

Internalization: Academic Construct, Political Question

While fear-of-success and attribution studies did take into account early gender-role socialization, sexual scripts, expectancies, interpersonal dynamics, and achievement settings, the focus continued to be upon psychic costs and/or gender-role related problems, and conflicts. Too often, as we noted earlier, the documented awareness of cultural stereotypes and gender attributes was presumed to lead irrevocably to internalization, enactment in behavior, and foreclosure of alternatives. The obvious academic, if not political, question is have the characteristics of the situation been duly incorporated into the personality?

The transformation of the cultural image to suit the social reality of the individual often has been overlooked or taken for granted. The particular reality of black women is a case in point. Ladner quoted Grier and Cobbs's 1968 description of the self-image of the black adolescent female:

> Born thus, depreciated by her own kind, judged grotesque by her society, and valued only as a sexually convenient animal, the black girl has the disheartening prospect of a life in which the cards are stacked against her and the achievement of a healthy, matured womanhood seems a very long shot indeed. The miracle is that, in spite of such odds, the exceptional love of parents and the exceptional strength of many girls produce so many healthy, capable, black women. (1972:84–85)

Ladner challenged Grier and Cobbs's assumption that a black woman does not have standards of her own and experiences self-rejection when she finds herself unable to do more than imitate the standards of white society. She cited evidence that black children, compared to their white counterparts, may fare very well. For instance, in a sample from a study of black and white junior high school students in a rural Southern town, Gaughman and Dahlstrom reported a stronger tendency for black children to describe their home life as happier than average and themselves as very satisfied with the kinds of people they were (1968). Ladner quoted the authors' conclusions: "Clearly if the self-concepts of these children have been unduly damaged, this fact is not reflected in their interview statements about themselves, nor in the educational and vocational aspirations which they report for themselves (and which they seem optimistic about realizing)" (p. 83).

Cobb and Grier assumed a deterministic harmony between culture and personality (1968). Pettigrew's 1964 work, suggesting that the psychopathological personality is an adaptive response to a stressful role, took a similar position.

> Being a Negro in America is less of a racial identity than a necessity to adopt a subordinate social role. The effects of playing the "Negro" role are profound and lasting. Evaluating himself by the way others react to him, the Negro may grow into the servile role; in time, the person and the role become indistinguishable. The personality consequences of this situation can be devastating—confusion of self-identity, lowered self-esteem, perception of the world as a hostile place, and serious sex-role conflicts. (P. 25)

While these formulations sought to focus on the environmental sources of pathology and low self-esteem, it is clear that individuals' psyches are the focus of analysis. Ladner, for instance, would certainly not deny that racism has taken a heavy psychological and physical toll on black men and women, yet she suggested that the degree and permanence of the impairment have been exaggerated and rarely approximated in real life (1972:81).

In any case, the degree and permanence of the individual's gender-related conflicts, like those related to race, are at issue in the achievement literature. Work on female achievement has focused on women's inadequate socialization for achievement, conflict with feminine gender-related traits, decline in motivation during puberty, and low levels of aspiration—as if all have in fact been truly incorporated into the personality. Inherent in these analyses is the assumption that the condition, once defined, is stable.

Conclusion

Thus far we have paid most attention to the processes of acquiring and maintaining the achievement motive. Numerous reliability and validity problems have plagued psychological and social psychological efforts to explain achievement behavior. Attempts to distinguish motives, internal standards of femininity-masculinity, and evaluations of self from cultural prescriptions have not been successful. Even the focus on the individual's environment has been hindered by assumptions about the degree and permanence of gender-related motives and dispositions. Yet we need not posit a stable personality disposition or motive acquired early in life to explain consistent expressions of discomfort. If motives seem fixed, they may be fixed to the extent that the social structure limits the expression of alternative ones. External factors can maintain behavior as well as internal forces.

Psychologists first questioned whether females had the functional prerequisites for achievement behavior. Studies of sex differences in ability, intellect, and cognitive style predominated. Although girls appeared to be achieving behaviorally, certainly in early academic work, researchers were concerned about underlying motives. Unless girls had the proper orientation to achievement, they might not continue to strive later in life.

Interestingly, while expectancy and incentive, both situational variables, were clearly part of the expectancy-value formula, the motive for success, an internal focus, received the most attention in the early need-achievement literature. Thus, despite its lack of predictive value in general and its particularly poor explanatory power with regard to females, the motive to achieve received primary attention through a good portion of the 1960s. We suggest that this focus arose out of the tacit assumption that the motive was pervasive and enduring, leaving incentive and expectancy secondary in the analysis. Moreover, until the first generation of scholars interested in female achievement, few had questioned whether it was truly a motive that had been tapped as opposed to a gender-role-stereotype or a socially scripted defense mechanism to cope with achievement-related situations.

Fear-of-success and attribution research, although concentrating on gender-related expectations and others' expectations, likewise has limitations. Coming out of the expectancy-value tradition, for instance, the motive to avoid success focuses on the presumed relationship between the motive to achieve and achievement behavior (but inverts the relationship). Likewise, attribution theory looks primarily at individuals' subjective interpretations of the causes for success rather than the conditions that reinforce gender-related perceptions. Both theories rely on early gender-role socialization experiences and, even more heavily, on the internalization of a unitary and rather limited gender-role script. Inherent in these theories is the assumption that individuals have internalized gender-role characteristics of an enduring nature. We then have a peculiar state of affairs: an actor who for the most part is not actively negotiating a present but reflecting a history and/or projecting a seemingly well-defined future. Time and change are noticeably absent from these presentations. The actor and the role are seemingly indistinguishable. The circumstances one faces, the timing of an event in one's life, and the historic moment, which sanctions only certain strategies to accomplish culturally acceptable goals, are not given their due weight. Individual striving remains paramount.

In chapters 3 and 4 we look at individual striving by young women in the domestic and occupational spheres, tracing the powerful interplay between the self and the social forces that have shaped and reshaped women's objective realities and their subjective views of probabilities for success.

Notes

1. In "The Problem of Feminine Masochism" Horney was careful to differentiate between attributes associated with gender role and the likelihood that women actually incorporate these qualities in their personalities (1979). Horney also questioned the tenacity of childhood experiences. Freud linked female masochism to woman's sexuality and morality. Horney raised the question of cause and effect, asking whether masochism is a sexual phenomenon that extends into the moral sphere or a moral phenomenon extending into the sexual sphere (Horney 1950, 1973). In her description of the surface structure of the masochistic personality we find many of the key concepts that recur in theories attempting to explain the development of achievement motivation in women. "Being loved" is the particular means of reassurance used by a masochistic person. Because the masochist has free-floating anxiety, s/he has an excessive need for attention and affection. S/he is very emotional in relations with people, easily attached because s/he expects others to give her/him reassurance, and easily disappointed because s/he never gets and never can get what s/he expects. The masochistic

person also mistrusts any affection for s/he feels unworthy of love. By display-ing inferiority feelings s/he elicits pity and thereby wins affection. This explana-tion helps to explain why the female in this model of development is so poorly equipped to achieve if she subscribes to a masochistic gender role.

2. Douvan and Adelson saw the dating situation as particularly troublesome for girls because of their presumed strong need for love and affection (1966). Tresemer, in a reanalysis of some of the dating data, argued that these findings were questionable in themselves and that important social changes had occurred since 1975. He suggested that dating presents some of the same problems to males as to females and elicits similar behavior. Tresemer thought a focus on the dating situation itself would better explain behavior than could gender-role at-tributes per se.

3. Most of the research on the relationship between self-concept and achievement has been conducted in the field of education. Studies typically have found a stronger correlation between self-concept and academic achievement among males than among females. Standardized rating scales have uncovered few con-sistent differences between males and females on self-esteem. Maccoby and Jacklin, in their 1974 review of the literature, concluded that the similarity be-tween the sexes in self-esteem is remarkably uniform across age levels through college age. They did report some changes over the life course, which we discuss in later chapters.

4. Stein and Bailey also emphasized possible sex differences in dealing with stress and fear: "The same cultural norm that permits females to express anxiety more easily may also lead them to experience it more readily and to defend against it less effectively" (1976:251).

5. Komarovsky, many years earlier, introduced the theme of conflict between femininity and success (professional, educational) and suggested that women may be disguising their real abilities (1946, 1950).

6. Atkinson has always seen his work in the tradition of social psychology. We are stressing here, however, that the environment seems to be given a heavier focus in the second edition of his book (Atkinson & Raynor, 1978). Horner, too, is moving toward a social psychology (1978). In an addendum aimed at clarifying some of the theoretical and methodological confusion surrounding fear of suc-cess, Horner noted that any sex differences found or predicted should be con-sidered a function either of sociocultural conditioning or prior learning of specific situational or contextual factors (1978). She identified age, as well as ethnic and racial factors, as significant moderator variables. She also argued that the motive to avoid success should not be confused with a particular sex-role orientation.

7. In our description of the low IO individual, we are reminded of McClelland's entrepreneurial young man—high on the need to achieve and pursuing standards of excellence that he has set for himself.

CHAPTER 3

Adult Roles: Links between the Private Script and Public Achievements

Historical times and individual timing have presented difficult problems in understanding achievement. Achievement motivation research, theories of gender-role development, and theories of personality have explained adult female achievement in terms of a well-defined past and stable future. Examining self-concept and personality traits as if they were rooted in early developmental stages (through the combined processes of identification, internalization, and socialization), researchers have described females as lifelong achievement casualties. As the permanence of "gender-related" traits has come under increasing attack, however, achievement researchers have been forced to recognize individual and historical timing as critical variables (Atkinson & Raynor, 1974).

Integration of these insights into achievement models has been slow. For instance, in most models of achievement although the individual lives in the present, future goals are assumed to enter into her/his daily calculations. Concepts such as risk-taking and delay of gratification rely on the actor's perception that there is a larger and more desirable payoff at some later point. In the gender-role literature, temporal concepts are even more future oriented. As suggested in chapters 1 and 2, little girls and female adolescents are thought to be influenced in their daily routines by roles (equated with goals) that they may (or may not) assume years or decades later. Both achievement and gender-related research assume that personal goals, once established are fixed and that alternatives along the way are limited in number and appeal.

By moving outward in our analysis, we hope to place expectancy and value in a historical, cultural, and economic context. By examining the social context in which achievement-related scripts are learned, we shift the focus from gender related passivity, dependence, and fear to dynamic historical and economic forces that open and close achievement opportunities. As we turn attention to such macro issues as cultural dictates and economics, we stress that changes in these areas are as complex and variously determined as are the motives of individual actors in experimental research.

But just as we rejected the psychological definition of achievement as autonomous striving, so we resist a definition couched in purely socioeconomic terms. Our focus on historical timing, represented in the fluid nature of the domestic and work spheres, clarifies individual achievement as process. Variations in the public and private spheres of life, and in their interrelationships, bring different structural conditions, limitations, and demands to individuals. For females, public roles traditionally have been linked to private ones. If young females have succeeded in questioning their cultural scripts and in gaining new freedom in the public sphere, they have done so through the reinterpretation, renegotiation, and redefinition of the long-term bargains and contracts they have made in the private sphere of life. This is part of the achievement process.

In chapter 2 we noted the roles traditionally linked to the establishment of a woman's identity and thereby thought to affect achievement expectations: girlfriend, wife, and mother. These sources of self-worth are embedded in the so-called domestic, or private, script. The roles inherent in the domestic script are critical in understanding differences in the achievement process for males and females. However, these roles have varied historically. By examining the variations, we highlight yet another macro issue important in the achievement process—the power differentials between males and females.

The Domestic Script

In chapter 2 we reviewed contemporary theories of the origins of the need to achieve, noting the unexplained discrepancy between women's apparently strong academic capabilities and their "underachievement" in other contexts. Social psychologists have suggested that achievement might jeopardize feminine identity: the very qualities that prepare a girl for the roles of wife and mother serve her poorly in the public arena. Who can blame the girl for being true to her gender roles since her future life chances depend most heavily on those roles? If statistics are any indication, women are indeed true to their gender roles despite the rising rate of divorce, increased maternal employment, and fertility declines. Rather than a rejection of marriage and family life, such demographic changes seem to reflect fertility delays and later-age marriage. Delayed marriage has been an almost continual trend since 1957. Young women now postpone marriage longer than did their mothers in the late 1940s and 1950s. And while census data for the mid 1970s indicated that singleness among persons under thirty-five had increased, they also showed that singleness had *decreased* for those over thirty-five years of age since 1960: only 6.3 percent of males and 5.2 percent of females aged thirty-five or over were never married (Scanzoni & Scanzoni, 1976:153). Other indicators suggest that most young people plan to marry. For instance, in 1974 the Institute of Life Insurance conducted a national survey of young people between fourteen and twenty-five years of age. Asked what lifestyles they thought most appealing, only 17 percent of the young women said they thought being single was the most desirable alternative. More recently the University of Michigan's Survey Research Center reported that 75 percent of 2,500 male and female high school seniors sampled planned to marry and thought it likely that they would have children (Herzog, Bachman & Johnson, 1979a, b).

Increases in the rate of divorce (from 2.5 per thousand in 1966 to 5.1 per thousand in 1977) ought not to deflect from the fact that remarriage rates are also on the increase. In fact, we might argue that the average couple is experiencing more of marriage at the end of this century than at the beginning. In 1910 marriages lasted, on average, for only twenty-eight years. With increased longevity, a typical married couple in the 1970s spends over twelve more years together than did the average couple around 1910 (Melville, 1980:439).

Similarly, although recent statistics indicate a sharp drop in the overall fertility rate, we get a different perspective on childbearing if we take a historic view. The incidence of childlessness among women in their early thirties is not higher than it was a few decades ago. Indeed, among women thirty-five and over the incidence of childlessness has declined since 1960. Glick noted that in the mid-seventies the percentage of child-free couples in the United States was less than a quarter of what it had been in the 1920s (1977a). Glick reported that even among women from whom we would expect the lowest birth rates (more education, later age of marriage, and employed), the average number of children was 2.0 for black women and 2.5 for white women (Scanzoni & Scanzoni, 1976). Motherhood is clearly a planned part of the future for most women. In fact, during the past few decades more women have been raising families than at any other period during this century.

To repeat, birth rate data indicate that the vast majority of women today have at least two children and that childlessness is on the decline. Table 3-1 shows the proportion in four birth cohorts, women who had become mothers by each birthday from fifteen through twenty-five. The cohorts were selected to represent four distinct reproductive patterns in twentieth century American fertility: pre-Depression, Depression, post–World War II, and post-Vietnam.

The span of time spent in childbearing has remained essentially the same throughout the century, ending for most women at about the age of thirty-five. While demographers assume that all women aged fifteen to forty-four are potentially pregnant, "ninety-five percent of all small families are completed before a woman reaches the age of thirty-five and about 90 percent of all large families (five or more) are also completed by this time" (Stellman, 1977:25). Stellman concluded that most women have had several decades of productive economic life available to them *throughout* the century (p. 5).

Table 3–1.   Proportion (per thousand) with at least one live birth, by age, for four selected female birth cohorts.

By exact age	Cohort 1902	Cohort 1917	Cohort 1932	Cohort 1947
15	003	003	003	004
16	010	010	014	015
17	031	028	045	042
18	067	066	103	091
19	143	125	184	163
20	242	192	292	258
21	232	260	396	348
22	396	327	494	431
23	466	386	583	513
24	526	443	660	580
25	576	499	721	630

Source: J. Coleman (ed.), *Youth: Transition to Adulthood* (Washington, D.C.: Government Printing Office, 1973), p. 62.

Therefore, perhaps changes in gender-role conformity over the century have not been reflected as much in the private arena (marriage and maternity) as in the steady increase of gainfully employed women (22 percent in 1948 versus almost 50 percent in 1979). The most dramatic changes have been among women with small children: the percentage of women with children under the age of five who work has tripled since 1948. Not only do young women plan to marry and bear children, but they also plan to work. (We explore the kinds of work women do and the rewards they receive for their public achievements in chapter 4.)

The Parameters of the Private Sphere

In the United States we live in a market economy. Our society's most valued achievements are measured in terms of market accomplishments.

Economic activities carried on outside the marketplace are not calculated in our national income estimates. The gross national product, for instance, does not include women's work either at home or in the community. Unpaid labor carried on in the domestic sphere (private arena) is, productively speaking and depending upon your analytic frame of reference, either "valueless" or "invaluable."

Admittedly, assigning dollar values to achievements within the private sphere is no easy task. Though both the public role of physician and the private role of mother require "stong motivation, a desire to achieve good results, and a disciplined, persistent application of skills and evaluative judgment" (Rossi, 1973:12), the standards of performance are far more clearly defined in the former case. Tangible and immediate results, along with financial and status rewards, usually attend the doctor's efforts. Success as a mother is not measured or rewarded in a straightforward fashion. Rich's recounting of her maternal experiences recalls many a mother's self-doubt: "Soon I would begin to understand the full weight and burden of maternal guilt, that daily, nightly, hourly, am I doing what is right? Am I doing enough? Am I doing too much?" (1976:223). As Coser and Rokoff suggested, the family is a "greedy institution," wherein one can never be too loving, too nurturing, or too expressive (1971). In housewifery, like motherhood, there are no specific standards or even social control mechanisms available to help define excellence:

> The physical isolation of housework, each housewife in her own home, ensures that it is totally self-defined. . . . Housewives belong to no trade unions; they have no professional associations to define criteria of performance, establish standards of excellence and develop sanctions for those whose performance is inadequate or inefficient in some way. No single organization exists to defend their interests and represent them on issues and in areas which affect the performance of their role. (Oakley, 1976:8)

Oakley added that the housewife role is so variable and personal that it "might well seem to contravene accepted definitions of what a 'role' is" (p. 8). As we see later in this chapter, the early home economists understood that "scientific" standards in the domestic sphere would be necessary if women were to receive personal and public payoffs for their private investments and achievements.

The increasing isolation of women in the suburbs reinforces the loss of standards, often making mothering and housewifery lonely occupations (Rich, 1976). Physically isolated from one another, suburban women lack the opportunity to form standards of excellence and perhaps to gain some unified control over their private lives (mechanisms available in the public sector). For the heroic entrepreneur of chapters 1 and 2, loneliness is self-imposed within well-defined arenas. The loneliness of the mother and housewife is structurally imposed.

How, then, are we to assess women's adult achievements? The measures and motives of achievement-oriented individuals have been geared to male roles in the public domain. No wonder that the best behavioral measure of the need to achieve has been energetic entrepreneurship. From the earliest formulations, the achievement oriented and motivated person stands in sharp contrast to the mother within the nuclear family:

> Institutional motherhood demands of women maternal "instinct" rather than intelligence, selflessness rather than self-realization, relation to others rather than the creation of self.(Rich, 1976:42)

Note that Rich was referring to *institutional* motherhood, that is, the patterns of behavior and feelings expected of mothers within the specific context of the modern, isolated, nuclear family. The heart of the problem is not with the self (individual mother) or with the function (mothering) but rather with the social structure (organization, dynamics and evaluation) of the family.

But the modern nuclear family had its origins in social processes begun well over a century ago, processes associated with the separation of the home from the place of work. Radical feminists at the end of last century understood that the separation (isolation) of the domestic sphere from the productive economy would render those relegated to that sphere not only isolated, submissive, and powerless but perhaps even a bit insane (Hill, 1979). Early in this century radical feminist Charlotte Perkins Gilman wrote prophetically of the isolated family in its isolated home and of motherhood within such a context (Gilman, 1910,1913).

Bell, reviewing some of Gilman's work, noted that the hallucinatory protagonist of Gilman's "Yellow Wallpaper" was Gilman herself (1980). Like the wife in her short story, Gilman suffered severe depression after the birth of her child. The advice Gilman received at that time from the leading nerve specialist for women, as Bell observed, was "unforgettable":

> Live as domestic a life as possible. Have your child with you all the time. Lie down an hour after each meal. Have but two hours intellectual life a day. And never touch pen, brush or pencil as long as you live. (p. 10)

The treatment reflected the very conditions of domesticity that had provoked the depression—"isolation, inactivity, submission of will, surrender of all desire and creative impulse" (Bell, 1980:10). However, unlike the protagonist in her story, who retreated to the domestic sphere and indeed went insane, Gilman took a trip to California (away from husband and child), began to write, and "recovered her cheer and self-confidence" (Bell, 1980:10):

> She broke then and forever with the conventional nuclear family. [For Gilman] female disadvantage had an evolutionary basis. It originated when man

monopolized social activity, thrust woman from her proper postion, and confined her to the functions of motherhood and household care. (Bell, 1980:13)

Historically speaking, woman's confinement to motherhood and household care is a fairly late phenomenon. The ordering of adult roles and the value of female labor have varied over time, and within the life course, with changing economic conditions. The separation of familial and work roles into private and public spheres is relatively recent (Brownlee & Brownlee, 1976). In the next section we examine the social processes that led to the emergence of the family as a private and isolated arena.

The Emergence of the Domestic Script

Achievement models generally imply that the gender-related traits associated with a female's socialization to the domestic script limit the extent to which she will be committed to and actively engaged in the public world of economic production (wherein we currently measure our valued achievements). But while these intrapsychic factors are assuredly intertwined with female achievement behavior, they leave us with a very narrow understanding of the social realities underlying the domestic role script. Economic decisions by both males and females have been made within the boundaries of their socially defined responsiblilities in relation to families. Such responsibilities have varied historically.

Family life has changed dramatically over the past few centuries:

> Historically, women have borne and raised children while doing their share of necessary productive labor, as a matter of course. . . . From the earliest settled life until the growth of factories as centers of production, the home was not a refuge, a place for leisure and retreat from the cruelty of the "outside world": it was a part of the world, a center of work, a subsistence unit.(Rich, 1976:44)[1]

Before family and economic life were clearly differentiated, women took an active role in the economic life of the community. During the seventeenth century,

> when spinning and weaving were household industries done primarily by women and children, each household provided its own raw materials and produced cloth chiefly to meet its own needs. But it was not uncommon for women to market part of their output, selling directly to their customers or to shopkeepers for credit against their accounts. With the expansion of the industry in the latter half of the eighteenth century, it became more common for women to be employed by merchants to spin yarn in their own homes under a commission system. The merchants would either sell the yarn or commission other women to weave it into cloth. (Blau, 1978:31)

Blau also noted that the "puritanical abhorrence of idleness" and the continual labor shortages of a frontier society opened up a wide range of business activities to women. They could be found working as tavern keepers, store managers, traders, speculators in commodities, printers, and publishers, as well as in the more traditional women's occupations of domestic servant, seamstress, and tailor. (p. 30)

In fact, in the preindustrial economy of the American colonial period "the lines around men's work and women's work were flexible" (Gordon & Buhle, 1976:280). According to Gordon and Buhle, "neither men nor women seemed concerned with defining what women were or what their unique contribution to society should be" (p.280).

Changes in the economic mode of production (industrial capitalism) produced changes not only in family-labor relations but also in the social value of women and children's economic contributions. Gordon and Buhle summarized the economic transformation:

As products previously produced at home came to be accessible in the common market, the prestige of women's labor inevitably declined. . . . Moreover, the increasing expression of products as commodities, defined not primarily by their use-value but rather by their exchange value upon the market, dichotomized those produced under market conditions by socially organized labor (i.e., almost entirely by men) and those produced privately for direct use (i.e., substantially by women and children) in the home. . . . To replace the spontaneous and relatively egalitarian division of labor in preindustrial society had come a mode of organization which far more than before thrust women into the role of caring for the home, while men engaged in activities to reshape the world. (1976:283)

Summarizing the general impact of modernization and industrialization upon women, Oakley noted:

With the coming of industrialization, the roles of married and unmarried women have been reversed. In the seventeenth century, domestic work proper—cooking, cleaning, mending and child care—would have been performed by the unmarried girl (and boy) under the supervision of the married woman, who herself worked in the family industry. Under modern conditions, it is the married woman who does the domestic work, while the unmarried female is employed in productive work outside the home. (1976:26)[2]

Therefore, Gordon and Buhle argued, "As the American economy capitalized its productivity, and as individual wage earners replaced families as the basic production units, women found themselves excluded from their earlier work experience" (1976:285). DuBois summarized this historical transition and its implications:

Adult women remained almost entirely within the private sphere, defined politically, economically and socially by their familial roles. Thus, the public sphere became man's arena; the private, woman's. This gave the public/private distinction a clearly sexual character. (1975:64)[3]

In the next section we see that the proper relationship between the public and private spheres of life and the consequences of change in either arena for women's achievements have long been feminist concerns. Heroic attempts by individuals and reform movements to gain access to and/or to bridge the gap between these spheres offer an important lesson in the achievement process. At issue, of course, is the power to control the boundaries and define the context of one's achievements. Without this power one cannot translate opportunity into advantage or effort into valued achievement.

Many of the issues raised by the pioneers in the suffrage, birth control, temperance, and home economics movements, for instance, have only recently resurfaced in political and academic debates about women's achievements (Carden, 1974; Deckard, 1975; Gould & Wartofsky, 1976; Jaquette, 1974; Martin, 1972). We include some of these early debates and others not only because they represent female achievements often lost or buried in history but also because they give us a historic case in point of women actively negotiating for control over the value of their labors, domestic and other. In both its intellectual and political analysis, the feminist consciousness has been sensitive to the complex relationships between the public and the private spheres,[4] resisting easy formulations about the impact of one upon the other. The issues raised well over a century ago persist as we assess the domestic barriers to women's achievements at various stages of adult life.

Strategies of Domestic Reform

Suffragists

The early suffragists did not directly challenge the feminine character of the private sphere; however, they did reject prohibitions on women's engagement in public, nonfamilial roles. Their demand for suffrage challenged the male monopoly on citizenship. The suffragist press for enfranchisement was radical in its insistence that women participate in society directly, as individuals, rather than through familial roles. Elizabeth Cady Stanton advocated this individualized identity for women: "Womanhood is the great fact in her life," she reminded her audiences . . . "wifehood and motherhood are but incidental relations" (DuBois, 1975:66).

The suffragists hoped the vote would bring women greater control over their lives in both the public and the private sphere. These nineteenth-century reformers used bargaining strategies that played upon the feminine character of the private sphere. It was common for them to use woman's "presumed special motherly nature" and "sexual purity" as arguments for increasing female freedom and status (Gordon, 1977:100). Elshtain summarized the strategy:

> Rather than rejecting the conceptual system from which these dichotomies were a predictable outgrowth, the Suffragists simply turned anti-Suffrage arguments upside down to serve as the basis for a pro-Suffrage plea. Yes, man was evil and bad and he had made something nasty out of politics. True, woman was purer and virtuous—look at the way she had ennobled the private sphere. What must be done, therefore, is to throw the mantle of private morality over the public sphere by drawing women into it. Women would be politicized and politics would be transformed in one fell swoop. (1974:463).

In effect, suffragists accepted and thereby, argued Elshtain, reinforced the assumptions underlying their powerlessness: "The majority of Suffragists did not "break the silence" by speaking with their real voices. Instead they made. . . a virtue out of historic necessity by celebrating the inequalities which arose from their oppression" (Elshtain, 1974:468).

Historically, women's achievements in both the public and the private sphere have been evaluated on scales of judgment not of their own making. In demanding revisions in these evaluations, reform groups have had to be cautious in their frame of reference. For instance, some scholars have argued that the suffragist "superior virtue" arguments were essentially a matter of expedience (Kraditor, 1974).

Although Elshtain blamed the suffragists for not rejecting the structural dichotomy, DuBois claimed that their demands for suffrage did challenge the sexual dichotomy between spheres:

> By demanding a permanent, public role for all women, suffragists began to demolish the absolute, sexually defined barrier marking the public world of men off from the private world of women. Even though they did not develop a critical analysis of domestic life, the dialectical relationship between public and private spheres transformed their demand for admission to the public sphere into a basic challenge to the entire sexual structure. (1975:65–66)

In lieu of seeking alternative vocations and sources of social value these women's rights advocates wished through political power to strengthen women's positions within marriage and the family.

Female economic dependence upon men (fathers or husbands) was a social necessity for most women; therefore,

> rejection of motherhood as the primary vocation and measure of social worth required the existence of alternative vocations and sources of worthiness. The women's rights advocates of the 1870's and 1880's were fighting for those other opportunities, but a significant change had come only to a few privileged women, and most women faced essentially the same options that existed fifty years earlier. (Gordon, 1977:115)

Accordingly, the early suffragists were duly concerned about a woman's control over her own body. Most especially they were concerned with women's legal rights within marriage. Paulina Wright Davis, at the National Woman Suffrage Association in 1871, attacked the law "which makes obligatory the rendering of marital rights and compulsory maternity'' (Gordon, 1977:104). Stanton staunchly argued that ''a woman owns her own body'' (Gordon, 1977:104). ''In their complaints against the unequal marriage laws, chief or at least loudest among them,'' Gordon noted, ''was the charge that they (laws) legalized rape'' (p. 104).

Interestingly, the issue for these early feminists was not birth control but a woman's right to refuse. The fundamental condition of birth control was the woman's right to establish the boundaries of her own decision making. Self-sovereignty was the key concern.[5] The social meaning of reproduction was foremost in the minds of these early women's rights advocates. For instance, their hostility to birth control devices despite their strong support for voluntary motherhood need not be seen as a contradiction (any more than their refusal to challenge directly the superiority of the public sphere). Gordon persuasively argued that the basis for their hostility toward artificial contraception lay

> in their awareness that a consequence of effective contraception would be the separation of sexuality from reproduction. A state of things that permitted sexual intercourse to take place normally, even frequently, without the risk of pregnancy, inevitably seemed to nineteenth-century middle-class women to be an attack on the family. . . . It did not seem, even to the most sexually liberal, that contraception could be legitimized to any extent, even for the purposes of family planning for married couples, without licensing extramarital sex. The fact that contraception was not morally acceptable to respectable women was, from a woman's point of view, a guarantee that such women would not be a threat to her own marriage. (1977:109–110)

Given woman's economic dependence upon marriage and family, traditional taboos against extramarital sexuality seemed to be in most women's best interests.

The suffragists' strategy turned on the enforcement of social norms. Rather than challenge cultural assumptions about the natural division of labor, they asked for legal control to reinforce existing rules. The strategy was also effectively used by groups like the Women's Christian Temperance Union.

Women's Christian Temperance Union

In promulgating the slogan that ''lips that have touched liquor shall never touch mine,'' the WCTU was training young women in sexual bargaining. If a young woman could make sobriety a prerequisite for marriage, she could then expect, in exchange, a middle-class lifestyle. Morality could not be assumed to be innate, natural, or well internalized; rather, it had to be carefully cultivated. Temperance was viewed as a means for acquiring economic and social rewards. Abstinence from drinking was held out as the solution to poverty.

The WCTU was promoting a moral world view that emphasized woman's power to control the public sphere through manipulation of her private roles (Gusfield, 1955). If she were limited to domestic roles, she should have control over her family investments. The WCTU formally endorsed the demand for female enfranchisement on the grounds that the role was necessary to protect the home and the woman within it from the influence of the saloon. As wives and mothers, women needed the power to control their husbands' worth—their prime investment (DuBois, 1975:69). Their motto reflected their goal: "Home Protection."[6]

Movements like the WCTU helped to build the base for the twentieth-century women's movement by familiarizing countless numbers of working-class women with a moral world view and thereby putting them in a better position to demand recompense for private violations. Social reform movements like the WCTU provided public information about the many ways in which women's expectations were violated. In this way private indignation could then be translated into a public issue.

Professional Domesticity

Yet another strategy for reform was offered by the founders of the American Home Economics Association. Unlike the social purity movement, this group openly questioned the "privatization" of the domestic sphere. Moreover, they did not believe that morality was the peculiar domain of women; rather, they saw the potential for transforming the life styles of both men and women, in both the public and the private sector, through education of the female (Bevier, 1911, 1918; Hunt, 1942; Richards, 1910). As reformers they appealed to the "scientific" rather than the "spiritual" modes of change:

> Specialization is necessary to develop skill. The domestic worker, wife, or servant is eternally unspecialized. . . . the specialization of those industries now lumped together as "domestic" will no more injure "the privacy of the home," the "sanctity of the "family," than has the specialization of the spinning wheel. . . .

> The professionalization of cooking, cleaning and laundry work should be hailed not only by the economist but by the hygienist, the eugenist, and the social psychologist as a long upward step in world progress. (Gilman, 1913:91–95)

In the early part of this century founders of the home economics movement, while differing considerably in their relationship to the feminist movement at the turn of the century, were united in the belief that women's labor in the home played a critical role in an industrializing economy. With this interpretation in mind, leaders like Ellen Swallow Richards, Emma

Willard, and Catherine Beecher insisted that scientific principles could be applied and refined through systematic study of labor in the domestic sphere. Thus, the early founders were stressing a scientific ideology that expanded the definiton of women's roles.

In her review of the family as a public and private institution, Laslett argued that the unintended impact of the home economics movement was further to segregate the private and public spheres (1973). Yet Richards, the founder of the movement, had intended by focusing on the domestic sphere not to reinforce sexual separatism but rather to emphasize that the domestic sphere was becoming increasingly drained of its intrinsic value for individual women as well as for the public sector:

> You cannot make women contented with cooking and cleaning and you need not try. The care of children occupies only five or ten years of the seventy. What are women to do with the rest? All of the movement for industrial education is doomed to fail unless you take account of the girls. You cannot put them where their great-grandmothers were, while you take to yourselves the spinning, the weaving, and the soap making. The time was when there was always something to do in the home. Now there is only something to be done.

> We are not quite idiots, although we have been dumb, because you did not understand our language. We demand a hearing and the help of wise leaders to reorder our lives to the advantage of the country. (Hunt, 1942: p. 91)

Richards urged that women retain control over their own labor through expert knowledge. By bringing science to bear on their efforts, women could, she felt, increase the value of their private investments.

The mental health of mature women also concerned Richards. She feared that alienation from work and social isolation were harming their spirits. She advocated "self-refreshment through knowledge" (Hunt, 1942: 91), specifically through home study courses:

> There are women in middle life, whose days are crowded with practical duties, physical strain, and moral responsibility, who need this last injunction; for they fail to see that some use of the mind, in solid reading or in study, would refresh them by its contrast with working cares, and would prepare interest and pleasure for their later years. Such women often sink into depression, as their cares fall away from them, and many even become insane. They are mentally starved to death. (Hunt, 1942:89)

Later in the century, Betty Friedan claimed that middle-class wives often suffer from the "problem with no name": frustration caused by their inability to use their talents and skills in a meaningful way (1963). A decade later, Yankelovich reported, "There are signs of frustration in the self-evaluation of young homemakers—centering chiefly on the feeling that they are somewhat inferior and that they are not getting the most out of life" (1974:155). The mental health data suggest that married women may be more vulnerable to mental illness than unmarried women and married men

(Bart, 1972; Bernard, 1973a; Gove & Tudor, 1973; Weissman, 1973, 1974). As late as 1977, Donley and Condry noted that women in their study (all between the ages' of thirty and forty) found homemaking "at best tolerable and at worst 'boring' and 'stagnating.' . . . The strongest need expressed was that of having 'a life of (one's) own outside the home' " (p. 3).

Bart's study of depressed menopausal women documented the bad bargain nineteenth-century home economists attributed to women's gender-role investments (1972). From the hospital records of 533 women between the ages of forty and fifty-nine who had had no previous hospitalization for mental illness, Bart concluded that role loss, including impending role loss, was associated with depression. Housewives were particularly vulnerable to depression in the menopausal years. The highest rates of depression were reported among housewives who had been intensely involved with their children. Bart suggested that lack of meaningful roles and the consequent loss of self-esteem, more than hormonal changes, seemed to account for their menopausal depression. She wrote: "...my data show that it is the women who assume the traditional feminine role—who are housewives, who stay married to their husbands, who are not overly aggressive, in short who 'buy' the traditional norms—who respond with depression when their children leave" (1972:184). She added that many women in her sample also felt their life situation to be unjust and meaningless because the implicit bargain they thought they had struck with fate did not pay off.

The early home economics leaders wished to upgrade the domestic sphere. They felt that the domestic field was worthy of study by both men and women and that the same academic standards used for the sciences should be applied to this area. In this way the social worth of the domestic sphere could be publicly valued.[7]

The Elusive Link between Cultural Constructs and Self-concept

Gordon and Buhle observed that women's loss of public value was directly linked to the rise of industrial capitalism (1976). According to these authors, cultural definitions of female worth and women's self-concepts were expressed in the "cult of the lady":

Not until the late eighteenth century did the lady become the *paragon* for *all* American women. . . . As late as 1890, nearly half of all American women lived and worked in (the) immediate social environment of a farm family, providing many necessities for the farm through daily hard work. Yet the farm wife lost her cultural standing to a new sector of women: the wives and daughters of the rising enterpreneurs and merchant capitalists of the urban Northeast. This new sector remained a numerical minority, while its ethos became *central* to American Woman's *self-definition*. Because of their class position, these women gained an hegemony over female cultural patterns never attained by the eighteenth-century elites. Taste, customs, religious and political principles, and above all, morality were reshaped in the nineteenth century through the cultural equivalent of the economic power that capitalists themselves wielded. Thus for all women in the society this *new ideal of femininity became the model*, however unrealizable in their own lives. (p. 284; emphasis added)

While Gordon and Buhle's link between the economy and the cultural definition of the lady was perceptive, we caution against the conclusion that this new ethos was central in American women's identity or self-definition. And although we have stressed that the achievement process must be understood in light of such macro variables as the economy, the dynamic interplay between cultural ethos and daily *reality* must not be neglected. If the new ideal of femininity was in fact the model for all women, it was so only in the sense that all women had to live within the dominant cultural milieu (Wertheimer, 1977).

What women actually felt and experienced and internalized may elude historians as much as it may elude sociologists and psychologists. Lerner argued that the prescriptive literature (sermons, educational tracts, women's magazines) may tell us less what women did, felt, or experienced than what men in the past thought women should do, feel, and experience (1975). And while Welter (1966) demonstrated fine scholarship in reconstructing the cult of the lady from sermons and periodicals of the Jacksonian era, interpretations of the cult's meaning differ. It may be that the cult did indeed represent reality. On the other hand, the media's earlier concern with woman's ornamental value, and later in the century with domesticity, may have represented a response to the opposite trends in society. As Lerner has suggested "idealization is very frequently a defensive ideology and an expression of tension within the society" (1975:7). Whatever their roots, the cult of true womanhood and the cult of domesticity were cultural expressions of the sexual character of the public and private spheres. That women had to deal with these cultural ideals was a reality; what they internalized is uncertain. As we have repeatedly noted, the relationship between self and role is a complex give-and-take between individual and circumstance.

Although the early suffragists did not directly question women's sphere, their insistence that women be "brought into direct relations with the State, independent of their 'mate' or 'brood' " (DuBois, 1975:66) made clear that women were more than wives and mothers. At the same time that middle-class women's rights advocates in the 1840s were insisting on civil rights, female labor leaders were challenging economic exploitation of women in the factories. Despite the fact that mill workers were not represented at the Women's Rights Convention at Seneca Falls in 1848, they, too, were responding to patriarchal assumptions about their "proper" sphere. As the *Factory Girls' Voice* proclaimed: "We rejoice in that convention as a significant indication of the tendencies of this age" (Foner, 1979:72).

In his fine recounting of women's active experiences in the American labor movement, Foner captured the tensions between prescribed roles and self, between what Lerner described as "prescribed patriarchal assumptions and women's efforts to attain autonomy and emancipation" (1975:13). Interestingly, Foner implied that patriarchal assumptions about the cult of the lady might have led men to underestimate the aggressiveness and persistence of militant factory women. For instance, William Schonler, a leading opponent of the ten-hour day expected that "maidenly modesty" would prevent women from appearing in public and giving needed testimony; however, not only did women address the congressional committee hearings, but they also provided a "dramatic picture of the working life of a female factory operative" (Foner, 1979: 75). So aggressive was the strike in 1848 by the Female Labor Reform Associations of Allegheny City and Pittsburgh that the *Pittsburgh Journal* described the women as "Factory Amazons" breaking "down the fences and walls" (p. 78). They won their strike, Foner noted, while "the men stood around waiting to help if needed" (p. 78).

Later in the century Leonora Barry, delegate to the 1886 general assembly for the Knights of Labor, warned women to put aside their "foolish pride" and "prudish modesty." Working-class women, she contended, realistically had to assess their futures and most particularly rid themselves of the

> hope and expectancy that in the near future marriage will lift them out of the industrial life to the quiet and comfort of a home, foolishly imagining that with marriage their connection with and interest in labor matters end; often, finding, however, that their struggle has only begun when they have to go back to the shop for two instead of one. (Flexner, 1968:200)

At the turn of the century Mary Harris ("Mother") Jones, who represented organized mine workers in Pennsylvania, West Virginia, and Colorado, was quick to point out that "politics is only the servant of industry. The Plutocrats have organized their women. They keep them busy with suffrage and prohibition and charity" (Brownlee & Brownlee, 1976:242). In her classic "You don't need a vote to raise hell" speech, Jones said:

> No matter what your fight, I said, don't be ladylike! God almighty made women and the Rockefeller gang of thieves made the ladies. I have just fought through 16 months of bitter warfare in Colorado. I have been up against armed mercenaries, but this old woman, without a vote, and with nothing but a hatpin, has scared them. . . . I did not believe in women's rights nor in men's rights but in human rights. (Brownlee & Brownlee 1976: 242)

How are we to assess these women's internal standards of femininity and fears according to expectancy models of achievement? Their active struggles show them as anything but passively internalizing the cult of the lady or of domesticity. They represent dynamic strategists whose identities appeared to withstand rigid gender-role stereotypes.

Female Educational and Occupational Pursuits: Only on Domestic Terms

In chapters 1 and 2 we noted that many of leading models of female achievement have focused on individual aspirations and expectations as central forces in shaping women's achievement behaviors. A complex mix of expectancy—the subjective assessment of the probability of attaining a goal—and value—the anticipated gratification associated with that goal—is commonly summarized in a single, static quantitative variable (for a good critique see Laws, 1976, 1978). The problem in these models lies not only in the shifting interactions in expectancy and value but also in the historical, cultural, and economic factors affecting the value of the goal itself. Debates continue, for instance, concerning the interpretation of women's increasing numbers in the educational and occupational systems. On the one hand, such increases can be interpreted as measures of heightened societal status and worth. On the other, women's unequal treatment within these spheres constitutes yet another measure of their societal worth.

Similarly, growing domestic power has been offered as a sign of the female's increased societal worth. Lerner cautioned, however, that the evidence for this development must be placed within an economic and sociological context (1975). She noted that Smith's argument that women's domestic power increased in the nineteenth century was provocative but perhaps misleading. According to Smith, the lower birthrates over the entire century suggested that women had increased power over their reproductive lives. Lerner offered another interpretation:

> One might, from similar figures, as easily deduce a desire on the part of men to curb their offspring due to the demands of a developing industrial system for a more highly educated labor force, hence for fewer children per family. (1975:8)

The timing and value of one's achievement efforts are heavily constrained by socioeconomic conditions. In addition, women's achievement efforts, especially in education and the labor market, have been consistently linked to their ascriptive roles in the domestic script. The question of who belongs at home cannot be divorced from the search for plentiful and cheap labor. As we shall see, women's entrances into and exits from the labor market and higher education are anything but random (very often their entrances into the labor market have been responses to demand for excess labor).

The New England textile mills provided the first opportunity for large numbers of women to work outside the immediate family in nondomestic jobs. Francis Cabot Lowell, a founder of the Waltham System, was particularly persuasive in his appeal to the young single daughters of farm families. He established boarding houses for girls "who would spend a few years before marriage at the mills, and he offered salaries which were to be saved for their trousseaus, or used to help pay off mortgages, or send a brother through college" (Kessler-Harris, 1976:333). Mill owners like Lowell argued that hard work and discipline would prepare young women well for their future roles of wife and mother. Assumptions about young women's private lives were used to justify lower wages: the argument that the women worked only for pin money was consistently invoked when laying them off or cutting their rates. Foner described the differences in wages between men and women working in the mills:

> Each male worker established his wages by negotiations, and they were in keeping with prevailing rates in the region for skilled or unskilled labor. In the case of women, however, there was no firmly established going rate. Wages were set at a level that was high enough to induce young women to leave the farms and stay away from competing employment, such as household manufacture and domestic service, but low enough to offer the owners an advantage in employing women rather than men and to compete with the unskilled wages of the British textile industry. Thomas Dublin's study of the Hamilton mill in Lowell reveals that women who had been in the mill for three to six years made only half of what was earned by men who had been there a comparable time. (1979:25)

If a young woman strove to increase her wages, she was not regarded as a high achiever but was instead chastised. Larenia Wright, secretary of the United Tailoresses' Society of New York, was rebuked for "clamorous and unfeminine declarations of personal rights, which it is obvious a wise Providence never destined her to exercise" (Wertheimer, 1977:97).

Foner argued that the early trade unions were hostile to women workers because changes in the mode of production made women appear as competition more than as potential allies:

> The 1790's marked both the beginnings of a national market and the rise of the merchant capitalists who furnished credit and materials to local producers and put pressure on them to increase their production. The small shops with skilled craftsmen producing for a local market soon gave way to larger shops with more and more workers and with one employer, manufacturing for markets in the South and the West. As competition for these markets increased, employers reduced wages and increased working hours. They also divided workers into teams in order to speed up the work through specialization and division of labor. And they began to replace adult men with young boys and girls and adult women to do the work at one-fourth or one-half the men's wages. (1979:49)

Therefore, the trade union men "saw the women as part of a reserve of cheap labor being used against them, and they often blamed the women instead of their employers for their plight" (p. 49).

In 1836, the National Trades' Union Committee on Female Labor expressed concern that female labor produced "ruinous competition . . . to male labor." Working women were seen as evading their natural responsibilities and moral sensibilities, which best suited them to domesticity. The committee explained:

> One thing . . . must be apparent to every reflecting female, that all her exertions are scarce sufficient to keep her alive; that the price of her labor each year is reduced; and that she in a measure stands in the way of the male when attempting to raise his prices or equalize his labor, and that her efforts to sustain herself and family are actually the same as tying a stone around the neck of her natural protector, Man, and destroying him with the weight she has brought to his assistance. This is the true and natural consequence of female labor when carried beyond the family. (Kessler-Harris, 1976:335)

From the late 1850s onward, most craft unions sought to bar women from membership and even from employment (Brownlee & Brownlee, 1976:213). Most of the arguments against women were couched in the cult of domesticity ideology. Edward O'Donnell, secretary of the Boston Central Labor Union, expressed the general tone:

> The growing demand for female labor is not founded on philanthropy. . . . It is an insidious assault upon the home; it is the knife of the assassin, aimed at the family circle—the divine injunction. It debars the man, through financial embarrassment, from family responsibility, and physically, mentally, and socially excludes the woman equally from nature's dearest impulse. (Brownlee & Brownlee, 1976:213)

Foner stated that two conditions prevailed in women's occupations of the 1850s: "Women in these trades were paid half of what men received for comparable work, often because it was assumed that women's wages were part of a family wage . . . women's wages rose little during the 1850's and in some trades acutally declined" (1979:85). Furthermore, sex-typing of jobs kept women in the weakest and lowest paid segment of the labor market. This was particularly true for the great waves of immigrants in the period 1890–1920:

> These "green" women entered a segment of the industrial work force that was clearly labeled female. Although a greater variety of industries employed them, women's status, wages, and working conditions designated a secondary status. The division of labor in the cigar factories of Pittsburgh at the turn of the century illustrates the kind of opportunities available to immigrant women. Many of the recent arrivals had skill and experience in rolling cigars, traditionally a woman's task in Slavic countries. In America, however, the well paying job of hand-rolling expensive cigars had become a male monopoly. The

second echelon of the cigar industry, mechanized rolling, was reserved for men and women of American birth or long experience in the United States. (Ryan 1979:121)

The same pattern prevailed in other industries:

> The first principle of the sexual division of factory work decreed that women would be relegated to unskilled tasks. In the garment factory this meant that men would cut out and usually press, while women finished garments, sewed on buttons, or worked with inferior materials. In the National Biscuit Company's Pittsburg plant in 1906 the baking was done by a handful of men, while 1,100 women packaged and frosted cakes. (Ryan, 1979:121-122)

Furthermore, this division of labor was not necessarily predicated on physical strength differences. Ryan noted that in the Pittsburgh metal trades "women carried sand cones . . . weighing ten to fifty pounds through dusty shops to fuming ovens" (p. 122).

During the nineteenth century educated women were systematically excluded from the professions. Foner observed that by the end of the Revolutionary War

> a male medical elite had begun to band together against women through a complex campaign for licensing and other legislation, harassment, restrictive medical school admission policies, propaganda about the alleged biological frailty and emotional instability of women, and the repeated assertion that women's proper sphere was home and hearth. . . . By the second half of the nineteenth century they were all but excluded from medical practice. (1979:38)

Most women who entered the nursing profession at the administrative and leadership levels in the nineteenth century were educated women who had been closed out of more prestigious professions. The occupations of nursing, teaching, and, later, clerical work were legitimate extensions of women's "natural" domestic roles. The patriarchal context of this situation was made clear in Ehrenreich and English's description of the nurse as the "ideal lady":

> To the doctor, she brought the wifely virtue of absolute obedience. To the patient, she brought the selfless devotion of a mother. To the lower level hospital employee she brought the firm but kindly discipline of a household manager accustomed to dealing with servants. (1973:39)

Clerical work is another area where we see how the economic need for cheap, plentiful labor allowed women into the labor force without sacrificing role priorities. In 1870 men constituted 97.5 percent of the clerical force. Clerkship at the time offered employees a lifelong career. However, with the rapid growth, consolidation, and bureaucratization of firms came a great change in the nature of clerical work. When clerical work became a low-level, dead-end job, it also became a female sex-typed occupation.

Thirty-five years after the editor of the *Ladies Home Journal* warned that women risked their morality when they stepped into an office (Davis, 1974:12), *Fortune* magazine asserted that women were by nature perfectly suited to the office. In a series of unsigned articles *Fortune* equated secretaries with wives, describing them as women who are "amenable, obedient, and devoted . . . capable of making offices pleasant, peaceful, and homelike" (Davis, 1974:17). A personal secretary was the "competent mother-wife who sees to her employer's every wish" (Davis, 1974:19).

The recruitment of women into schools and particularly higher education also was closely related to the need for low-paid workers with particular skills. The fifty years following the American Revolution saw great economic changes and even greater changes in institutions of education—most particularly, a widespread movement advocating secondary education for both girls and boys (Howe, 1972). Lerner (1969) and Roby (1972) suggested that the egalitarian ideology of the Jacksonian period promoted the spread of common schools and consequently created a new need for teachers. Roby argued that these schools were seen by the working class as a guarantee of social and economic equality for their children (1972). However, the growth in women's higher education stemmed not so much from the egalitarian ideology of the time as from the critical need to train teachers to instruct a growing number of school children. Roby noted that men were not readily available for this function since they were either already gainfully employed or heading west. Schooling for women, then, was in part a by-product of ideological changes but even more the outgrowth of economic events. Training female teachers meant filling a critical shortage at relatively low cost. As Lerner wryly noted: "America was committed to educating its children in public schools but it was insistent on doing so as cheaply as possible. Women, available in greatest numbers, were willing to work cheaply" (1969:7).

There was no paradox in the active recruitment of women into the occupational world at the same time that the ideology extolled their virtues within the home. For example, who was better equipped *by nature* to teach children? Ideology and economic need neatly dovetailed. Teaching, like factory work, was considered a prelude to marriage rather than a lifelong career. Women's publically achieved roles in nursing, factory, teaching and clerical work were seen as extensions of their private familial roles.

The Civil War gave great impetus to female higher education in our country as the financial pressures generated by the war and declining male enrollments forced many institutions to become coeducational. In 1866 the University of Wisconsin was reorganized so that all departments were officially open to men and women. As the state superintendent of higher education explained: "[The] expense of carrying on the institution would be greatly lessened if both sexes were generally to recite together" (Roby, 1972:123–124). Women were seen as sources of tuition badly needed to keep schools open, particularly in the poorer Western states of Kansas, Indiana, Minnesota, Missouri, Michigan, and California.

Importantly, these coeducational advances were always delimited by debates about women's proper, if not natural, roles. The 1860s and '70s heard heated discussions about whether women's schools should imitate men's in their curricula. Henry Fowle Durant, the founder of Wellesley College, believed that women's education should be as thorough as men's but "regarded an hour of domestic work a day as an integral part of the educational program" (Roby, 1972:124). The presence of women in Oberlin College was essential for "the well being of men (Hogeland, 1973:167). Women students not only provided a pool of educated potential marriage partners but also served men directly while in college. Hogeland reported that female students were required to wash and "repair the clothes of the 'leading sex,' care for their rooms, and take charge of the dining hall tasks" (p. 167).

In sum, while women's personal goals have been varied, as social actors they must always be understood in relation to culturally assigned roles. Economic systems as well as ideological beliefs contribute to defining and maintaining achievement behavior and the achievement process.

Conclusion

In this chapter we have focused on the economic origins of the private sphere of life and the consequent sexual division of labor. The split between public and private spheres was early recognized as critical in defining the value and scope of women's achievement roles. Feminists astutely recognized that women's inextricable ties to the private arena could easily lead to both a personal and a public devaluation of their labors, domestic and other. The fight to reintegrate the female into the public sphere and/or to upgrade the private sphere has emphasized women's unique power disadvantage.

Attempts to make the achievements of women visible, attempts to redefine productivity, and attempts to expose patriarchal assumptions about adult women's achievements all have aimed to include the female reality in our understanding of the world. In the next chapter we explore adult women's economic subordination in today's labor market and in the organization of professional life. In so doing, we wish to redefine the public script to include the female occupational reality and thereby to expand our definitions of the achievement process.

Notes

1. See Hareven (1977, 1978a,b), Kanter (1977a, 1978a), Pleck (1976), and Tilley and Scott (1978) for detailed discussions of the family's economic role.
2. Brownlee and Brownlee focused on ecological factors that may have increased

women's relegation to the private sphere, suggesting that agricultural opportunities encouraged colonists to marry earlier and thereby led to an increase in family size (1976). Furthermore, they argued that as a result of more favorable agricultural and climatic conditions, mortality rates, particularly for infants and children, were lower in America than in Europe. The low infant mortality rate eased some of the "psychological anguish" of childrearing and therefore emotional investment in childbearing probably increased. The authors inferred that childrearing was becoming concentrated in the hands of women from the colonists' strong attachment to the value of the marketplace:

The impulse to maximize pecuniary return, the impressive profits to be made from expanding production, the acute scarcity of labor (including family servants), and the fact that the productivity of women working in the fields was less than that of men, all joined with the growing emphasis the colonists placed on childrearing to tie women increasingly to the tasks of infant care and child training. (p. 9)

3. In her recounting of the political analogue of moral woman and immoral man, Elshtain contended that the modern concept of moral woman developed with a shift in the work of postmedieval political theorists, specifically Bodin and Machiavelli (1974). Elshtain suggested that unlike Aristotle, Plato, and the Stoic philosophers, who ultimately connected knowledge and the pursuit of good with politics, the postmedieval theorists saw politics as divorced from moral considerations. These political distinctions match those we have touched upon in this chapter:

Woman is totally immersed in the private, nonpublic realm and is judged by the single standard appropriate to that realm alone. [Therefore] she does not share in public life. . . . According to this system, if a woman should "go public" (or attempt to), she is still to be judged as a private person. All that women were in private (kind, virtuous, loving, responsible) men could attempt to become with the aid and succor of women; but women could not "become" what men were (responsible public persons) without forsaking their womanhood by definition. (pp. 459–460)

4. The public-private split continues to be debated within feminist political circles. Most critics argue that women still have scant control over the factors underlying their assignment to and investment in private roles. Radical feminists see biological capacities as a major source of women's subjection in family roles. Socialist feminists focus on the woman's economic dependence on males and her inability to control the value of her labor. Moral elements are also used to account for the boundaries on women's private decisions. This view emphasizes early socialization. Women are thought to have acquired special skills appropriate to the private sphere, for which they are more highly motivated and trained. Proponents of this view also stress the value of "female culture." They are divided with regard to the desirability of encouraging males to participate in the domestic sphere and prefer the separation between the public and the private realm. In fact, the feminine domestic realm is thought to be superior on a variety of grounds. There is, finally, a movement for a merger between public and private. This approach is often equated with calls for androgyny and the elimination of all gender roles. Nostalgia for an integration of home and workplace is found among both conservative social reformers and radical feminists.

5. Elizabeth Cady Stanton, while unfamiliar with current models of attribution and achievement, understood that social power plays a critical role in the maintenance of self-esteem: "Nothing strengthens the judgment and quickens the conscience like individual responsibility. Nothing adds such dignity to character as the recognition of one's self-sovereignty" (DuBois, 1975:67).

6. DuBois noted that the

   WCTU spoke to women in the language of their domestic realities, and they joined in the 1870's and 1880's in enormous numbers. The WCTU's program reflected the same social reality that lay beyond suffragism—that the family was losing its central place in social organization to nondomestic institutions, from the saloon to the school to the legislature, and that woman's social power was accordingly weakened. (1975:69)

7. Walker and Gauger were among the first to provide economic measures for domestic services in the private sphere (1973). In her statement to the Congress's Joint Economic Committee hearings on economic problems of women, Walker convincingly argued that economic discrimination against women prevails in *and* out of the labor market.

CHAPTER 4

Adult Roles: The Public Script

Help Wanted

Requirements: Intelligence, good health, energy, patience, sociability. *Skills:* At least 12 different occupations. *Hours:* 99.6 per week. *Salary:* None. *Holidays:* None (will be required to remain on stand-by 24 hours a day, 7 days a week). *Opportunities for advancement:* None (limited transferability of skills acquired on the job). *Job Security:* None (trend is toward more layoffs particularly as employee approaches middle age. Severance pay will depend on the discretion of the employer). *Fringe benefits:* Food, clothing, and shelter generally provided, but any additional bonuses will depend on financial standing and good nature of the employer. No health, medical, or accident insurance; no Social Security or pension plan. (Chesler, 1976:97)

Most people would readily recognize this ad as a summary of the modern domestic roles of wife and mother. Women's private achievements still receive little recognition. Like virtue, such achievements ("labors of love") are often said to be their own rewards. To appreciate the irony of the ad, however, is to recognize that women's achievements in the private sphere make an important contribution to an industrial capitalist economy (and consequently to men under capitalism) and to patriarchy (and consequently to individual men as husbands and fathers).

What value, for instance, do biological reproduction, education and care of children, care of the sick and the elderly and the daily chores of meal

preparation, laundry, and cleaning—all typically done in the private sphere
of the home—have in the productive, wage-earning public sphere? Can
household labor be transferred to the wage labor force?[1] As Fee noted,
household work is a "wageless form," which accounts for its appearance of
triviality. Our interest here is not to resolve whether housework is productive labor in the specific context of capitalist production. Rather we wish to
note how distinctions between public and private achievements affect the
questions we ask and consequently the answers we receive about achievements in the public world of work. At issue is whose reality do the academic
models we use to evaluate achievement in the public sphere represent.

Academic inquiries in the sociology of work are bound by definitions
of "labor force." Acker suggested the implications for understanding
female achievement over the life course when labor force means only those
working for pay and those actively seeking work (1978). She noted that we
typically exclude from inquiry

> those doing unpaid work such as housework or volunteer jobs. These activities
> are, by implication, defined as nonwork. Thus, the analytic category labor
> force is much more consistent with the work experience of men than with the
> work experience of women. When we discuss work as labor force participa-
> tion, we are much more likely to encounter the significant elements of male
> lives than the significant elements of female lives. (p. 139)

Acker concluded that except for research on professional women (we address the shortcomings in this literature, too, at the conclusion of this
chapter) "the description of women's life-time careers and how they take
action to ensure their economic survival in a competitive, individualistic
society has never been a major focus of sociological study" (p. 140).
Therefore, until we include women in our models we have an incomplete
understanding of the achievement process.

This chapter introduces the concepts of occupational segregation, dual
labor markets and internal labor markets to elucidate the structural conditions and the restrictions and opportunities affecting adult women in pursuit of public achievements. In this way, wage inequities and blocked opportunities may be seen as related to the structural world of work and not
primarily or even necessarily to women's internalized fears or standards of
femininity. Consistency in female achievement behavior must be analyzed
as much in macro as in maturational and personality terms. If we fail to
recognize the constraints the organization of the public world of work
places upon women's potential mobility, we tend to see the sources of con-
straint as individual and thus within the woman's personal control. We
specifically focus on professional women to show how male-oriented
models of organization within the labor market shape and control the conditions under which women labor. By indicating how in almost every particular women are connected to the public world of work differently from

men, we emphasize the need to revise our models of achievement. We cannot generalize from men's experiences if we are to characterize authentically women's achievements. We begin by discussing some of the male based assumptions underlying the dominant theoretical framework in social stratification studies—the status attainment tradition.

Status Attainment Theory

Status attainment is to social mobility and stratification research today what McClelland's need achievement was to achievement motivation research several decades ago. Just as introducing females into achievement models spurred major critiques of McClelland's work, so introducing females into the male-based model of status attainment has caused some important reappraisals.

The history of the status attainment model in some ways parallels that of need achievement research and theory. Just as McClelland worried that we might need a whole new psychology to explain women's achievement motivation (Lesser, 1974), Duncan, Featherman, and Duncan identified a similar problem for status attainment.[2] In explaining why women were excluded from their original empirical model, these authors noted: "Our strategy does indeed rest on the assumption that patterns of achievement for men and women are quite distinct; different variables may be relevant, or the same variables may have different weights" (1972:15).

Yet despite such forewarnings, researchers in the status attainment tradition continue to ignore the different realities men and women face in the world of work and education. Lenski, in his classic book on stratification in America, noted that it was virtually impossible to ignore sex when looking at the distribution of power (1966), yet power dimensions are virtually absent in status attainment theories. Blau and Duncan, for instance, while conceding that the reward structure can sometimes be influenced by men in controlling positions, dismissed this insight by asserting that such influences are basically random and not built into the occupational system in any systematic fashion (for an excellent discussion see Stewart, 1977a:7). The individual is the focal point for control and change in both the achievement motivation and the status attainment literature. More often than not the individual under analysis is male.

As with the need achievement model, the status attainment model's explanatory power is not very strong. By 1976 some authors were suggesting that "even with the tremendous growth in the number and visibility of status attainment researchers, the present hypothesized paradigm is inadequate; how can we conclude other than this with total explained variances of approximately 50 percent?" (Falk & Cosby, 1976:314). Falk and Cosby added: "This points to an obvious need for a continued search for variables of importance in understanding the status attainment process" (p. 314).

In our view, women are influenced by significant others and institutions *first* and *directly* as members of a subordinate sex and secondarily as individuals. Sex as an intervening variable makes their individual realities quite different from men's. Since current status attainment theories generally do not directly account for the effects of gender role, men and women are not differentiated in order to explain their public achievements. No wonder when operationalized the model yields variables that explain so little of the variance. In the next section we suggest that some of the missing variables in the status attainment model had long been present in the gender-role literature.

Gender-Role Contributions

The very variables that Falk and Cosby (1976) claimed are so important in understanding the status attainment process for *all* workers, though explored in the gender-role literature, remained unaddressed in status attainment models. Myrdal emphasized that gender posed the same problems as racial status when he compared women to blacks in our society (1944). In 1944 Hughes described in some detail the complex interplay between race (ascribed status) and professional attainment (achieved status). Interestingly, Hughes was later to place nontraditional career women in the role of "marginal men" (1949). Hacker pursued the same analysis, suggesting that formal discrimination against women "whether in the form of being barred from certain activities, or if admitted, being treated unequally, arises from the generally ascribed status of 'female' and from the socially ascribed status of 'wife,' 'mother' and 'sister' " (1951:62).

When women were included in the analysis, the occupational research of the 1960s and 1950s strongly implied that women's occupational realities were clearly different from men's (Caplow, 1954; Ellis, 1952; Etzioni, 1969; Orzack, 1959). Likewise, Bernard's 1964 portrait of the academic woman and her later work on the different priorities of women and men and the different realities they faced (1971) were not integrated into the studies of stratification. Rossi's important article on the transition to parenthood, while presumably relevant only to family scholars, offered a critique of occupational research as well (1968). She noted how impoverished concepts about work and parenthood were, primarily because most writers assumed a priori that men preferred and derived primary satisfaction from work, and women from marriage and motherhood. Oppenheimer's detailed monographs on the sex labeling of jobs (1968, 1970) and Gross's on the sex segregation of the labor market (1968), showing clear differences in work realities for males and females, appeared to have gone unheeded as well. So, too, Epstein's (1970a, b) and White's (1970) fine insights into the different collegial interaction patterns men and women faced within the professional setting offered a sophisticated analysis of the subtle barriers to achievement. Epstein's *Woman's Place* was one of the first books specifically describing women's distinctive and unequal place in the professional world (1970b). She noted that women carried an extra handle as professionals—lady lawyers, women doctors, female professors—that implied different treatment, different evaluation, and ultimately unequal rewards.

Although power differentials were implicit in most of the early discussions of male and female work realities, Collins (1971) and Goffman (1959) were among the first to call explicit attention to the mechanisms maintaining those power differentials. They wrote about the power relationships behind ordinary customs and personality traits, as well as about changes in these systems over the life course. In 1973 the *American Journal of Sociology* devoted a whole issue to essays on women. Huber warned in her introduction to that issue: "Social conflict is likely to occur when some group feels that it is not getting its fair share of rewards. Sociologists often fail to spot probable sources of conflict because our stratification theories are outmoded. We need new theoretical spectacles" (1973:764). She pointed to the need for a new analysis that understood the special plight of women given their association with the family:

> The preoccupation with the family as the primary agent of stratification has . . . led to the idea that we live in an achievement society, even though a substantial majority of all Americans suffer restricted opportunity because of an ascribed status. Any woman, for example, whose daily routine includes changing diapers and dishing out the applesauce is doing semiskilled blue-collar work, regardless of her own educational attainment or the SES level of her husband. A trick of definition—the work is unpaid—allows us to maintain the fiction that this kind of outcome doesn't really count. The anomaly that half of all Americans are expected to do blue-collar work regardless of talent and training is not discussed in the stratification texts. (p. 764)

In the same issue Bernard concluded that "Sociology is in crisis because the old paradigms are overburdened by anomalies and satisfactory new ones are not available" (1973:776).

Despite the overwhelming evidence available and the remarkable insights of these writers,[3] three years later *Signs* published a special issue on women and the workplace in which many of the same insightful comments were still being offered and still, for the most part, remaining unheeded. The next section details how the current status attainment model (frequently referred to as the "Wisconsin model") insufficiently accounts for female status aspirations and attainments.

The Wisconsin Model

At the end of the sixties Rosen summed up years of cumulative study with an almost apologetic note: "For good or ill 'achievement' in the U.S.A. means achievement in work" (1969:359). Despite the many changes apparently wrought by the countercultural outbursts of the 1960s, ample evidence from the Yankelovich data indicated that the work ethic was alive and well in the 1970s. For most Americans work was still the most valued measure of success.

The fifth of a series of research projects on American youth revealed that among a rather heterogeneous group of people aged sixteen to twenty-five, the work ethic was quite strong (Yankelovich, 1974). College youth actively pursued "a career as a means to self-fulfillment, with money, security, and possessions in the overall scheme, partly taken for granted, partly demanded as a matter of right, but subordinate to the main goal of finding just the right life style for expressing their psychological potential" (Yankelovich, 1974:22). Noncollege youth in 1973 were just about where the college population had been in 1969, wanting self-fulfillment as well as money and security in work. The desire to do self-rewarding and interesting work is one sign of a vital work ethic. Kanter noted that meaningful work (work that gives a feeling of accomplishment) has been the first-ranking answer in the Detroit area surveys since 1958 (1978b).

In the status attainment tradition, both educational and occupational attainments are conceptualized as part of a general status attainment process. Educational attainment is seen as a means toward the valued goals of occupational and financial success. In the Wisconsin model, aspirations and attainments are joint functions of socioeconomic background and individual differences in ability and performance (Duncan, Featherman & Duncan, 1972). Among the attempts at modeling the status attainment process, the works of Sewell and of Haller stand out (Haller & Portes, 1973; Sewell, Haller & Portes, 1969; Sewell, Haller & Ohlendorf, 1970; Sewell & Hauser, 1975, 1972). In these works, status attainment is treated within a "three-phase causal model [see figure 4-1]. Relatively fixed contextual variables, such as parental socioeconomic status and intelligence, exert influences on attainment which are mediated by such social psychological variables as academic performance, significant others, educational aspirations and occupational aspirations" (Falk & Cosby, 1976:308).

Note that although the Wisconsin model stresses the dynamic interplay between individual and environment, thus portraying attainment as a developmental by-product of early as well as current influences, the ordering and the impact of causal variables (timing within the model itself) present problems for the analysis of female achievement. For instance, in the Wisconsin model as described by Falk and Cosby (1976), aspirations (attitudes) have an indirect but causal relationship to attainments (occupational and educational). Aspirations mediate the effect of antecedent variables such as parents' social origins, academic ability, significant others, and academic performance. For our purposes we wish to question the "easy link" often made between aspirations and motivation. Frequently, aspirations are considered indicators of personal or individual striving. In this sense the Wisconsin model has incorporated the psychological attributes important in need-achievement models (individual striving).

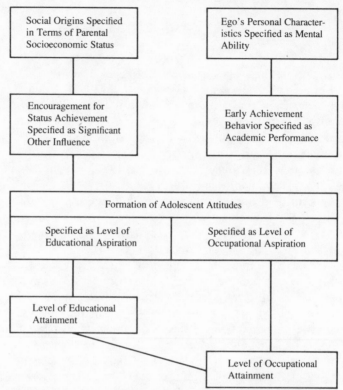

Figure 4-1. The Wisconsin Model in Block Diagram Form. Source: William W. Falk and Arthur G. Cosby, "Women and the Status Attainment Process," *Social Science Quarterly*, 56, 2, September 1975, p. 312. Reproduced with permission of the author and University of Texas Press.

In a perceptive critique Meixel noted that beyond the first stage of the Wisconsin model, no social structural or cultural inputs have any causal impact on status attainment: "After consideration of placement in the social structure as an antecedent to status attainment, the rest of the process is essentially an individualistic one; attainment depends on the individual's ability, motivation, and self-assessment" (1976:12). Yet throughout this book we have stressed the problems in linking individual motivation to control of outcome. Therefore, any analysis of individual aspiration and motivation must take into account gender-role related aspirations and expectations, limitations, and opportunities.

Keller and Zavarolli discussed the critical distinction between individual motivation and aspiration:

Any given success goal has both an absolute and relative value, the first reflecting its cultural desirability, the second, its social class accessibility. The "relative distance" of a social class from a given goal thus determines an intervening variable between individual ambition and social achievement. We can thus anticipate differences in the frequencies of certain educational or occupational aspirations in various social classes without postulating differences in extent of individual ambitiousness among their members. (1964:58)[4]

The parallel to women is readily apparent: women's occupational aspirations and life achievements are conditioned by accessibility and opportunities.

The Wisconsin model includes social structural variables (e.g., social origins of parents), but their impact is limited in both time and scope. Other social structural variables (e.g., the sex-segregated labor market) and their impact on aspirations and expectations are not taken into account. In her critical review of the work motivation literature, Laws suggested that motivation is a function of two forces: expectancy, the subjective probability of attaining a goal; and value, the anticipated gratification associated with that goal (1978). She argued that the two must be measured independently. As we have shown, in the achievement motivation research, gender role affects both value and expectancy, which in turn affect aspiration. In addition, over time and over the individual life course both value and expectancy change. However, the dynamic relationship among these variables is *not* generally accounted for in the Wisconsin model; that is, an individual's goals, values, and perceptions of both the opportunity structure and her/his ability (at any particular point) are combined in a *single* measure. This combination of qualitatively different and changing variables in the single dimension of aspiration at one point in time is at best suspect.[5]

Trying to measure work aspiration levels over the short term is misleading. Citing data collected by Harmon, Laws noted that occupational outcomes can rarely be attributed to early expressions of aspirations (1978). For instance, high scores on the Strong Vocational Interest Blank did not predict the occupations pursued by Harmon's subjects who had worked most of the time following graduation from college. Comparing Birnbaum's 1975 data on homemakers, married professionals, and single professionals, Laws concluded:

> The three groups showed little difference in the occupations they reported having considered as children. All had considered wife and mother (homemakers most frequently); and all had considered professional careers (the married professionals most). The most career-oriented (single professionals) had the highest proportion undecided at the early stage, suggesting that their career choices entered their life later than the standard female occupational map. (p. 31)[6]

Including the female gender-role script makes clear how many factors in the complicated process of development lead to and interact with status attainments.

In an attempt to correct some of the problems in a model originated for and basically applied only to males, Falk and Cosby offered an expanded status attainment model (1976). The improvements of this representation, shown as figure 4-2, over the one presented as 4-1 are clear. Inclusion of mother's education and occupation broadens the concept of structural impact. Heavy consideration is given to the interaction process and to the gender roles women play, such as sister, girlfriend, wife, and mother. Finally, the temporal ordering of events is addressed. The authors cautiously sug-

Figure 4-2. An Expanded Status Attainment Model Incorporating Status Contingencies for Women in Block Diagram Form. Source: William W. Falk and Arthur G. Cosby, "Women and the Status Attainment Process," *Social Science Quarterly*, 56, 2, September 1975, p. 313. Reproduced with permission of the author and University of Texas Press.

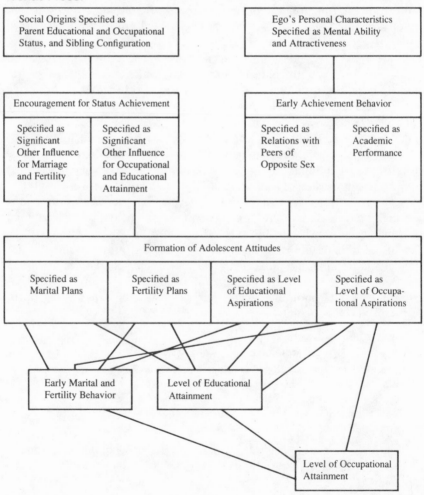

gested that socialization into gender roles may or may not precede aspirations; they left this problem for empirical testing. In this sense they did not assume that socialization has some fixed effect on individuals from early on. By including the private gender script in status attainment, they explicitly recognized that sex makes a difference. In addition, they put individual striving into a social context.

Nevertheless, status attainment theorists influential in the late seventies seem not to have expanded their models but rather to have narrowed them. For instance, while recognizing the emphasis on individual process, Featherman skirted aspiration and motivation in the status attainment model by stressing worldly success: "The relevance of values to this work is in its essential assumption that achievement is credibly indexed by worldly success—by work and graded performance rather than by some personal, self-relevant standards" (1978:1). Success in this model is attendant upon individual effort. Individual effort, however, either as aspiration or as motivation, is in continual and dynamic interplay with the social structure. Because this interplay differs for the sexes,[7] we would expect the variables measuring individual efforts and abilities (e.g., academic ability) to interact with ascribed variables (e.g., socioeconomic background) differently for women and men. Some empirical data seem to support this argument.[8]

Interestingly, while status attainment theorists recognize that a fundamental handicap to women's occupational chances rests in "the subtle normative practices of sex socialization and the current institutions of childrearing and homemaking" (Hauser & Featherman, 1977:215), these variables have been neglected in testing the theory. Two of the major comparative studies on educational and occupational attainments for both sexes excluded gender-role variables and social psychological variables from analysis (McClendon, 1976; Treiman & Terrell, 1975).[9] Even researchers interested in mobility patterns note that while they "can document the presence of sexual inequality of opportunity," they "cannot explain it with their data" (Hauser & Featherman, 1977:116). However, the problems encountered in explaining the links among socioeconomic background, gender-related issues, occupational and educational attainments pale by comparison to the problems encountered in explaining occupational attainment and earned income. There is now little disagreement about the different realities males and females face with regard to earned income (U.S. Government Joint Economic Committee, 1977). In the next few sections we consider why most women cannot expect hard work to bring them an adequate income or jobs that mean autonomy and/or power.

Sex and Status in the Marketplace: The Female Reality

One reason for the male-oriented reality reflected in our academic models is the belief that work roles are still nearly synonymous with the husband and father roles. Therefore, significant aspects of the occupational script relevant to females generally have been excluded. "Comfortable assumptions that women exist within the confines of the family enjoying the economic support of men and that this existence is not problematic" (Acker, 1978:141) neglect the statistics: over half the women from eighteen to sixty-four are now in paid employment, as are half the women who have children over six years of age (U.S. Department of Labor, 1977), and working wives contribute over one-quarter of the earned family income (Bureau of Labor Statistics, U.S. Department of Labor, 1978).

In neglecting women's reality, we tend systematically to underestimate the economic contributions they consistently have been making. At the turn of the century, for instance, taking in boarders was one of the most common forms of work for women, especially among immigrant populations. In 1910, 5 percent of the country's population, or 4.5 million people, lived with families to whom they were not related. However, this work was considered unpaid housework and was ignored in census reports (Baxandall, Gordon & Reverby, 1976:150). Smuts argued that census reports prior to 1940 (except that of 1910) made no regular effort to include women workers (1959).

In a perceptive article on women's work history, Branca explained:

> The application of the male model has led to serious interpretive problems. For one thing, it has misplaced our time focus, by forcing women's history into the periodization presumed appropriate for men. Since men's labor history for the industrial period has focused on factory industry . . . women's labor historians have consistently sought their subjects in the same milieu. The fact is that even to the present day factory labor comprises only a small part of women's work history, and that in general it is fair to say that factories and women rarely mixed, which is not the same thing as saying that therefore women didn't work or that their work did not change. (1975:130–131)

Branca suggested that looking for women in the wrong places distorts our understanding of female economic contributions:

> We cannot fully document the actual occupations of the very large number of women who did not work in factories. Much female part-time labor went unrecorded. Women who worked beside their husbands or fathers, whether on the farm or in the shop, might not show up as employed in the census returns. (p. 132)

During most of the nineteenth century, women's economic contributions were fundamental to "agriculture, domestic manufacturing (mainly but not exclusively in textiles and dress), domestic services, retailing, and to a slight extent textile factory labor" (Branca, 1975:133).

In earlier chapters we alluded to the complex interplay between patterns of female employment and the supply and demand of the market. However, contemporary increase rates for new types of female workers should not obscure the historical and demographic fact that women steadily have contributed to the economy. What is new to the latter half of the twentieth century is not women's labor force participation per se but their *increased* labor force participation:

> Although there was a 23.5 percent increase in the recorded proportion of women 14 and older in the labor force in the forty-year period between 1900 and 1940, there was a much greater increase in the period half that long between 1940 and 1960—a 35.8 percent change. (Oppenheimer, 1970:5-6)

The most significant increase—from 28 percent to 38 percent between 1951 and 1963—has been in

> the proportion of women in the labor force who had children under 18. . . . What all these changes in the labor force composition add up to is that, at least with regard to age, marital and family status, the female labor force today is not very different from the adult female population as a whole. (Oppenheimer, 1970:19)

The value of women's economic contribution has been underestimated because female income is seen as secondary to men's: currently only 7.3 percent of wives substantially outearn their husbands (Hacker, 1979:3). Oppenheimer offered an interpretation of women's economic contribution that does not underestimate its real value. She noted that even if a wife's income is not comparable to that of the husband, her impact on the family's socioeconomic status may in fact be sizable: "The most important issue is not whether her earnings equal those of her husband's but the extent to which her earnings provide a functional substitute for upward occupational mobility on his part or a counterbalance to downward mobility" (1977:400).

Finally, we should not neglect the economic though unremunerated contributions of wives whose husbands' careers depend upon their active participation. Epstein described corporate and government jobs so demanding that men need "able wives to entertain, soothe, make contacts, and offer ballast. Most top careers, in fact, have been cooperative efforts, but husbands hold the titles and power and their wives serve as statusless, unpaid partners" (1975:12). Early on, Papanek described this "two-person one-career syndrome" (1973),[10] as most prevalent in large, complex organizations and in political careers. Wives of men in such occupations are expected, if not actively directed, to help their husbands (Hochschild, 1969; Lopata, 1971; Moore, 1962; Seidenberg, 1973; Taylor & Hartley, 1973; Whyte, 1956; Young & Willmott, 1973). According to Papanek, the two-person single career is structurally part of the domestic role rather than a matter of "choice, accident, or conflict" (1973:857). As such, it is "real" occupational labor that takes place in the private sphere.

Clearly, then, occupational labor (paid or unpaid, counted or uncounted) is a part of the adult female reality. Furthermore, the data strongly indicate that this pattern will not change, at least not in the near future.

Young women expect to work: 95 percent of the females in Rand and Miller's combined samples of junior high, senior high, and college students intended to work after finishing school (1972). Herzog, Bachman, and Johnston, reviewing the research of others and their own national sample of female high school seniors concluded that "many women plan to combine work with marriage and childrearing" (1979a:9).

We have argued repeatedly that the dynamic interplay between the individual and the social structure is different for the sexes. Academic models based only on male experiences cannot take these different realities into account. Subsequently we run the risk, as in status attainment models, of attributing females' realistic expectations about what kinds of jobs await them in the labor market to their personal aspirations or ambitions. However, women's expectations should not be confused or equated with personal ambition.

A study based on a random sample of eleventh-grade students in Pennsylvania produced convincing evidence that aspirations and expectations are uniquely linked for the sexes (Marini & Greenberger, 1976).

> For boys, there was virtually no difference between the mean percentage of women (or conversely, men) employed in the occupations aspired to and expected. For girls, on the other hand, the mean percentage of women employed in occupations which were expected to be attained was significantly greater than the mean percentage of women employed in occupations which were aspired to. On the average, girls expected to enter occupations which were more highly female-dominated than those they aspired to. (Marini & Greenberger, 1976:20)

Furthermore, among students who aspired to male-dominated occupations, a smaller proportion of girls than boys expected to obtain an occupation in this category. In addition, girls perceived the male-dominated jobs they aspired to as less accessible than the female-dominated jobs seemed to aspiring boys (p. 22). Perhaps this is not unrealistic given Gross's 1968 analysis that sex desegregation is evident primarily in the male influx into female occupations and Oppenheimer's 1970 analysis that women do not replace men in the labor market.

Next we explore the structural realities women face in the labor market. As we have suggested, structural realities affect both female aspirations and attainments. The interaction between gender and structural reality is missing in most status attainment accounts of women's achievements.

The Female Occupational Structure

At the beginning of the 1970s Oppenheimer described the labor market as so sex segregated that one could speak of two nonoverlapping markets, one for males and one for females. In the early seventies approximately 40 percent of the labor force was female. Cahn documented that the vast majority of women at that time were secretaries, bookkeepers, domestic workers, elementary school teachers, waitresses, typists, cashiers, sewers and stitchers, registered nurses, or retail trade and sales workers (Cahn, 1979).

Men and women inhabit distinct occupational worlds. Most female dominated jobs are white-collar, with clerical work accounting for roughly half of this labor force (McClendon, 1976; Howe, 1977). Furthermore, the range of female dominated occupations is narrower than that of male dominated ones: female dominated occupations are underrepresented at the highest and lowest levels of the occupational prestige distribution. Occupations such as nurse, social worker, and teacher (the "semiprofessions") command fairly high levels of prestige, but not the highest levels, which male dominated professions, such as doctor, architect, and lawyer, enjoy.

This labor market condition is described by economists as a "dual labor market model" (or "dual economy model") wherein there are two markets—primary and secondary. Female dominated occupations (and hence a large majority of women) tend to be located in either the secondary market or the nonenterprise component of the primary labor market. Jobs in the secondary market tend to have low wages and fringe benefits, poor working conditions, high turnover, little chance of advancement, and often arbitrary and capricious supervision (Wolf & Rosenfeld, 1978:826). In the nonenterprise component of the primary market "training is brought to the job, skills are not specific to firms, there is little on-the-job training, the market includes a large geographic area (or nation), and there is not much likelihood of occupational advancement" (Wolf & Rosenfeld, 1978:872).

But while sex segregation of occupations and market location explain different attainments by emphasizing distinct opportunity structures for men and women, some interesting data show that sex, too, mediates the process whereby we translate individual achievements into attainments. For instance, sex segregation and market location do not alone explain why within any one generation women do not seem to rise to the first level of supervision and management at the same rate that men do (Acker, 1973; Cole, 1979). Nor do these factors explain why women earn less for equivalent work and effort (Suter & Miller, 1973; Treiman & Terrell, 1975). In short, why are women unable to translate their individual resources and achievements into professional advantage or higher earnings? We explore this question next.

Translating Resources into Economic Gains

According to Deitch, "Traditional explanations of women's lower wages tend to concentrate on women's lower 'human capital investments,' and lower 'commitment to labor force activity' " (1980:1). In her summary of the human capital approach to income differentials, Deitch captured an important link between status attainment and need achievement models. The "human capital model"

> implies that if women's work histories and qualifications become more like men's, women's wages will rise accordingly. The human capital model implies that the earnings gap problem is one of unequal qualifications and investments rather than an inequitable distribution of rewards and inequality of opportunity. (P. 2)

As in the need achievement and status attainment models, the focus in the human capital model is on individual performance and competitive effort.

Alternatives to human capital models have been offered that shift the focus from individual commitment and qualifications to inequality of opportunity and gender-role impact. The work on wage inequities is particularly pertinent. Bib and Form, for instance, concluded that their structural theory, which encompasses stratification of economic sectors, sex segregation of occupations, and sex status, better explains variance in earnings for their national sample of manual workers than does human capital theory (1977). They found the lowest incomes among workers in the economically weak sectors of the labor market and in unorganized occupational groups disproportionately composed of females:

> The low income of blue-collar women cannot be explained by individual variables in a human capital model but by the merging of three low strata: economically weak enterprises in the peripheral sector, occupational groups with weak organizational power, and the subordinate estate of women in society. (P. 979)

Bibb and Form called all three factors critical in understanding income differentials, which reflect social structural rather than individual constraints. Referring to the income determination process, the authors concluded that "men appear to be at a considerable advantage in capitalizing on education, vocational preparation, and lengthy tenure" (p. 987). Blue-collar women cannot translate their resources into advantage in the same way blue-collar men can. Finally, the authors suggested that the full extent of the stratification process was not reflected in their data: "Within both core and peripheral sectors and within major occupational groups, blue-collar women usually occupy the lowest paying, least desirable postions, a nuance not reflected in our aggregate measures" (pp. 991–992).[11]

Deitch also noted that unequal pay is clearly related to unequal opportunity *and* to sex status (1980). She, like Bibb and Form, argued that models including structural variables (e.g., location in the market and unionization) in earnings equations explain more of the total variance than do models with only human capital variables. She emphasized that sex has its own impact: men, for instance, benefit more from unionization and from supervisory status than do women; men also receive, on the average, much higher rates of return than women in dollars for each additional year of education and experience. In effect, women do not appear to earn as much on their human capital investments (education and experience) as do men. According to Deitch, the sex differential in return for education is one of the strongest explanations for the wage gap between men and women:

> When all the other factors are controlled for, women receive $273 for each additional year of education while men receive $686 for each year completed. This is true despite the fact that women in the sample have an average of 12.02 years of education and men have 11.86 years. . . .

> If the women in the sample were to receive the same rate of return for education as men do, $684 instead of $273, for each of their twelve years of education, women's average annual earnings would increase by $4,964. This difference would reduce the total male-female earnings gap in this sample by 84%. (P. 17)

Deitch added that if men benefit more than women from unionization, supervisory status, and years with one employer, merely moving more women into better-paying jobs would not eliminate the wage gap.

Other researchers have challenged the human capital theory, especially with regard to accumulated resources over the work cycle. Reskin and Hargens found status attainment differences for male and female chemists (1977). They challenged the notion that men and women are rewarded equally for "accumulated advantage." According to their data, men did better than women in converting predoctoral publications into prestigious postdoctoral fellowships. And having held a relatively prestigious fellowship aided the men, but not the women, in obtaining a tenure-track first job. Moreover, women did not improve their chances of ultimately securing a tenured university postion by increasing the number of their scholarly contributions to the same degree that men did.

An earlier study by Reskin of chemists showed important differences between the sexes (1976). As is not uncommon in status attainment models, the male subjects exhibited the expected pattern of relationships; that is,

> calibre of professional training and graduate school performance were associated with receipt of a prestigious award, which in turn was associated with high-status positions and scientific productivity, illustrating the accumulation of advantages. (P. 609)

"In contrast," Reskin noted, "the female chemists accumulated no advantages with respect to the postdoctoral experience" (p. 609). If achievement norms govern status attainment,

> predoctoral background characteristics should covary with award prestige, which in turn should covary with occupational outcomes. The major finding of this analysis—the existence of sex interactions in the predoctoral determinants and occupational consequences of the postdoctoral experience—

seriously questions whether achievement norms govern status attainment for female scientists. (P. 610)

Reskin and Hargens suggested that "the explanation often advanced that women are less committed to their careers and therefore may not *try* to convert their early resources to later advancement has not been supported by evidence" (1977:18; emphasis added). In fact, commitment is not fixed for either sex by the time the Ph.D. is awarded but "more plausibly is a function of both the opportunities for and institutionalized barriers to scientific performance" (Reskin & Hargens, 1977:18).[12]

Such arguments are particularly important in light of Cole's 1979 book, *Fair Science: Women in the Scientific Community.* Cole found that the scientific community basically treats women fairly. Our purpose is not to criticize the book: any quantitative study assessing discrimination among academically employed scientists that claims women academicians suffer little discrimination (Cole did not consider financial remuneration but noted substantial sex based discrimination in promotion to high rank) will receive its share of attention (see especially Mason, 1980). Perhaps more important than his claim that women suffer little discrimination is Cole's evidence that, at least as far as rank, women are not treated equitably within the scientific reward system. Their failure to accumulate advantage was readily acknowledged by the author. Cole further acknowledged that academic rank has important consequences for scientists' careers, particularly with regard to salary and access to the "means of scientific production." This latter observation is critical. Since Cole rested his "fair science" argument largely on evidence that women's lower productivity accounts for most of the observed differences between men and women with regard to status and reputation, access to the means of production becomes an important issue. Lower productivity might well be related to poorer access. The discriminatory processes that limit women's access to the means of production are crucial in understanding their work world attainments. As Acker suggested: "Unless we know how the conditions of women's work are controlled and shaped in male-run organizations, work inequalties may persist under even a radically changed economic and political system" (1978:154). In the following section we investigate the organization of professional life.

Barriers to Women in the Professions

As Epstein astutely noted: "No matter what sphere of work women are hired for or select, like sediment in a wine bottle they seem to settle to the bottom" (1970b:2). Although written over a decade ago, these words still ring true today: the upper strata of almost any profession are devoid of women. Kanter found that women do not hold positions of power and authority in organizations, especially in American industry (1975, 1977a). The

few women in management tend to be concentrated in lower-paying positions and in less powerful, less prestigious organizations (Kanter, 1975:35).
The overrepresentation of women in ancillary positions and specialties
within universities, law, or medicine is striking. Lorber, looking at the
medical profession, noted:

> The fault may not lie in their psyches or female roles, but in the system of pro-
> fessional patronage and sponsorship which tracked them out of the prestigious
> specialties and "inner fraternities" of American medical institutions by not
> recommending them for the better internships, residencies, and hospital staff
> positions and by not referring patients to them. (1975:82)

Gates suggested that the legal profession

> remains a stronghold of male chauvinism despite the recent influx of young
> women into law schools. Few women lawyers have yet found their way into
> legislatures, onto judicial benches, or into the upper echelons of law firms.
> Women students lack role models because of the dearth of female law pro-
> fessors. Recent graduates still have trouble obtaining clerkships with judges
> and positions with prestigious firms. Those who do secure jobs are often
> restricted in the kinds of cases they are assigned—typically they are denied
> court room experience and contact with important clients who are believed to
> prefer a male attorney. Women lawyers tend to know their rights better than
> do other women workers, however, so they have been able to practice their
> skills against employers who disdain them. More than one prominent firm has
> had to defend itself against an attorney alleging sex discrimination in hiring or
> other conditions of employment. (1976:73)

And lest one suspect that academe is any different, the National Education
Association reported the following percentages of female faculty: professors, 8.9 percent; associate professors, 15.2 percent; assistant professors,
24.1 percent; and instructors, 44.8 percent (U.S. Department of Labor,
Women's Bureau, 1975:152). As other professions are studied, the same
picture emerges. A recent breakthrough is the focus on structural causes to
explain the poor representation of women in upper-echelon positions. Attention has shifted away from "women's problems" to the social organization of the work setting and to gender-related dynamics.[13]

This new focus has produced some exciting theoretical and empirical
work, especially on the social dynamics of tokenism (Kanter, 1977b; Laws,
1975) and on networks (Kaufman, 1977, 1978; Lipman-Blumen, 1976).
Lipman-Blumen started from the premise that from early childhood and
clearly as an *ongoing process*, men seek and enjoy and/or prefer the company of the same sex:

> The stratification system which ranks individuals and groups in terms of their
> value to society, systematically places males in more highly valued roles than
> females. . . . The pragmatic recognition that males controlled economic,
> political, educational, occupational, legal and social resources created a situa-

tion in which men identified with and sought help from other men. Women, recognizing the existential validity of the situation, also turned to men for help and protection. (1976:16)

Lipman-Blumen's conclusions differ somewhat from ours, however. She argued that as women have gained more resources, they have developed a homosocial world of their own and consequently have turned to other women for help rather than to men. Yet Kaufman warned that although such female networks exist and are increasing, they are not yet as strategically located or as powerful as those of men (1978). Exclusion from male networks may be as important a structural barrier today as it was when Epstein identified this problem over a decade ago (1970a).

Several informal features of the professions and professionalism almost by definition work against women's mobility. One, for instance, is the clublike context of professional life (Epstein, 1970a:968). Hughes noted that the "very word 'profession' implies a certain social and moral solidarity, a strong dependence of one colleague upon the opinions and judgments of others" (1962:125). People who bear certain ascriptive statuses (black, female, etc.) are at an immediate disadvantage in the collegial context. As Hughes suggested long ago, ascriptive statuses condition the set of characteristics necessary to gain acceptance by one's peers as a professional (1944). He said that "auxiliary characteristics" are "the bases of the colleague group's definition of its common interests, of its informal code, and of selection of those who become the inner fraternity" (p. 355). Hughes' fraternal imagery is apt: like fraternal societies, the collegial group depends upon "common background, continual association and affinity of interest" (Epstein, 1970a:972). Accordingly, women and other low-status individuals are unwelcome in such associations. And the more informal the setting, the greater the likelihood that ascriptive variables will be important:

> In a collegial body such as the board of directors, a staff conference, or an administrative committee, the atmosphere of formality and the short duration of contact facilitate cooperation without reference to sex roles. But where the cooperating group is unorganized, where contacts are more or less continuous, and especially where the relations between equals . . . are personalized, we encounter once more the barriers which hinder men and women from free mutual participation. (Caplow, 1954:243)

Presumably, then, persons who lack certain auxiliary characteristics face problems in collegial groups. The significance of colleagues cannot be overestimated. White, a social psychologist who studied women scholars at the Radcliffe Institute, revealed how important collegial contacts are for professional identity and self-evaluation (1970). The women interviewed had all been awarded fellowships so that they might continue their professional interests on a part-time basis. The findings suggested that although the opportunity to be intellectually engaged in a project was important to the women's sense of professional identity and competence, equally critical was the access to stimulating colleagues. White concluded that "appraisals of their work by others, coupled with acceptance and recognition by people whose professional opinions were relevant and appropriate, made a significant difference in determining whether a woman felt like a professional, and whether she in turn had a strong sense of commitment to future work" (p. 413). White added: "Challenging interaction with other professionals is frequently as necessary to creative work as is the opportunity for solitude and thought" (p. 414; see also Daniels, 1980).

Male-female collegial situations are difficult for women's role partners, too. Take, for example, the protégé system, whereby one's name and work become known in the upper echelons of one's profession. Epstein (1970a), White (1970), and Keller (1974) suggested that since the top levels in most professions are almost entirely male, problems arise in dealing with female protégés: "A man may be hesitant about encouraging a woman as a protégé. . . . He may believe that she is less likely to be a good gamble, a risk for him to exert himself for, or that she is financially less dependent upon a job" (White, 1970: 414). If she is less likely to receive sponsorship than her male peers, a woman is more likely to be excluded from crucial arenas wherein professional identity and recognition occur. In her study of academic women, Kaufman quoted a respondent who felt clearly left out of the mentor system:

> Although my research interests are clearly in line with one of the older males in my department, he has never asked me to share my ideas with him or even to read some of his research proposals. I wouldn't feel so badly but I have a male colleague who is my age and whose dissertation was much further removed from this senior professor's area of interest. My young friend has just been asked to help formulate a new research proposal with our older colleague. . . . My main contact with my older colleague is that his oldest daughter attends the same university I graduated from and that remains our main topic of conversation. (1978:16)

Because women are excluded from male networks, or the "informal brotherhood" in which experiences are exchanged, competence built up, and the formal code elaborated" (Hughes, 1944:356), they are not only marginal but invisible when important professional decisions such as selection for promotion, tenure, research grants, co-editorships, summer teaching, and departmental privileges are considered (Hughes:1973). If women are denied access to established male networks (even if they have formed their own), they most likely will remain outside the power centers of their professions. Moreover, if women and men operate in different arenas, gender-role stereotypes will stand unchallenged.

Surely, women who have overcome the innumerable educational and cultural barriers to their attaining professional status have acquired coping

mechanisms and maneuvering techniques. Why, then, do so few professional women make it to the top? We already have suggested an answer:
limited access to the power centers of the professions. Here we wish to
elaborate on this pattern and suggest that inclusion in old boy networks may
create as well as solve problems. For instance, inclusion in old boy networks
may yield tokens rather than role models for future female professionals.

Kanter's research focused on what happens to women who occupy
token statuses or, more specifically, to women who are alone or nearly
alone in a peer group of men (1977b). The term "token" goes beyond
numerical scarcity. As Kanter said:

> Lone people of one type among members of another are not necessarily tokens
> if their presence is taken for granted in the group or organization and in-
> corporated into the dominant culture, so that their loneness is merely the ac-
> cidental result of random distribution rather that a reflection of the rarity of
> their type in that system. (P. 969).

The data attest to women's token status in prestige professions.

Kanter noted that tokens, because of their rarity, often find that attention is directed at their gender roles rather than at task-relevant behavior
(1977b). She suggested that tokens respond to this pressure either by
overachieving or by attempting to limit their visibility. Most take the latter
route, attempting to keep a low profile—avoiding public events and
meetings and, even more important, occasions for performance. However,
by keeping their visibility low, they also hide their competence.

Kept on the periphery of colleague interaction, tokens not only remain
outsiders but also miss the informal "caught" information White called
necessary for survival and mobility (1970). Furthermore, the price the token
may eventually have to pay for being "one of the boys" is occasionally to
turn against "the girls" (Kanter, 1977b). Laws also argued that by allowing
herself to be treated as an exception, the token preserves the illusion that
women in general are not really up to the professional task (1975).
However, the most devastating effect of tokenism may be the caricatured
roles women are offered within the professional setting. The four role traps
Kanter identified for women have a familiar, if not comfortable, ascriptive
ring: mother, seductress, pet, and iron maiden (1977a).[14] All these roles
focus on a female's sex status first, allowing ascribed roles to encompass
(and delimit) achieved ones. In effect, the roles available to women allow
them to *fulfill*, not challenge, gender stereotypes, preventing women from
exhibiting their own competence. "Fear of success," Kanter suggested, may
really be "fear of visibility" (p. 986). The most important point, however,
is that the structure of the professional setting *elicits* such behavior. It is not
necessarily a reflection of long-standing personality traits and internalized
gender-role attributes.

More subtle forms of maintaining traditional gender roles have been less researched but deserve attention. Research on the use of physical space and touching informs us that the "nonverbal elements of behavior such as body position, location in space, facial cues, voice tones and sensitivity to these behaviors in others, are often overlooked but highly important aspects of interpersonal communication" and that male and female experiences are quite different in this area (Frieze & Ramsey, 1974:1). For instance, the male boss often has physical access to his female secretary, which is not reciprocal. He may come quite close to her in giving instructions, "but she would not be expected to have equal or such easy access to his office, his desk, or his physical presence when asking a question" (Frieze & Ramsey, 1974:3). Although it might be argued that this discrepancy is a result of subordinate/superordinate relationships and not gender-role related, some evidence suggests that women's physical space is violated more often than that of men (Frieze & Ramsey, 1974; Henderson & Lyons, 1972; Somner, 1959). Henley (1973) and Jourard and Rubin (1968) have demonstrated that women tend to be touched more than men by both men and other women.

Control of verbal space is another sex distinction Frieze and Ramsey emphasized (1974). They noted that men tend to talk more than women participants in both dyadic and group interactions; furthermore, "detailed analyses of verbal transcripts also indicate that women may have trouble getting a group's attention and that when they do get attention, it may be lost by male interruption" (p. 5). Even intonation can imply gender and status differences: "An intonation pattern common to women is rising pitch at the end of an utterance; this is often taken to communicate hesitancy, insecurity and shyness" (Frieze & Ramsey, 1974:5).

While no one behavior pattern by itself seems particularly important in relaying an image of self, these gender-role expectations as a group defeat the image of an achieving woman. A growing body of empirical data suggests that gender based differences affect almost all aspects of the work situation. Rosen and Jerdee found that evaluations of the efficiency of certain supervisory styles were influenced by the sex of the supervisor and subordinates: reward style was rated more effective for male supervisors than for female supervisors, while a friendly, dependent style was rated more effective for supervisors of either sex when used with subordinates of the opposite sex (1973:47). In a 1961 study Gilmer found that over 65 percent of male managers believed that women would be inferior to men in supervisory jobs (Rosen & Jerdee, 1973:44). Similarly, Bowman, Wortney, and Greyser found that although a minority of men (41 percent) were antiwoman executive in principle, only 35 percent were pro-woman executive (1965). In their research on male managers' attitudes toward working women, Bass, Krusell, and Alexander documented the pervasiveness of cultural norms about male-female interaction in the workplace (1971).

Managers felt very strongly that women would not make good supervisors; capability was not the issue, but rather the managers' feeling that other men and women would prefer having male supervisors.

Kaufman and Fetters's 1980 study of accountants provides some insights into the work world of women on the executive climb:

> "One vice-president at a client's office called me a 'nosy broad' when I was doing exactly what I should, . . . trying to gather more information about their internal audit system," claimed one senior-level woman. Another quoted a client: "Oh look, the (firm) sent in the secretaries." A female supervisor complained: "I was actually kicked out of a client's office when I arrived because he refused to give 'privileged' information to a woman." Another staff-level woman said: "One client told me I wasn't 'for real.' He claimed that I was on the audit for social reasons, not for career reasons. He actually said I was probably looking for a husband or maybe a 'pat on the head' for being so bright." (pp. 11–12).

Conclusion

In this chapter we have seen that a woman's economic status is greatly affected by a whole constellation of variables and assumptions about her worth. An important step forward has been made by those who are attempting to explain economic inequities in terms of structural features of the labor market and the organization of occupations therein. While these efforts have shifted the focus away from the individual woman (and thereby away from "female deficiencies"), the organization of the labor market and of the job structure also are based upon assumptions about woman's biological, sexual, psychological, and intellectual functioning. Consequently, analyses that attempt to explain the differences between males and females on the basis of structural conditions in the labor market but without reference to the gender hierarchy outside that realm are also somewhat limited.

Just as theories based on the need to achieve had trouble accounting for women, so do status attainment and human capital theories. For all these theories presuppose a model that generally excludes social structural variables thereby viewing the individual actor, either economic man or achieving man, as the source of eventual economic or achievement outcomes. If success is not forthcoming, the fault rests with the individual. We cited evidence in this chapter that challenge such assumptions. We need not necessarily resort to individual characteristics (or deficiencies) to exlain sex differences in the marketplace. Work force conditions can account for such differences as well. In the next chapter we see how the woman at midlife and thereafter fares. Any analysis of her achievements must simultaneously include a complex individual actor, her potential for change, and the many barriers, including age, that obstruct her achievement path.

Notes

1. Whether woman's domestic labor is, in fact, nonproductive labor has become a major subject of debate. Benston's "Political Economy of Women's Liberation" posited that the central, inherent, issue revolves around "use" and "exchange" values (1969). Dalla Costa and James claimed that women provide not only use value but also exchange value: "The community of housewives is the . . . hidden source of surplus labor (1972:7).

   These modern feminist economists are concerned with the same questions debated by feminist domestic reformers a century ago. They are trying to bring the achievements of women into the visible productive world. This awakening to the hidden value of women's labor has been strong among feminists in the field of social stratification as well (Acker, 1973, 1978; Bose, 1973; Huber, 1973).

2. We focus on the status attainment literature in the Blau and Duncan tradition rather than works we feel are richer in theoretical explanation (Dahrendorf, 1959; Parkin, 1971; Sorokin, 1927) because of the current predominance of status attainment in the social stratification and mobility literature.

3. The gender-role writers whose work we have mentioned in this section represent only a small part of the literature.

4. In reviewing this chapter, demographer Melanie Martindale perceptively noted that gender creates an increased relative distance or perhaps even a new kind of distance with, she suggested, higher transportation costs.

5. Parallel arguments can be found in the literature comparing common-value theorists to class-specific theorists, especially with regard to working-class adolescents' ambitions. For instance, while common-value theorists frequently ask respondents what they would like to do for a living, class-specific theorists focus on expectations. The former generally find that Americans affirm the success value of social advancement and economic achievement; the latter generally find that the expectations of Americans are limited by race, class, or sex. What one hopes for may be quite different from what one expects (Han, 1969).

   Empey identified other methodological issues that he felt *underestimated* the strength of the working-class adolescent's ambitions (1956). If we take middle-class aspirations as a single criterion for aspiration level, we tend to focus on professional and managerial occupations as indicators of high aspirations. Not surprisingly, then, Empey found that the higher one's socioeconomic class, the higher one's occupational aspirations tend to be. However, such measures underestimate the aspiration levels of lower socioeconomic status students. Almost all such respondents in Empey's study preferred and anticipated having a higher occupational status than their fathers', but not necessarily professional status.

6. Stewart noted a similar problem in the temporal ordering of events for female mobility:

   Because data limitations prevent the comparison of the entire span of a father's career with those of all of his offspring (which would enable us to detect different patterns for women), most studies compare a single point in the careers of a sample of sons or daughters (first job or current job) with a point in the careers of their fathers (usually job at daughter's age 16). The assumed relation of first job to the completion of educational preparation for work, to the life cycle, to a career pattern or even to later job is clearly not the same for most working women as it is for men. The question of whether a father's occupation is the appropriate point of comparison when studying female occupational mobility, especially given that daughters' occupations are found in a different occupational distribution and in a different life cycle pattern, is not asked. (1977b:10)

7. For instance, Meixel noted that "Hout and Morgan (1975) apply a variant of the Wisconsin model for educational expectations and find that the model fits white males the best" (1976:17). Similarly, males and females have different mobility patterns (Havens & Tully, 1972; Tyree & Treas, 1974).

8. Early research suggested that female educational attainments were more closely tied to the ascribed criteria of family background while those of males were more strongly related to academic ability (Sewell & Shah, 1967, 1968). Similarly, Alexander and Eckland found in a national sample of youths taken in 1955 and followed to 1970 that for females, sex interacted with educational attainment factors in such a way that family status was a stronger determinant of educational attainment than was ability; for males, the opposite was true (1974). Alexander and Eckland argued that sex had a direct, unmediated depressant effect on female educational attainment. In fact, for females, sex (an ascribed status) was a better predictor of educational attainment than was socioeconomic background, academic performance, educational aspirations, academic self-concept, curriculum enrollment, or influence of significant others (Meixel, 1976:17).

9. We have deleted from our discussion two major comparative studies of male and female educational and occupational status attainments that found the status attainment process similar for the sexes. Treiman and Terrell (1975), as well as McClendon (1976), stated that the process and level of status attainments were similar for males and females. However, these researchers used a restricted Wisconsin model, excluding from analysis the social psychological variables. They employed only the socioeconomic variables in accounting for educational and occupational attainments. Importantly, they could explain only some 30 percent of the variance by parental education and occupation. Therefore, Meixel argued, "less of the variance in status attainment is explained by the model than is left unexplained" (1976:16). McClendon suggested why so little of the variance was explained:

   The reader should be reminded that the variables in the basic model of occupational status only explain a little over one third of the variation. The addition of intelligence scores is known to significantly increase the explained variation, but still leaves over half the variation in status unexplained. . . . Thus it is possible that the presently unmeasured variables which explain the remaining variation might be different for males and females. They might also show the present model to be misspecified in such a way that variables presently in the model may show sex interactions. (1976:61).

Similarly, Treiman and Terrell noted "that the complex interaction between norms governing sex role and family relationships and institutional arrangements governing occupational opportunities and rewards for women . . . is obviously the next important order of business" (1975:198).

10. Mortimer, Hall, & Hill, questioned how long women will continue to accept this kind of vicarious achievement (1976). A growing consciousness of exploitation—spurred by expanding educational opportunities, by the women's movement, and by growing labor force participation—may make this role a thing of the past.

11. In addition, protective legislation that restricts women to lower-paying, unskilled jobs in industry further reinforces stratificational boundaries. Shortridge argued that occupational stratification may be a function more of job title than of the nature of the work itself (1975). A man, for instance, doing a charwoman's work may be called a janitor, a caretaker, or an industrial cleaner and consequently be paid more for his labors. Outright discrimination occurs even when title differences are not present: "At the bottom of the economic spectrum discrimination is not even illegal for the provision of the Fair Labor Standards Act requiring equal pay for equal work applies only to jobs that are covered by the minimum wage" (Shortridge, 1975:247).

12. See Persell for comparison of rewards for research in education by male and female researchers (1978). Research papers, anonymously rated by a national panel of judges, revealed no differences in quality between males' and females' work, but there were substantial differences in the incomes between the men and women who were rated.

13. In 1974 Acker and Van Houten reanalyzed one of the most famous studies in organizational behavior, the research now known as the Hawthorne studies (Roethesberger & Dickson, 1939). They suggested new explanations for the rise in productivity in the all-female group, indicating that differential experimental treatment of the male and female groups, rather than gender-related attributes, led to many of the findings. Acker and Van Houten showed that people in the generally higher output group were for the most part young unmarried women from traditional and usually economically disadvantaged families (all except one were living at home in first-generation immigrant families) and suggested that one would expect little risk taking or assertiveness from such women, given the powerlessness of their position:

For the women's group, the relationship was between powerful males and weak females; that is, the females, being weak, had to please the supervisors if they wished to stay in the test room, so they adopted the norm of increased production. Their attempts at developing some self-protection resulted in reprimands and eventually exclusion; compliance led to special rewards. (P. 154)

This perhaps is one of the clearest examples of the way in which female behavior is interpreted as personality based despite the structural variables that are shaping and evoking women's responses. Persons, male or female, placed in normatively sanctioned powerless positions might well match their behavior to the conditions they face on the job.

Acker and Van Houten also examined Crozier's (1964) study of two French bureaucracies. Once again they pointed to control mechanisms within the work setting that varied with sex of the worker:

Control mechanisms for women may more often resemble those used with children. . . . adult women were frequently referred to as girls. The use of this word shaped the construction of reality for both the men and the women, and allowed for control. Also, organizational rewards offered women may be often products or services stereotypically thought to be preferred by women, while rewards offered men are not so sex linked. For example, women may be frequently rewarded with such things as flowers, trinkets, and so forth. Women may be subjected to more personalized control arrangements than men. Men may usually face impersonal rules and regulations that are fairly universalistic for men occupying similar positions, while women may more often be required to adjust to rules that are particular to their relationships with a male supervisor. (1974:161)

Some researchers have argued that the very structure of low-level white-collar positions encourages behavior that is stereotyped as female; for example, clerical and secretarial jobs "require" passive and/or compliant behavior. Syzmanski noted that personal loyalty and subordination are critical requirements for those worker roles; thus "corporations have a major stake in perpetuating the 'feminine' qualities of such jobs and do so by rewarding and encouraging meekness and subordination" (1974:724).

14. Of course, power over men through any of these roles is at best limited. For instance, if a woman plays seductress, she may be regarded as an attractive female but not necessarily a skilled colleague. If a woman plays pet, she reinforces her dependence on males. In both cases she undermines her individual abilities or actions. Epstein noted that of the twenty-five women corporate presidents and vice-presidents studied by Hennig in 1971, most were either widows or daughters of men who had led these firms or had other ties with a man in command (1975). However, rising to the top on the strength of affectional and kinship ties is risky: positions thus won are nontransferable and leave in the woman in a poor bargaining position (Epstein, 1975).

CHAPTER 5

The Mature Woman: Calculating Her Worth

We have repeatedly emphasized that definitions of women's achievements reflect social norms and expectations concerning female public and private roles. As we have traced women's contributions historically, we have noted the rhythms of life course achievements women share as a consequence of their sex. In this chapter we look at variations, across groups of women, based on age and experience. While all women's achievement schedules are subject to social control, each age group is uniquely affected by the historical moment. This chapter largely concerns the mature woman, over thirty-five, born prior to the baby boom and currently swelling the ranks of the labor force. More than half of American women today are over thirty-five: 30 percent are thirty-five to fifty-four and an equal proportion are fifty-five or older. (U.S. Dept. of Labor 1976, 1977). No wonder the mature woman is of growing interest to social analysts and the subject of countless self-help books and conferences. The "midlife crisis" has created a new focus and worry for Americans.

The volume of material published at the close of the seventies on the midlife crisis has made even the fear-of-success literature pale by comparison. Debates concerning people thirty-five years of age and older clearly have struck a sensitive chord in both women and men. The recent journalistic and academic outpouring about individuals at midlife has shaken popular stereotypes about aging. It has also challenged theoretical assumptions about the developmental process and the potential for growth and change in later life. As we review the issues related to aging, we shall see how the reconsideration of women refines and revitalizes old methods and theories by generating more dynamic concepts of maturation for both sexes.

In chapter 1, we addressed the issue of developmental fixity, criticizing the undue focus in need-achievement models on early experiences—on individual drives, motives, and needs as opposed to social and cultural influences (Goslin, 1971). The original gender research called early experiences pervasive and enduring. Hoffman's analysis of need affiliation in women was directly linked to a different early developmental pattern for young girls:

> If the child's own resources are insufficient, being on her own is frustrating and frightening. Fears of abandonment are very common in infants and young children, even when the danger is remote. Involvement in mastery explorations and the increasing competence and confidence that results can help alleviate these fears, but for girls, they may continue even into adulthood. The anticipation of being alone and unloved then, may have a particularly desperate quality in women. The hypothesis we propose is that the all-pervasive affiliative need in women results from this syndrome. (1975:144)

If development, achievement oriented or otherwise, is characterized as process, the exact stage of life is less important than the ongoing interactions between the individual and the social context. As Gewirtz (1971) and Kagan (1976) argued, the developmental point in time for implementing change may be irrelevant since the environmental circumstances needed to facilitate development may be a juncture in a sequence of experiences and only incidentally a moment in historical time. This issue of timing, while debated in the developmental literature (Butler, 1977; Clarke & Clarke, 1976; Gewirtz, 1971; Goulet & Baltes, 1970; Harris, 1957; Lerner, 1976; Moos, 1976; Skolnick, 1976), remained unaddressed until recent gender-role research.

In this chapter we argue that most theories of achievement fail to account for the life experiences of the older woman, whose current status is powerfully influenced by institutionalized sex and age discrimination. Feminists are increasingly politicizing the value of the labels attached to mature women's contributions in domestic and familial roles. They are insisting that older women get a better legal, social, and economic return for their private investments as wives, mothers, and community leaders.

In chapter 3 we suggested that during the life stage periods in which women were most actively involved in familial roles, they were often confronted with a seemingly normless situation. It is hard to assess and compare one's achievements and accomplishments in areas that lack clear benchmarks. Accordingly, women have found it difficult to bargain or negotiate, except through informal means, from their private roles. In chapter 4 we looked within cohorts and emphasized the importance of women's location in the marketplace. Because of women's segregation within and between occupations, female public labor, though its worth can be measured, is underestimated.

Chapter five continues this analysis by focusing on current attempts to reevaluate women's public and private worth. By examining the attitudes, values, and behaviors of mature women, documented in longitudinal studies, and by making cross-generational comparisons, we expand our analysis to include the accumulated costs and long-term consequences of specific life events and sociohistoric conditions. This chapter ends by addressing some issues now receiving attention in the courts and legislatures. These issues—displaced homemakers, retraining for nontraditional careers, and equal pay for work of comparable worth—typify concerns that are prompting scholarship on achievement which is more sensitive to the female life experience.

Theories of Aging: Assessing the Potential for Change

Most theories of life course development have emphasized the early years as a period of growth and the later ones as a time for turning inward for personal consolidation (Bischof, 1976; Goulet & Baltes, 1970; Hess, 1976; Rebelsky, 1975; Troll, 1975). Jung, sometimes called the spiritual father of life cycle theory, broke away from Freudian emphasis on childhood by focusing on youth and maturity (1933). Although he described it as psychologically positive "to discover in death a goal towards which one can strive," aging in his view was an "inexorable inner process [that] enforces the contraction of life" (p. 17). Jung introduced several ideas that have been elaborated in other models. He suggested that the task of youth was to learn to abandon the dream of childhood, while that of the later years was to turn inward and sometimes to become more like the opposite sex.

Jung based his hypotheses on aging on clinical work; other researchers active at the same time set out to document his views empirically. Later, Kuhlen's research brought new attention to the midlife period. His descriptions of this stage included individuals motivated by anxiety and the threat of losing past gains (Kuhlen, 1964, 1968a, b). He suggested that personality changes in this period reflect conservatism, intolerance of ambiguity, and rigidity; in addition, certain motives (such as achievement, power, creativity, and self-actualization) are on the decline (Lowenthal, Thurnher & Chiriboga, 1976).[1] According to Kuhlen, midlife represents a shift from active, direct gratification of needs to vicarious living. Citing her own investigations, Neugarten pointed out that in advancing age people may seem less happy, view themselves more negatively, have lower self-esteem, and show less self-confidence. In summarizing these results, she commented:

> It should come as no surprise to the reader that this particular interpretation of aging is not well accepted by people in the middle-aged or older categories. Indeed, when the writer presented these views at an adult education conference some years ago, it was denounced as "a theory of decay." (1968b:125)

Neugarten carefully observed that the motive for an individual's contraction can be generated by external sources. Contraction may result from the satisfaction of earlier motivations; physical or social loss; a sense of being locked into a situation; or even the changing time perspective that comes with having lived over half of one's life (Hochschild, 1973b; Levinson, 1974).

The belief that there is a decreased investment in living from midlife onward has been incorporated into a controversial *theory of disengagement*, most explicitly articulated by Cumming and Henry (1961). These whisperings of mortality and the impending doom models of development received academic attention in Jacques's "Death and the Mid-life Crisis" (1965) and popular attention in the work of Sheehy (1974) and Levinson (1978). Yet these early formulations of the aging process were based heavily on male patterns and tended to treat as natural, if not universal, events that were the product of the historical moment as well as of chronological age (Hareven, 1978a). Brim closed his 1974 address to the American Psychological Association with the following comments:

> It is certain that some men have crises at some time in their mid-life period, and it seems that this must be when men get hit with multiple demands for fundamental personality change in the same year, or month, or week. As one person summed it up: "the hormone production levels are dropping, the head is balding, the sexual vigor is diminishing, the stress is unending, the children are leaving, the parents are dying, the job horizons are narrowing, the friends are having their first heart attacks; the past floats by in a fog of hopes not realized, opportunities not grasped, women not bedded, potentials not fulfilled, and the future is a confrontation with one's own mortality. (1976:177)

Of course, male midlife stresses in some ways resemble women's (Dohrenwend & Dohrenwend, 1974; Gould, 1972, 1978). Endocrine changes are taking place in both sexes. From about the age of thirty, males experience a gradual decline in testosterone and cortisone production and a slowing in the secretion of androgens. And somewhere between her late forties and early fifties, the woman experiences hormonal changes leading to menopause (Troll, 1975). However, research on women has sensitized us to the problem in generalizing from developmental literature. Gilligan noted that educator John Dewey long ago summarized the difficulty succinctly: "Writers, usually male, hold forth on the psychology of women, as if they were dealing with a platonic universal entity, although they habitually treat men as individuals varying with structure and environment" (1980:11). Citing Levinson's 1978 book, *The Seasons of a Man's Life*, Gilligan observed that Levinson justified his study of only males by recognizing that although sex differences in "biology" and "social circumstances" did exist, he was sure that his approach "offered a basis for the study of women" (1980:12).

Gilligan's critique of the moral development literature is similar to our analysis of the achievement literature.[2] She argued that the approach to gender has focused heavily on one question—"How much like men do women think?"—with the underlying assumption that there is but one path of development (1980:12). In particular, Gilligan referred to the scales typically used in studies of moral development. When measured by these scales (derived from Kohlberg's study of adolescent boys), females appear to have a less developed sense of justice or, more negatively, some form of developmental failure (1967). In such studies, the moral judgments of females range around Kohlberg's stage 3, where good is defined in terms of interpersonal relationships. On the other hand, the judgments of males appear to advance in a more linear fashion toward stages 4 and 5, where good is defined in terms of society's rules and universal principles. In accounting for these patterns, Kohlberg noted: "Stage 3, personal concordance morality, is a functional morality for housewives and mothers; it is not for businessmen and professionals" (Gilligan, 1980:16).

Gilligan's work on adult professional women suggests that the interpersonal orientation noted by Kohlberg is not simply "a functional morality for housewives and mothers" but a different perspective, an additional frame of reference on justice and moral decisionmaking, held more often by women than men. Gilligan has followed a tradition in moral problem solving that moves beyond mere knowledge of society's rules to the implications of their enactment (Beard, 1946; Elshtain, 1974; Gould & Wartofsky, 1976; Jaquette, 1974; Scarf, 1978). This frame of reference makes the concept of justice more complex, emphasizing the capacity of the individual to raise questions about the origins of rules and definitions in relationship to the realities of interpersonal obligations and introducing seemingly irrational, but clearly morally relevant, emotions such as "compassion, love, and sympathy" (Gilligan, 1980:17) into the moral decisionmaking domain. Gilligan thus has moved us past a moral orientation based on the male adolescent's understanding of justice to a more complex model that addresses adults and includes women.

Although we do not wish to dismiss the commonalities shared by the sexes in the aging process, the focus on the female developmental process has challenged and expanded our concepts of aging and development and, our assumptions about the capacity for change. In the case of moral development, the focus on women has extended the moral decisionmaking domain to include the "moral passions" and highlighted the more complex thinking that comes with age. In personality development, the focus on the female has uncovered the potential for change over the life course. Neugarten, one of the pioneers in life course research, using the Thematic Apperception Test on different age groups, found that as they age men become increasingly passive and dependent, while women become increasingly active and dominant (1968a). To explain these findings, she coined the phrase "return of the repressed."

In an analysis that drew on Neugarten's data, Hochschild speculated that social reasons dictate what is repressed in younger women (dominance and mastery) and younger men (passivity and dependence) (1975b). Hochschild explained Jung's description of the "change into opposites" (1933) and Neugarten's "return of the repressed" (1968a):

> The crossing of paths in old age may be an unconscious expression of equally unconscious social conditioning. Thus, when we examine data which tells us about unconscious social processes in youth, we are not necessarily discovering innate or intrinsic psychological givens. Rather, we may be seeing the unconscious expression of social conditioning. We cannot automatically equate social conditioning with conscious behavior, nor innate tendencies with the unconscious. (1975b:558)

Even when theorists agree that the sexes share certain experiences as they grow older, the interpretation of these experiences varies. While many theorists concede that aging may be associated with increased vulnerability and crisis (Bart, 1972; Bischof, 1976; Woodruff & Birren, 1975), others see these changes as positive (Bühler, 1935, 1961; Neugarten, 1968; Janeway, 1971, 1973, 1980; Lowenthal, 1975; Erickson, 1976; Hochschild, 1976; Jackson, 1977). Bart went so far as to suggest that "withdrawal (or disengagement) is as inadequate a response to aging as it is a means of contraception" (1975:4). Bühler also described midlife and beyond as a time for growth and expansion (1935, 1961). She noted that this period often succeeds a crisis, by which she meant a renewal of interest in life. The growth potential of crises has been explored by more contemporary theorists as well (Erikson, 1976).

Neugarten noted that although leaving school, parents, and children behind are events as predictable as menopause, grandparenthood, and retirement, they are not crises but punctuation marks along the life course (1968a). We should keep in mind, however, that the timing of "normal" life course events differs not only by sex but by generation as well (Elder, 1974, 1978; Friedman & Shade, 1976; Kanter, 1978a). Recent demographic scholarship has reminded us that our views of normal development are rooted as much in the demands of the social and historical moment as in biology (Conger, 1971; Foner, 1976, 1978; Hareven, 1977, 1978a, b; Rossi, 1977). In his analysis of family portraits in medieval France, Aries pointed out that children were presented as miniature adults and expected to partake in and enjoy adult activities (1962, 1978). Childhood had yet to be conceptualized as a separate stage in the life course. Marriage, parenthood, and work were lifelong activities in preindustrial America (Boocock, 1978; Sawhill, 1978; Smelser & Halpern, 1978). Movement into and out of these roles did not necessarily represent transitions into adulthood: children and adolescents were shuttled between school and the labor force depending on the seasons and the needs of the economy (Hareven, 1978:19). At the turn of the century, careers were terminated more often by sickness and death than by retirement.

One of the functions of socialization is to motivate people to follow the current prescriptive timetable (Troll, 1977). Expectations regarding age-appropriate behavior are embedded in daily and social interactions, and most of us are aware of these expectations. As Neugarten put it:

> Age norms and age expectations operate as prods and brakes upon behavior, in some instances hastening an event, in others, delaying it. Men and women are not only aware of the social clocks that operate in various areas of their lives, but they are also aware of their own timing and readily describe themselves as "early", "late" or "on time" with regard to family and occupational events. (1968a:143)

Sometimes, socially prescribed limitations imposed by age norms conflict with actual capabilities and throw us off schedule. In her sixties, Janeway described her sense of conflict between chronological age and her individual professional life cycle:

> I keep waking up in the morning and thinking I'm 31. It makes me feel like the woman in the laxative ads on TV: "You're not as young as you feel." I do not find her an acceptable role model, but here I am, missing my real age by a generation. It's not that I want to be 31, nor that I think anyone else imagines me to be 31. . . . In fact for someone who likes to think she's reality-oriented, it's a mighty silly feeling. So why do I have it? (Harris, 1975:185)

For Janeway, fresh professional challenges brought a sense of newness, youth, and productivity:

> When I wrote *Man's World, Woman's Place*, in my fifties, it was like writing a second first book. I had to read enormously, of course, but I also had to learn quite a new way of writing, with no help from the fictional skills I'd developed in the past. In a way, I think that the willingness to do something like this, to go on learning, is why I don't mock myself more for that silly wake-up delusion that I'm 31. I shall certainly be proved wrong one day, but until I am I shall think of the work I want to do, the work that lies ahead, as if I were 31; I shall be as ready to plan vast projects and tangle with new ideas. (Harris, 1975:185)

Janeway's is a vigorous assertion that aging need not limit ambition, learning, or productivity.[3]

Of particular interest to people studying women is the possibility of reviving or developing capacities at later stages in the life course. This issue has received increasing attention as generations of older persons are challenging notions of irretrievable loss. Research is suggesting that a good deal of human capability can be activated or reactivated when the social situation is receptive (Goulet & Baltes, 1976; Hulicka, 1977). Capacity to achieve is not the same as opportunity to do so: while the human may possess a genetic basis for a wide range of learning, such genetic equipment does not in any way insure that such potential will be realized (Clarke & Clarke, 1976). Psychologists refer to the gap between inherited capacities and demonstrated abilities as the "loss of potential." The absence of a behavioral characteristic in a population need not imply permanent extinction:

> Some persons interpret the maturation process as a series of irreversible decisions that produce an adult with a pattern of fixed responses or traits. But there is an important difference between what is true for cell or tissue or organ and what is true of the organism as a whole. In the exceedingly complex nervous system, a great many potentialities can be "stored." Each one separately, we can assume (exaggerating the probable truth) is an irreversible pattern, but seen collectively they make up a repertoire of potentialities for behavior, only some of which can be expressed at any given time. So complex is the storage system that new patterns can be learned and old patterns can be extinguished thoughout life. . . .

> But *extinction* does *not mean* the *elimination of potential.* (Yinger, 1965:44–45; emphasis added.)

Interestingly, then, unlike the early development literature, the burgeoning body of work on development in the later years assumes considerable potential for change and variation over the life course. In the next section we explore attitude and value changes over the life course by comparing different generations of women. Such comparisons place assumptions about developmental patterns in a sociohistoric context. By so doing we hope to emphasize not only the human capacity for change but also the rich effect of life experiences on our measures of worth and, consequently, achievement.

Changes over the Life Course: Maturity, Mental Health, and Gender-Role Attitudes

When we speak of mature or aging women, females commonly grouped into the age range of thirty-five to sixty-five, we are in fact referring to several chronological and historical cohorts. Each generation of mature women shares a distinct frame of reference and set of responses to role transition as a function not only of date of birth but also of stage in the family life cycle (length of marriage and number of children), career history, and life experiences. These factors make it difficult to separate patterns of healthy and disturbed aging, distinguish age-specific problems versus lifetime conditions, and identify sources of stress that are endogenous (physiological or personal) as opposed to exogenous (social or environmental).

As researchers have come to appreciate the value of distinguishing between age differences as a function of developmental versus historical time, the models guiding inquiry have become more complex. In particular, growing emphasis has been placed on specifying the particular cohort, or generational age group, under discussion (Elder, 1974; Foner, 1976, 1978). In our discussions of women born during the same period, we must also remain mindful of variations within the cohort group, such as race, socioeconomic class, employment status, and stage in the family life cycle.

Increasing methodological attention has been given to the problems of gathering and analyzing socioeconomic life course data. In 1977 the Social Science Research Council convened a conference to review research based on the National Longitudinal Surveys of Labor Force Participation (NLS) data and to suggest directions for the future. In his report on this conference, Peterson pointed out the difficulty in distinguishing between changes caused by age and those caused by specific cohort experiences—an especially hard distinction in the area of gender roles. By way of illustration we turn next to a discussion of aging, mental health, and mature women.

Researchers agree that at all ages, more women than men are diagnosed depressed. Earlier we cited Bart's groundbreaking work relating middle-aged female depression to maternal role loss (1972). Using Human Relations Area Files, hospital records, and intensive interviews, Bart compared women between the ages of forty and fifty-nine who had been diagnosed depressed with a control group of nondepressed women. She reported that the middle-aged depressed women were more likely to have suffered maternal role loss (objectively defined as at least one child out of the home), particularly when they had had an overprotective or overinvolved relationship with their children. She concluded that with few positive roles to move into beyond menopause and no rites of passage to ease the transition, many women who have committed their lives to family lose much of the central meaning of existence as they grow older.

Striking a similar theme, other observers have focused on the older woman's loss of sexual appeal (Sontag, 1972). De Beauvoir (1972) called the post menopausal stage the "dangerous age," the "dying of women's youth" (1972a). And Preston's explication of "old bag" leaves little room for ambiguity: the term means sexless, useless, shapeless, and worn out (1975:41).

Just as a male model of development cannot explain female achievement because it ignores the life experiences specific to women, so, too, sources of crisis and stress identified in any one generation of women's experiences can also be misleading. For example, the first generations of women experiencing an early end to childrearing and an increased life expectancy are having to deal with the nature and meaning of family commitment over an extended lifetime without the benefit of institutional or normative help (Angrist and Almquist, 1975; Osipow, 1975). Old models of womanhood, as Troll noted, may no longer be useful (1977).

We have already noted that the key life events for most women have remained the same across the generations (Conger, 1971; Rich, 1976). They marry, have children and grandchildren, work outside the home in either paid or unpaid labor, obtain some schooling, and survive their spouses. Nevertheless, the timing of certain life events has altered considerably, with a sharp decrease in childbearing among women in their thirties and a ten-year rise in life expectancy since 1930 for women in their twenties (Gordon; 1978:203). Who is the "average" mature woman today? If she is a member of the cohort born between 1930 and 1939, she is likely to have married at the age of twenty; had her first child about a year later, and to have born her last child at thirty-one. By the age of fifty-two she can expect to see her last child married and within the next twelve years to attend her husband's funeral. She can anticipate five to ten years of widowhood.

Recent research on mature women's lives has challenged many assumptions about aging and introduced new variables for investigation; today the biological orientation of much early work on older women is giving way to a longitudinal approach. Guttentag and Salasin designed a project to investigate the long-term consequences of stress in women's lives (1977). Questioning the data and theories that showed menopausal women particularly vulnerable to depression, these researchers explored sources other than specific age-related events (e.g., menopause and maternal role loss) to account for this vulnerability. Guttentag and Salasin suspected that stress accumulated over years of occupying powerless roles might explain the high incidence of depression in this population. They found that rates of depression indeed were associated with stresses from life conditions such as single parenthood, low income, poor education, and responsibility for young children.

Belle also reported that cumulative life stress seems to put one at risk for depression (1979). However, the daily reality is critical:

> when we look at the column that controls for Life Conditions Stress (feelings associated with current difficult life conditions) compared to the column that controls for Family History Variables, there is a much welcomed find. Feelings about current life circumstances are a more powerful predictor of poor mental health than events from childhood. This indicates to us that while there

exists an association between past and present stress and depression the *present* is a more powerful predictor of mental health. (1979:138; emphasis added)

Satisfactions Over the Life Course: Work and Family Roles

Other investigators interested in age-related changes have suggested that both men and women may use a wider range of reference points in evaluating their life achievements and accomplishments than is commonly supposed (Dohrenwend & Dohrenwend, 1974; Lowenthal, Thurnher & Chiriboga, 1976). Douvan (1978) and Iglehart (1979), in reanalyses of changing attitudes toward family and work roles, noted new ways in which work and achievement are being reintegrated into women's assessments of their lives —and ways in which such integration has changed over the past few generations. Douvan reported on normative shifts in marital attitudes (1978). In both the 1957 and 1976 national studies all respondents were asked, "Suppose all you knew about a man/woman was that he/she didn't want to get married. What would you guess he/she was like?" In 1957 four-fifths of all respondents apparently thought such a choice indicated that the person was either too selfish or too neurotic to marry; about one-fifth gave reasons that were relatively neutral. In 1976 less than 25 percent of the population considered a person who chooses not to marry either sick or morally flawed and 14 percent viewed the choice positively.

The last bit of evidence requires me to skip ahead of my data presentation a little, but it is such a compelling and poignant reflection of the moral force of pro-marriage norms in 1957, that I cannot resist using it here. Many of you will remember that Jessie Bernard used the 1957 data as evidence for one of her inimitable, provocative generalizations: to wit, that marriage was good for men but bad for women. She based the assertion on symptom data and general life satisfaction which indicated that single men had more negative mental health symptoms than married men, but that, in general, single women were more symptom free than married women. . . . I decided to look at attitudes toward marriage by marital status to see whether married women were more negative in their attitudes than married men or single women. I found that indeed, they were, but the findings were particularly striking about single women. In every marital status in which people had experienced the married state—that is, among the married, widowed, divorced and separated—women were always more negative about marriage than men were. Only among those who had never been married were women more positive about marriage than men. And they were extraordinarily positive . . . more than any group except widowed men. By 1976 their positive evaluation of the marriage state had dropped more dramatically than any other group. (Douvan, 1978:5-6)

Douvan concluded that these findings reflected the normative climate in 1957, when marriage was defined as the only legitimate status for a woman. She identified two factors that may have contributed to the idealization of matrimony: on the one hand, if marriage is the only status valued by a society (particularly for women) and refusal of marriage is thought to reflect on one's good sense or morality, then unmarried people obviously will want to marry; moreover, women who prefer the single state will be reluctant given such normative expectations to reveal that they reject the idea of marriage.

This is a fine example of the way in which culturally dictated expectations may differ from internalized sentiments and preferences. Douvan was suggesting, as we did in our analysis of early achievement and gender-role acquisition, that when the time is ripe, the sentiment will out."[4]

However, unless new institutional supports appear, normative changes do not occur comfortably:

> In 1957 two groups in the population showed notable symptoms of stress: divorced women and single men. Our data reveal that in 1976 single men and divorced women are still exceptionally stressed. The divorced woman—particularly if she is raising children alone—faces realities like poverty and role overload which are so oppressive that they make social stigma pale by comparison. . . .
>
> The unmarried male in our culture has still not experienced a socialization which prepares him with adequate social and interpersonal skills to create and maintain a reasonably integrated and satisfying life with people on his own— that is, without a wife to initiate and maintain friendships and kinship ties. (Douvan, 1979:2)

Thus, even if individuals are psychologically ready to entertain new career and family patterns, the successful integration of these changed perspectives into everyday life demands institutional reorganization.

Manis and Markus studied women who had come to the University of Michigan's continuing education program between the years 1963 and 1973 (1979). They were especially interested in attitudes about combining work and family roles for both career and non-career oriented women. Respondents were asked to recall their attitudes at various ages and to report what they would do differently if they could start all over again. Women who had gone the furthest with their careers were the least likely to claim they would do something differently. The authors stressed that real-life experiences best explained the older women's current frustrations with work and family roles:

> The women who say they would wait longer to marry did indeed marry earlier than the mean for this group. The women who say that they would wait longer to have their first child had their first child at an earlier age than did the rest of the women in the sample. Those who say they would have fewer children have

larger families than the other women. Those who say that they would finish their education, or get started on their careers before marrying and having children are less likely to have a college degree than the other women, or, if they have a B.A., they earned it at a later age than did the other women. (p. 5)

Iglehart, drawing on the same data set as Douvan (1978, 1979), compared married women's attitudes toward housewivery and paid work across two generations (1979). Most theories of female achievement assume that women must be "pushed," "pulled," or "lured" into employment (Iglehart, 1979:100). Iglehart noted, however, that the cultural norms placing women in the home are most relevant for middle-class white women; other groups, such as black, blue-collar, or rural women, are expected to digress from traditional norms and have been commonly described as "overrepresented" in the labor force—sometimes they are even treated as a "social problem" (p. 100). Iglehart used a subsample of white, currently married females. The 1957 subsample consisted of 628 women who were full-time housewives and 149 who were full-time employees. The 1976 sample included 337 wives who were full-time housewives and 231 who were working full-time outside the home. In 1957, 74 percent of the wives were full-time homemakers; by 1976 the percentage had decreased to 55. The percentage of wives participating full-time in the labor force rose from 18 percent in the 1957 sample to 37 percent in the 1976 sample. In both years, 8 percent worked part-time.

The decrease in the percentage of employed women reporting that they would rather be home on a full-time basis, from 22 percent in 1957 to 3 percent in 1976 indicates that work may be a welcome choice for women rather than a necessity (Iglehart, 1979:28). Although employed wives in 1976 clearly preferred to be in the world of work full-time, they also would have preferred another type of occupation—from 24 percent in the fifties to 41 percent in the seventies (see also Manis & Markus, 1979; Osipow, 1975). Iglehart also reported work preference by occupation and education. Among college educated clerical and sales workers the percentage preferring another kind of work nearly doubled.

Contemporary housewives are more dissatisfied with their work than were their counterparts in the fifties. In 1957, 68 percent of the housewives expressed a positive opinion toward their daily chores; this percentage had decreased to 50 percent in 1976 (Iglehart, 1979). The percentage of homemakers expressing neutral or ambivalent feelings rose from 27 percent in 1957 to 44 percent in 1976. Iglehart suggested that while the percentage expressing positive feelings had decreased, dislike of day-to-day tasks and not dissatisfaction with the domestic role explained this decline. The relationship of education to views on housework also changed significantly from 1957 to 1976. Education was related to housework in both studies but the contemporary relationship was much stronger, especially among younger and older mothers (children under five or over nineteen). Though each income level showed a significant decrease in the percentage of housewives expressing positive opinions of housework, for both time periods low-income housewives were more positive. Women with less than a high school education were generally older and they appear to have retained a more positive orientation toward housework across time; in Iglehart's sample this older, less educated group was also far less likely than any other to have plans to seek employment in the future. (Though such women neither anticipate working nor will find jobs easily, they are highly likely, especially in the later years, to be forced to seek employment.)

As Iglehart reported, housewives are not necessarily unhappy with their role but rather with particular aspects of it (1979). She added:

> [It] becomes crucial to identify the reasons many wives spend their present and plan to spend their future in the housewife role. If it is a sense of duty that compels them, then writers can continue to degrade the role of women in the home. If it is by choice that they are in the home, then a more realistic appraisal should be made of the social rewards contained in homemaking. (p. 83)

Clearly, social rewards attend women in both sets of roles. And recent data indicate that under the right conditions, working may enhance a woman's mental well-being (Belle, 1979).

The Stress and Families project, looking at "the total number of jobs women had held in their lives, the highest salary received in the past three years, and the duration of work experience in the last three years," found that the greater the total number of jobs a women had held during her lifetime, the lower her scores on anxiety and depression (Belle, 1979:352). Similarly, the highest salary received in the past three years, though not related to income or education, was significantly related to many measures of well-being—most particularly, few depressive symptoms. Finally, the longer the duration of work experience in the past three years, the lower the reported depressive symptoms and the higher the respondent's self-esteem (Belle, 1979:354).

> In summary, while current work status bears little correlation with either psychological well being or long term work trends the more longitudinal indicators capture a strong relationship between the total number of jobs ever held and well being and similarly between having had work in the past three years and well being. (Belle 1979:354)

The powerful relationship between total number of jobs (strongest longitudinal variable) and general well-being led the researchers to speculate about just what such a variable measures. They concluded that total number of jobs indicates flexibility of movement into and out of the paid labor market. The ability to obtain employment when this option is expedient or desirable and to stay at home when the occasion warrants may be critical in women's employment (Smith, 1979). Power over the timing and sequencing of one's roles may be a key to mental well-being.

Turning now to an analysis of mature women as neglected, we will reemphasize themes we introduced earlier in this chapter. To pursue the issue of timing, we must take into account the costs of institutionalized discrimination over the life course and the woman's changing orientations toward work and family after she has accumulated life experiences and a broader comparative perspective. Our review of social policy issues surrounding older women stresses the potential for change on both the social and the personal level, tracing links between women's public and private roles. Here again we see how the nineteenth-century feminist analysis of the value of domesticity has resurfaced in the twentieth century.

The Costs of Vicarious Achievement

In 1977 the National Advisory Council on Women's Educational Programs undertook an investigation of the educational needs of three groups of disadvantaged women: displaced homemakers, single mothers, and older women, an estimated 26 million females. Displaced homemakers, after years in the home, have lost the support of their spouses through death, desertion, divorce, or separation. Single mothers are caring for and supporting children in the absence of the fathers. Older women, that is, women over sixty years of age, are more likely to be widows than wives (National Advisory Council 1977:24). It is a sign of women's growing political influence that this population is currently referred to by social policy analysts as "neglected." As a group, neglected women illustrate the arguments we have been making concerning the cumulative costs of discrimination. Moreover, they dramatize the risks involved when women depend primarily upon their spouse's achievements for their own economic support.

Elsewhere we noted that in order to explain women's personal commitment to various roles we must also understand the social processes, normative and institutional, that help maintain their commitment. Current policy debates about neglected women are the first step both toward normative and institutional change and toward helping older women establish new priorities, values, and satisfactions. Such changes would enable women in their later years to pursue meaningful public achievements. Neglected women are generally poor in an economic sense and have suffered accumulated disadvantage. Moreover, they face a tough dilemma:

> Women are *thoroughly conditioned* to want to be good to and to sacrifice themselves for male children and for adult men. (Not for other women.) This inhuman sacrifice of self has a dangerously *shortsighted altruism* at its core; an altruism that ensures the female's eager *complicity* with the status quo. And

the status quo is one in which marriage and motherhood do not "pay off," economically and psychologically, as we think they should. Nevertheless, *women feel even more threatened* when marriage and motherhood as basic female survival mechanisms are taken away from them. They fear, as usual, that something "worse" will happen, if they leave an abusive husband or abandon their children. And they are right. The *nonpayoffs* of divorce and of market place employment do, in all reality, match many women's nightmare expectations. (Chesler, 1976:110; emphasis added)

Chesler has followed the tendency of the academic literature to present an "oversocialized" view of the female personality. As we have stressed many times, notions that women are permanently conditioned to anything are suspect. While we agree with Chesler's assertion that most women are threatened when marriage and motherhood seem in jeopardy, this tells us little about their behavior when "nightmare expectations" occur, nor does it tell us how well women adapt as single parents, displaced homemakers, or widows over time. We are just beginning to develop longitudinal data that might help us make such evaluations.

Corcoran examined changes in marital and economic status experienced between 1968 and 1975 by a national sample of 1,050 married women aged thirty-five to fifty-four in 1968 (1976). She noted that the highest incidence of divorce occurred among women in the middle years of the age group studied. She added: "By 1975, 12.2% of the women aged 35–54 in 1968 were no longer married to their original spouse. Of these 12.2%, less than one-fifth had remarried by 1975 so that 9.9 percent of the original sample of married women were still unmarried in 1975" (p. 2). Although divorced women's major supports are alimony, child care payments, and welfare, about 55 percent of all divorced women receive neither welfare nor alimony and child care payments. Corcoran reported an average annual welfare payment of $1,930 in her New York sample. Only 14 percent of the divorced women said they had been awarded alimony; however, collecting is difficult and after five years most of the women gave up seeking the payments due to them. Only 44 percent in Corcoran's sample received child support.

Divorce may weigh heavily on women with young children, but it is crucial to recognize the increasing heterogeneity not only of the female labor force but also of the general population of women responsible for their own economic survival. Nonmarried older women—single, separated, divorced, or widowed—comprise a growing segment of today's communities: about 10 percent of the 22 million women between the ages of forty-five and sixty-four live in female headed households; another 25 percent live alone or with unrelated persons. The widowed female now outnumbers widowers four to one (Nye & Berardo, 1973:600). Nonmarried women in their later years represent a particularly vulnerable part of this population. Women who lack partners at this point often face a series of role changes and their personal discontinuity is compounded by inadequate institutional responses. Problems of reentry into and mobility within the labor force, of retraining or obtaining further education, of finding adequate health care and housing, are formidable. Welfare, alimony, and retirement plans provide inadequate compensation for income losses when marriage ends (Barrett, 1979a, b). Nye and Berardo noted that 70 percent of widows over fifty-five are left with assets under $10,000 and 40 percent, with assets under $5,000. The growing incidence of divorce at all ages and the financial hardships faced by older women, however their marriages end, make the notion of vicarious achievement through matrimony suspect at best.

Shields described displaced homemakers as altruistic achievers: "the women who bought the home-and-hearth package and believed our life was about keeping Dad glad and *kinder* clean; we are the women who fulfilled our role as full-time homemaker, dependent on our husbands for source of income, and who, in our middle years, have lost that income through widowhood and divorce" (1976:1). According to Shields, Sommers coined the phrase *displaced homemaker*, "knowing. . . . that older women who *have* to work because they have lost their 'job' as wife and mother are literally 'forcibly exiled' from the economic mainstream of society, cut off from meaningful opportunities to be economically independent" (p. 2). The displaced homemaker is a woman in her middle years (generally thirty-five to sixty-four) who has been deprived of her traditional role by the loss of her spouse through separation, divorce, abandonment, or death (Sommers, 1976). When she finds herself alone after twenty to thirty years' support by her spouse, she has neither financial nor personal resources to rely upon.

Current social security provisions reflect an image of the homemaker as an appendage to, rather than a fully equal partner in, marriage. And until recently, a woman divorced after less than twenty years' marriage had no social security protection based on her husband's employment; married more than twenty years prior to divorce, she was eligible for benefits only when her ex-husband retired or died. The growth of no-fault divorce has eroded the economic protection of dependent spouses and children, always minimal at best. Working together with the National Conference of Commissioners on Uniform State Laws, many women's groups are calling for accountability in the economic provisions of divorce laws. They have pressed state legislatures, for instance, to adopt statements of intent similar to this one introduced in the Wisconsin Legislature in 1975. Women's organizations want the following statement included:

> It is the intent of the legislature that a spouse who has been handicapped socially or economically by his or her contribution to a marriage shall be compensated for such contributions at the termination of the marriage insofar as possible, and may be reeducated where necessary to permit the spouse to become self supporting at a standard of living reasonably comparable to that enjoyed during the marriage. (National Commission of IWY 1976:231)

Such demands represent an effort to win benefits for homemakers as workers, a view incorporated in the California Displaced Homemakers Act and in legislation pending before the U.S. Congress.

The New Home Economics

In chapter 4 we illustrated various ways in which the value of women's labor in both the private and the public sphere often has gone unrecognized and/or unrewarded. We gave as one example the turn-of-the-century census practice of calling the taking in of boarders unpaid housework. Recently, within academia, as in the legislatures, we have witnessed attempts to provide more meaningul measures of women's lifetime contributions to the economy. We are referring here to the emergence of the *new home economics*, a reconsideration of the value of domestic time and labor.

The new home economics shares the usual set of economic assumptions that individuals are rational, that they attempt to maximize their own welfare, and that they have information with which to evaluate and choose among alternative courses of action (Boulding, 1970). When studying decisions about the use of both time and goods within the household or family, the new home economists examine choices about marriage, divorce, childrearing, and female employment (Schultz, 1974). One of the best-known illustrations of this approach is Becker's model of marriage and divorce (1973). In this model, the motives for entering into marriage include the desire to have children, the efficiency of sharing a household with a loved one, and the efficiency associated with the specialization of male and female time within marriage:

> If women's market productivity and wages are lower than men's, but women are at least as productive within the household as men, then marriage permits a substitution of the wife's less expensive time for the husband's more expensive time in household activities and a corresponding substitution of the husband's time for the wife's time in the labor market. . . . Men "hire" women to bear and rear children and to do housework because they are physically incapable of the first and because their time is too valuable to devote to the second and third. Women "hire" men to be breadwinners and to earn the wages which they are generally not able to command. Thus, each marriage partner gains by teaming up with the other. (Sawhill, 1978:119)

This analysis does not consider the costs—psychic or otherwise—of lower earnings in the marketplace to women. In her critique of Becker's approach, Sawhill noted that the motives attributed to the rational economic actor in the family setting reflect care and love rather than conflict, bargaining, hate, fear, or power struggles. Yet the very concept of a *household utility function* rests on the assumption that family members carefully weigh each others' preferences in order to arrive at consensus: "It is not particularly instructive simply to assume that people do what they want to do. Boulding's (1970) statement that the economist's indifference curve (representing individual preferences) was 'immaculately conceived' gets at the heart of the matter'' (Sawhill, 1978:121). How much room is there for bargaining and negotiation?

We have repeatedly emphasized the inadequacies of concepts like "choice" as they are used to account for women's achievements. Neglected women, like displaced homemakers or single mothers, are sometimes described as though they had made an unfortunate or ignorant series of bad choices in planning for their futures: they neglected education or training; they selected a spouse unwisely; they timed the births of their children inconveniently; they invested their energies in the wrong commitments. In this model, explanations for female achievements seem to be a search for women's mistakes. But good decision making demands institutional support as well as individual effort. For instance, the National Advisory Council on Women emphasized, the importance of providing stipends to women of all ages for education and retraining programs: "Unless these women can be assisted while they learn more marketable skills, they are doomed to the treadmill of underemployment" (Eliason, 1977:5). The council also recommended that "tax reform legislation be revised to provide nontaxable assistance by employers for career advancement to displaced homemakers, single mothers, and older women" (Eliason 1977:5). At present the Internal Revenue Service requires employees to pay tax on any financial support received from employers for career advancement; preparation for better-paying occupations falls into taxable income categories. This regulation illustrates the way in which existing policies may perpetuate discrimination that is clearly immune to individual corrective efforts. It is clear, then, that the bargaining tactics learned in adolescence are better aimed at direct rather than vicarious achievement. Girls must be redirected to learn from mothers and grandmothers as they confront the realities of aging—often, as the statistics show, without a husband or other source of support.

Retraining Vicarious Achievers:
Issues of Equal Pay and Comparable Worth

Describing marriage patterns familiar to many mature women, Lipman-Blumen and Leavitt describe three points along a hypothetical vicarious achievement continuum for spouses: altruistic, contributing, and instrumental. For the altruistic achiever the relationship with the husband and his accomplishments are primary. Other styles are more common. There is the contributing vicarious achiever who derives pleasure "primarily from the belief that she has contributed in some measure to the success of the direct achiever, if only by maintaining the relationship" (1976:26).

Although she is like the altruistic achiever in that she obtains pleasure mainly from her relationship to her husband, the contributing achiever is more
likely to accept responsibility for the family's socioeconomic success by
becoming a secondary wage earner. This financial effort occupies most of
her marital life. This type of woman demonstrates the accumulated costs of
institutionalized discrimination in the labor market; the rationale for paying
her less and placing her in low-mobility jobs falls apart when the older contributing vicarious achiever may be the sole support of herself and/or her
family.

In contrast to altruistic and contributing achievers, the instrumental
vicarious achiever appears more interested in the extrinsic rewards of success. She is more likely to perceive her marriage as a means to security,
status, love, money, achievement and even other relationships (Lipman-
Blumen & Leavitt, 1976). This wife may manipulate the marital relationship
in order to achieve other ends, "including those which the vicarious individual may feel unsuited to attempt on his/her own" (Lipman & Leavitt,
1977:6). (In the 1950s the mate selection literature was full of studies of
"hypergamy" and characterizations of women battling competitively over
eligible males.) Although such an achiever might be happy with the extrinsic
rewards related to alimony, child support, and inheritance, the statistics
suggest that she will not have much success in these arenas. The statistics
also suggest that in her later years remarriage is unlikely.

Most older women cannot afford to be vicarious achievers. However,
their gender-role socialization may have left them unprepared for the
economic and social realities of aging. At the same time they also may be
overqualified for many of the jobs currently targeted in training programs
for older women. The National Advisory Council on Women's Educational
Programs recommended:

> These women need training for well-paying jobs that offer advancement op-
> portunities. They need education to remedy their ignorance of such economic
> realities as money management, credit, insurance, and banking. They also
> need access to financial aid for tuition, child care, transportation, clothing,
> and frequently, living expenses. (Eliason, 1977:4)

This proposal points up the realities surrounding women's secondary status
in the labor market. Female occupational patterns, often attributed to
women's peripheral commitment to jobs (as vicarious achievers), in fact
reflect labor market constraints.

In 1977, 25.4 percent of adult women between the ages of twenty-five
and fifty-nine who had stopped work in the previous year did so because
they could not find jobs; this was true of only 17.7 percent of men (Barrett,
1979b:70). Moreover, the female unemployment rate rose more than the
male rate over the past decade (Barrett, 1979b:64). New attention is being
given to *discouraged workers*, people who after months of fruitless job

searching are no longer counted as unemployed even though they are out of a job and want work, and to unemployed persons who take part-time positions out of desperation. The U.S. Labor Department estimated that the number of discouraged jobless women in 1977 (694,000) was more than double that of men (317,000) (Barrett, 1979b:68). In summary, then, the female is more likely to be jobless, discouraged, or involuntarily working part-time than her male counterpart. We are becoming increasingly aware that this is the result of labor market conditions and not necessarily of lesser commitment to public roles. Other beliefs about women's achievement patterns are coming under scrutiny as empirical research accurately describes female labor market participation. For example, employers traditionally underestimate women's labor force attachment by expecting that wives will move in accord with their husbands' career opportunities. However, when account is taken of job status, men and women differ very little in job attachment (Women's Bureau, 1976).

In a recent report Barrett claimed that: "education and training do not pay off in higher earnings for women to the same degree that they do for men" (Barrett, 1979a: 43-44). The life cycle income profiles of men and women by years of education show that for men in their mid-forties, the income of the average college graduate exceeds by about $9,000 a year that of the high school graduate. For women (in their mid-forties) the annual difference in earnings between high school and college graduates is about $4,000. Furthermore, women who have finished college earn less money than do male high school graduates of all ages; their median income about equals that of male high school dropouts. These statistics, reflecting sex discrimination in the labor market—not lesser commitment—explain women's relatively flat life cycle earnings profile.

In an effort to describe human resource utilization, the U.S. Commission on Civil Rights developed measures of overqualification and underemployment (1978). Their indicators showed that the payoff for an education (measured in terms of occupations and earnings) was significantly less for most women and minority men than for majority males. The overqualification indicators used by the commission demonstrated that majority males with high school educations were more likely to find jobs suited to their educational level than were most females and minority males. Majority females with a high school diploma or some college were more likely than majority males to find jobs comparable to their education in 1960 than in 1970, but by 1976 the positions had reversed. Among individuals who had finished college—approximately 11 percent of minority males and females, 22 percent of majority females, and 34 percent of majority males—the financial payoffs continued to vary by ethnicity and sex (U.S. Commission on Civil Rights, 1978). Minority males earned approximately 85 percent and minority and majority women less than 70 percent of what comparably educated majority males earned.

Federal employment programs have periodically attempted to address some of these persistent inequities. Many of the programs that proliferated in the 1970s were consolidated in the Comprehensive Employment and Training Acts of 1973 (CETA). CETA provided public service jobs, training, and other services for economically disadvantaged, unemployed, and underemployed persons (Barrett, 1979b:91). A related but smaller program, the Work Incentive Program (WIN), was designed to place welfare recipients—persons receiving Aid to Families with Dependent Children (AFDC)—in jobs and training.

Most CETA participants were white males between the ages of twenty-two and forty-four with twelve or more years of education (Barrett, 1979b:92). Women were clearly underrepresented relative to their eligibility: Harlan noted that in 1977 only half the women eligible for the nonsustainment portion of Title VI public service employment were participating in the program. Research indicates that, in general, federal guidelines explicitly or implicitly leave room for local programs to give clear preference to male family heads. Although in 1976 female family heads represented 90 percent of AFDC recipients and thus belonged to the WIN target population, they accounted for only 73 percent of WIN participants and only 65 percent of those who eventually found jobs (Barrett, 1979b:93).

Perry, Anderson, Rowan, and Northrup, in summarizing the patterns of training for women in manpower programs prior to CETA (1965–1972), reported that "female trainees were heavily concentrated in programs having a limited emphasis on the acquisition and development of marketable occupational skills" (1975). Similarly, female participants in CETA have been less likely than males to be enrolled in on-the-job training, which entails occupationally specific training in an actual work setting, often with a private employer. Instead, women have tended to be enrolled in short-term or part-time adult work experience, with no required training components (Harlan, 1980:6). Barrett reported that in WIN programs three-fourths of the women, compared to one-third of the men were placed in jobs paying less than $3 per hour (1979b:98).

While public service programs other than WIN do not explicitly favor men, the family income limit for eligibility has the same effect (Herman, 1979). For example, a woman with an employed husband whose earnings exceed the family income limitation would not be eligible for job training. In 1977 the Carter administration proposed a comprehensive welfare reform program, the Program for Better Jobs and Income (PBJI), that eliminated any uncertainties about who should get preferential treatment. According to the U.S. Department of Labor:

> Only one job or training opportunity will be offered to each family. That opportunity will be available to the sole parent or, if there are two parents, to the family's usual "principal earner." The principal earner is defined as the parent

who either has worked the most hours or had the highest earnings in the past 6 months (Barrett, 1979b:93).

Although the language was carefully chosen to appear sex neutral, it supported a policy reflecting a somewhat outdated view of family support systems. The program deprived couples of deciding for themselves whether the wife or the husband should participate in the labor market (Wilder, 1980). (While this chapter is especially concerned with the needs of older women in the displaced homemaker category, it is important to bear in mind that such policies deprive younger women in intact families of important achievement opportunities. Such opportunities might prepare them for meaningful job training prior to losing a husband or slipping deeper into poverty in their later years.)

Other inequities persist. For instance, although since 1974 WIN has made efforts to reduce occupational segregation, over 60 percent of the female participants in 1978 were in clerical, sales, and service occupations (Harlan, 1980:7). While WIN training for women emphasizes basic education, clerical skills, keypunch operations, licensed practical nursing, and nurses' aid training, male enrollees can find jobs in the whole range of occupations normally found in the labor market. Such sex-typing in training is receiving political attention as the Vocational Education Act comes up for reauthorization in the 1980s (Dunkle, 1980; Wilder, 1980).

One way to break sex-typing in training programs is to channel women into nontraditional occupations. American Telegraph & Telephone and the Union of Electrical Workers have followed this route. As Falk-Dickler noted: "Women in midlife must begin to think of themselves as car salespersons as well as car drivers, as typewriter repair persons as well as clerk-typists, and as accountants as well as bookkeepers" (1976:3). However, the strategy of urging women to move into nontraditional careers is often based on the assumption that a woman performing a male sex-typed job will receive equal pay for work of comparable worth (see, however, Deitch, 1980). As we have seen, the market generally proves this assumption false.

While some advocates for women's equity advocate retraining in non-female stereotyped jobs, others argue for a reevaluation of women's present occupational worth. Behind the comparable worth argument is the assumption that whole classes of jobs are traditionally undervalued because they are held by women and that this inequality, in the form of lower wages (among other indicators), amounts to overt sex discrimination. This analysis goes considerably further than the prohibition of wage discrimination under the Equal Pay Act, which applies only to jobs requiring the *same* skill, effort, responsibility, and working conditions. But, as Hagglund noted, to circumvent charges of sex discrimination, growing numbers of employers are changing job evaluation systems, redesigning jobs, and rewriting job descriptions to avoid paying women equitably for jobs that are identical to those of men (1980). While the law is clear with regard to equal pay for equal work where jobs are identical, there is still debate about recompense for jobs that require *similar* skill, effort, and responsibility (Hagglund, 1980:181).

The comparable worth issue is especially relevant to mature women for several reasons. First, for people who have been in the labor force a long time, back pay and double indemnity can represent large sums of money. Second, as noted in our discussion of CETA and other training programs directed toward women joining or rejoining the labor force, low-mobility and low-paying jobs are at the heart of this debate. Third, as Lenhoff observed, many mature women presently in traditional female occupations do not want "men's jobs" and think that the women's movement threatens their freedom to choose a "woman's job" (1980). In fact, as we have noted in other chapters, a vocal segment of the women's movement has repeatedly stressed the value of women's traditional labors in both the public and the private sphere and has resisted efforts to devalue these roles in contrast to those of men. The early home economists and many feminists today share an appreciation for the intrinsic merit, as well as internal strength, of women's traditional endeavors. Roles embedded in a female subculture within the world of work may offer greater psychological satisfaction and less stress to many women—particularly older women who have grown comfortable in this subculture—at this period in history (Lopata & Steinhart, 1971).

For these reasons, then, both today and in the past there has been strong support for political changes that would increase the value attached to women's traditional labors rather than demand that women move in directions for which they have not been prepared:

> For every first woman construction worker there are thousands of secretaries. For every first woman electrician and first left-handed, blue-eyed female bus driver there are hundreds more working on a line with other women like them. In fact, 80% of the women in the country work in 25 job categories and those are overwhelmingly "women's jobs."

> And so, those who want to improve women's lives by improving their paychecks, those who are looking for equity have begun shifting their emphasis. They are less ardent about trying to urge women out of the jobs they hold—and often like—and more concerned with getting women's jobs reevaluated according to their real worth. (Goodman, 1978:39)

Conclusion

A woman's achievements are characteristically measured against standards derived from typical middle-class, middle-aged, white male's schedules and timetables. Social historians have made us aware of cohort differences that go beyond male/female distinctions to emphasize variations among women. The new home economics recognizes the value of domestic labor but neglects actors as sentient and negotiating individuals. Social policy must take into account such negotiating actors; actors who find themselves in a public and private script that is under revision and reevaluation.

Notes

1. Lowenthal,Thurnher & Chiriboga's research supported the notion that there is an apparent value shift with age (1976). Their data suggested that earlier stages of the life cycle have an expansive orientation on achievement, coupled with high expectations. Middle-aged and older persons, however, tend to focus inward.

2. In reviewing research on sex differences, Gilligan noted patterns of explanation similar to those in achievement critiques (1980). For instance, even when sex differences are not reported, researchers suspect that there may be yet undiscovered explanatory sources that make the results different—just as need affiliation was invoked to explain young girls' achievement behavior.

   Gilligan also questioned the scoring of various cue responses (1980). Holstein, in her longitudinal study of moral development in adolescents and their parents (1976), also reported being troubled by a scoring system based on the Kohlberg measures. This system implies that the often sensitive responses of mature women place them in a category with children.

   In a strongly cognitive scheme such as Kohlberg's . . . emotional response to conflict which is exemplified by females more than males results in adult female reasoning being categorized with children's. . . . The problem of where to categorize irrational but morally relevant emotions such as compassion, sympathy, and love will remain a problem, especially in the light of consistent sex differences produced by scoring standards for these moral passions. (Gilligan & Murphy, 1979:17)

3 It has become almost axiomatic that intellectual ability begins to decline rather sharply in middle adulthood. Cross-sectional studies have shown that intelligence peaks somewhere between adolescence and the middle twenties. Troll noted, however, that longitudinal studies (more reliable in reflecting change over time) do not reflect this inverted-U age curve of intelligence (1976:33). She reported that general intelligence scores appear to increase slightly up to about age fifty.

4. Douvan's data also indicated that the norm against divorce is neither as strong nor as absolute as it once was. In a subsample of the 1976 group, 20 percent of the respondents said that divorce was never a good solution to marital problems, while 80 percent thought that under some conditions it represented the best path (Douvan, 1978:7).

CHAPTER 6

Achievement, Moral Commitment and Life Choices

In social science the concepts of achievement and moral commitment have paradoxically remained isolated from one another, analyzed as if they operated in a social vacuum. Female achievements are often treated in terms of women's moral commitments. Acquisition of the motive to achieve, gender identity, and a moral conscience supposedly occur early in childhood. Once internalized, need achievement and gender identity are seen as stable and permanent. Once established, moral judgement in its "autonomous" form is thought to be sustained across a lifetime. But social and moral learning are neither acquired nor maintained in a historically static or economically just atmosphere.

Often when analyzing women's achievements, we lose the important distinction between free choice, as in moral commitment, and forced choice, as in social powerlessness. Choice and decision for women, as for all social actors, must always be viewed within a social context. Boundary conditions and systems of rewards and punishments are ever present, externally, as well as internally. Rarely are the motives attributed to women conforming to culturally prescribed sequences of events linked to their social powerlessness. Rather, women's commitment, especially to gender roles, is located within a developmental model that stresses not only cognition (knowing what is expected) but also sentience (feeling that what is expected is appropriate). While maturational and developmental forces clearly operate, what often maintains these commitments for women are ubiquitous and powerful cultural and structural sanctions against those who deviate.

Conscience, its acquisition and maintenance, exists in a social context. Allport (1937, 1955, 1961), in discussing the "functional autonomy of motives," accepted a learning theory explanation for the origin of conscience. He rejected, however, the view that its maintenance depends upon reinforcement. Therefore, he underemphasized the many social determinants in adult life that keep conscience from fading. Parsons (1964), relying on reinforcement as an important factor in the acquisition of conscience, equivocated with regard to the forces necessary for its maintenance. We view the growth of conscience as similar to the internalization of a norm. In social psychological terms conscience is internal only in the sense that there is a predictable response at some remove from the stimulus: "The internalization of a norm is the propensity to conform to the norm—to behave in the way the norm reinforces—at a spatial or temporal remove from its sanction" (Scott, 1971:88). What we call "moral commitment," or the internalized response to a norm (moral consensus), is the same behavior in Scott's model that follows upon learning a response to any conditioner. As Boring noted, "When learning is established, extinction of the response by stopping the reinforcement is slow" (Scott, 1971:87). Commitment will dim, if not disappear, without sanctions. Sanctions remain critical throughout the life course; they represent the boundaries of behavior, the pathways to achievement.

Control over these boundaries is part of the power politics of the gender system we have described throughout this book. The contemporary social science literature typically presumes that aspects of the female role naturally, inevitably, or (at the least) probably will conflict with achievement but accord with domesticity. Yet this assumption seriously overestimates women's satisfaction with the status quo and underestimates their capacity for renegotiating the value of their labor and the direction of their commitments.

Vicarious Achievement: The Sociopolitical Context of Marriage

In her analysis, especially of the Brontës' and Eliot's nineteenth-century heroines, Spacks pointed to women's inherent moral dilemma in accepting the dependent roles offered to them through marriage (1975). Spacks explained that in "exercising a Victorian woman's only important choice—of whom, or whether, to marry—they risk[ed] the integrity of inward vitality" (p. 95). The marital institution required dependency and therefore "the appearance of irresponsibility or of responsibility defined by others" (p. 95).

Claiming responsibility for oneself is but a single issue in the analysis of moral commitment. The selection of any set of roles that demand dependence and, in the most literal sense of the term, selflessness cannot be equated with feminine virtue or greater moral commitment until we examine the political-economic context of such a choice. Marriage is as much an economic necessity at the end of the twentieth century as it was at the beginning. In the last half of this century, a woman alone (especially given the returns on her marketplace endeavors) still risks not only the stigma of social deviance but, clearly, economic deprivation as well.

Even the most recent research on intergenerational socioeconomic mobility suggests that women are less likely than men to step into the occupations of their fathers (Featherman, 1978). Although the expectancies, sentiments, and motives described in expectancy-value and status attainment theories are theoretically linked to the attitudes and attributes of individuals, women's achievements are still linked to familial others. Featherman summarized the literature with the recognition that

> vicarious achievement (through spouse) remains as a major mechanism for intergenerational continuity or change in status for women, supplementing or complementing the opportunities for achievement through independent economic pursuits outside marriage and the home economy. (P. 53)

Under these conditions the decision to marry reflects economic necessity as much as an enduring moral commitment to the private gender roles associated with marriage. As one of Austen's characters recognized, spinsterhood is a bitter fate only for those who cannot afford it.

The sociopolitical context of marriage helps us to understand what maintains commitment. In an insightful and witty summary of marriage today, Hacker analyzed the power politics of marriage (1979). Using Bernard's notion that there are two marriage realities for every one marriage, Hacker suggested that marriage is clearly different and unequal for the sexes (see also Gillespie, 1975). In reviewing Pietropinto and Simenauer's 1979 survey of marriage in America, Hacker placed their data in a political context. Not only, he argued, do men and women choose marriage for different reasons—he "to settle down," she "for love"—but also "he loves her as a creature not quite his equal, and the endurance of his affection requires maintaining that disparity. . . . Men may say they want wives who are accomplished and independent. But they also want them docile" (pp. 23-24).

In *The Dilemmas of Masculinity*, Komarovsky noted that even males in her sample who had for the most part rejected the notion of differential social and intellectual attributes based on sex and who would look for male and female friends with the same attributes expressed concern about the combination of motherhood and career for their future wives (1976). The majority saw no substitute for the mother during a child's pre-school years. Komarovsky listed the inconsistencies in the men's responses: "The low status attached to housewifery but the conviction that there is no substitute for the mother's care of young children; the deeply internalized norm of male occupational superiority pitted against the principle of equal opportunity irrespective of sex" (p. 37).

That marriage is different for men and women in "every major particular" (Hacker, 1979:24) has been well documented and has found one of its best discussions in Bernard's *Future of Marriage* (1973a). Hacker continued his analysis by noting that marriage means more to women than to men, that they think about it more, and finally that what they have to say about marriage is ultimately more interesting and insightful. Since women's major complaints revolve around communication problems with their husbands, Hacker wondered how many men are prepared to treat their wives as equals: "Being asked to talk with women as equals is an experience at odds with most of their prior training" (p. 24).

Hacker's belief in women's ability to get beyond the "I" in the marital relationship fits with our analysis of women's presumed greater ability for selflessness or, as Hacker termed it, the "collaborative self." He stated firmly: "Women are indeed less bound up with 'I' than men, more willing to define themselves through a collaborative life" (1979, p. 24). His hopes for men were not very sanguine: "Most men feel threatened by such a prospect and by the time they marry it is too late for most to create that kind of capacity" (p. 24). While we do not necessarily agree with Hacker's analysis of men's and women's capacities (perhaps women are less bound up with themselves because they are more constrained than men), we do agree with Hacker that marriage is an unequal bargain for women.

Using census statistics, Hacker aptly addressed the unequal bargain facing women in the marital institution:

> To begin with, women have fewer marriage opportunities than men. Things start out well enough, as young people pair off. By the age of thirty, nine out of ten young men have been married at least once. Their problems begin when divorce and widowhood set in. What happens can be illustrated by looking at how matters stand once people reach the ages of 40 to 44. By that time there are 300,000 fewer men, due to death or disappearance. As a result, among 2.1 million unattached Americans in this age range, there are 137 women for every 100 men. (1979:25–26)

Within the unattached category Hacker found sharply varying groups. Among those who have been divorced and are not yet remarried, "there are 141 women for every 100 men. For those who are separated, the proportion is 213 to 100. And there are 644 widows for every 100 widowers" (Hacker, 1979:26). Hacker employed the census statistics skillfully to show that as she ages a female has a diminishing chance of remarrying; children make a difference as well:

> A childless divorced woman stands a 73 percent chance of remarrying. With two children, her odds are 63 percent. With three, 56 percent. However age is a more important factor than whether a woman has children. A woman in her twenties with three children has a better (72 percent) chance of remarriage than a childless woman in her thirties (60 percent). (p. 26)

Hacker added that

> in the typical first marriage, the husband is about two and a half years older than his bride. However when he remarries, he looks for someone at least five years his junior, a preference that holds even when his second wife has herself been married before. . . . Most remarriages take place not long after youthful divorces, with the couples closer in age. Men who divorce later—say, in their forties—are more apt to pick brides ten years younger than themselves. (P. 26)

Hacker's final point, demonstrating that women get the short end of the marriage statistics stick, was that the more successful a woman, the less likely she is to marry. Not only are women with graduate educations more than twice as likely as men with similar schooling to get divorced but "among women between 35 and 44, with some graduate education or incomes exceeding $20,000, 20 percent have never married—almost four times the rate for other women of their age" (p. 26).

Any analysis of woman's commitment to private gender roles (especially those that interfere with her ability to pursue and perform well in public achievement roles) must be made within the context of the sociopolitical factors that maintain her commitment. Any shifts in women's options would, as Hacker noted (1979), entail major changes for men. This recognition is not new. Scene 9 in Brecht's *Galileo* is a particularly appropriate dramatic rendition of our analysis of power, politics, marriage, and morality. In this scene, a ballad singer in a carnival-like atmosphere (a sign of social upheaval) reaffirms with mock sincerity the established order of the universe and of society. He charges that if people were to believe in Galileo it could lead to disruption not only of the universe but of the social hierarchy as well. According to Kaufman, this Brechtian view stresses that any kind of thinking that investigates the transitory and changeable aspects of things and processes threatens the ruling class (1979). At the height of the merriment the ballad singer's wife is attracted to a dwarf astronomer. The wife, who heretofore has been circling her husband as the earth does the sun, notes that she "could do with a change." Recognizing that his egalitarian views could jeopardize his own personal domain, the ballad singer then rejects revolution and the new moral order. The obvious message that the ruling or dominant group will resist change raises the point that unequal relations are inherently unstable. Such conditions (as we suggested in chapter 5) ultimately hold little moral force for people most oppressed within the system and set the conditions for manipulative behavior.

Renegotiating the Boundaries and Definitions of Achievement

Earlier we described the bargaining and negotiating skills young females may learn in adolescence. We suggested that these skills might be employed in developing interpersonal competence and achievement strengths often undervalued in expectancy-value models of achievement. Now we wish to emphasize that since gender inequities persist over the life course, these skills are often sharpened in adult heterosexual exchanges. The research literature on mate selection is rich with descriptions of feminine "posing," "manipulation of comparison levels," and sometimes even Machiavellian strategies. However, these interpersonal techniques should not necessarily be confused with moral and long-standing commitment to normatively prescribed gender roles.

Feminist scholars, aware of these different skills, have repeatedly called for a broader definition of both women's and men's achievements. Whether women's skills at interpersonal negotiation are an asset or a liability to status attainment remains apart from the sociohistorical fact that the achievement goals for most young women are still embedded in an institution in which a husband's occupational prestige remains clearly superior. Thus the research on dating patterns described by Douvan (1972), the need for affiliation identified by Hoffman (1972) and Bardwick (1971), and the fear of success diagnosed by Horner (1968) portray forces in contemporary female achievement which take their meaning from a cultural and structural context that puts women in an unequal position vis-à-vis men.

Is it any wonder that a feminist academician surveying the achievement literature on women would suggest that a woman's description of her ideal husband might yield useful projective data for the assessment of an achievement motive? Tangri justified this choice:

> We should also note that marriage is the *only kind of status* for which women may legitimately strive, though there are mores guiding the subtlety and style of striving; it is at any rate legitimate to want to get married, to try to get married, and to marry as well as possible. Marriage, or a particular kind of marriage, may be thought of as an achievement goal for women in much the same sense as a man's vocational choice serves as an achievement goal for him, and as such, the nature of this choice may reflect women's motivational dispositions. Furthermore, it does not arouse the countervailing fear of success in competing with men.
>
> Second, for most women the determining influence of life style, opportunities, and limitations derives from the men they marry. Therefore, pro-

jective descriptions of this man might serve to define a woman's desired style of life the way a man's description of his future vocation would define his. (1975:242)

Marriage as an economic institution continues to set the boundaries and definitions women and men use to shape and guide their life ambitions. Our understanding of individual achievement motives and expectations in women calls for continued examination of gender-role relationships in both the public and private spheres. Even as we begin to study the personal aspirations and goals of new generations it is critical to bear in mind the historical and political legacies they inherit. For it is the changing attractiveness of cultural rewards that stimulates the role innovation necessary for social change.

Conformity to roles requires a strict schedule of rewards and punishments to insure stability of behavior over time. However, the cultural sentiments about conformity to roles constantly change. For example, role qualities thought to be intrinsically motivating for one generation may not activate the next, necessitating adjustments in the mechanisms that maintain the status quo. At the same time, public and political revelations of the private costs of social conformity may alter the incentives and expectations for public achievement in succeeding generations. This is reflected in the apparently freer reexamination and discussion of gender roles, especially about marriage and parenting going on among most young people today. Scholars are just beginning to describe the new incentives and pathways to achievement being explored by women and men who are often as puzzled and surprised by their life choices as the researchers studying them.

The current decade of research on female achievement has been conducted in a political climate critical of the values attached to traditional masculine achievement roles. Along with the rewards, the costs of success in competitive careers are being more openly considered. Both feminists and their critics are quick to warn ambitious women of stress disorders often associated with those in pursuit of power, prestige and fame. Countless self-help magazines publish articles on the false promises of success along with advice on salary negotiating and dating among executives in competing companies. We regard this openness to the complexities and inconsistencies surrounding women's emerging achievement patterns as a refreshing antidote to the narrow formulations which have characterized achievement definitions in the academic literature to date.

Feminists have pointed to the importance of differentiating between real and ideal behavior; between manifest and latent sanctions; and among conformity, consensus, and institutionalized deviance. As we complete our review of women's feelings and attitudes about achievement, particularly in the later years, it is critical to recognize the sanctions that may keep them committed to a set of life "choices." The consequences of their investments are not in fact inevitable. New meanings can be attached to old sentiments, and old bargains can be renegotiated. The first step is identifying the rewards and sanctions operating over time in the woman's private as well as public spheres.

In our introductory chapters, we criticized the undue determinism in models of gender-role learning. We close by contrasting the related issue of free will and its associated concepts of moral autonomy and responsibility. We have chosen to emphasize woman's capacity, if not willingness, to question and reinterpret her roles and achievements through history and across the life course.

Bibliography

ACKER, J. "Women and Social Stratification: A Case of Intellectual Sexism." *American Journal of Sociology 73*, 4 (1973):936–945.

_____"Issues in the Sociological Study of Women's Work." In A. Stromberg and S. Harkess (eds.), *Women Working*. Palo Alto: Mayfield, 1978.

ACKER, J., and Van Houten, D. R. "Differential Recruitment and Control: Sex Structuring of Organizations." *Administrative Science Quarterly 19*, 2 (1974): 152–163.

ALEXANDER, K., and ECKLAND B. "Sex Differences in the Educational Attainment Process." *American Sociological Review 39*, 5 (1974):668–682.

ALLAN, V. R. "Economic and Legal Status of the Older Woman." In Proceedings of the 26th Annual Conference on Aging. Institute of Gerontology, University of Michigan and Wayne State University, 1975.

ALLPORT, G. W. "The Functional Autonomy of Motives." *American Journal of Psychology 50*, 1-4 (1937):141–156.

_____*Becoming: Basic Considerations for a Psychology of Personality*. New Haven: Yale University Press, 1955.

_____*Pattern and Growth in Personality*. New York: Holt, Rinehart, 1961.

ALPER, T. G. "Achievement Motivation in College Women." Paper presented to the Meeting of the Eastern Psychological Association. New York City, April 1971.

_____"Achievement Motivation in College Women: A Now-You-See-It-Now-You-Don't Phenomenon." *American Psychologist 29*, 1 (1974):194–203.

ANASTASI, A. *Differential Psychology*. 3d. ed. New York: Macmillan, 1958.

ANGRIST, S., and ALMQUIST, E. *Careers and Contingencies: How College Women Juggle with Gender*. New York: Dunellen, 1975.

ARIES, P. *Centuries of Childhood*. New York: Random House, Vintage, 1962.

_____"The Family and the City." In A. Rossi, J. Kagan, and T. Hareven (eds.), *The Family*. New York; Norton, 1978.

ASTIN, H., and MYINT, T. "Career Development of Young Women during the Post–High School Years." *Journal of Counseling Psychology 18*, 4 (1971):369–394.

ATKINSON, J. W. "Motivational Determinants of Risk-taking Behavior." *Psychological Review 64*, 6 (1957):359–372.

_____(ed.). *Motives in Fantasy, Action, and Society*. Princeton: Van Nostrand, 1958. (a)

_____"Thematic Apperceptive Measurement of Motives within the Context of a Theory of Motivation." In J. W. Atkinson (ed.), *Motives in Fantasy, Action, and Society*. Princeton: Van Nostrand, 1958. (b)

_____*An Introduction to Motivation*. New York: Van Nostrand, 1964.

ATKINSON, J. W., and FEATHER, N. T. (eds.). *A Theory of Achievement Motivation*. New York: Wiley, 1966.

ATKINSON, J. W., Heyns, R. W., and VEROFF, J. "The Effect of Experimental Arousal of the Affiliation Motive on Thematic Apperception." *Journal of Abnormal and Social Psychology 49*, 3 (1954):405–410.

ATKINSON, J. W., and RAYNOR, J. O. (eds.). *Motivation and Achievement*. Washington, D. C.: Hemisphere, 1974.

_____*Personality, Motivation, and Achievement*. New York: Wiley, 1978.

BANDUCCI, R. "The Effect of Mother's Employment on the Achievement, Aspirations, and Expectations of the Child." *Personnel and Guidance Journal 46*, 3 (1967):263–267.

BANDURA, A., and HUSTON, A. "Identification as a Process of Incidental Learning." In P. Mussen, J. Conger, and J. Kagan (eds.), *Readings in Child Development*. New York: Harper, 1965.

BANDURA, A., ROSS, D., and ROSS, S. "Imitation of Film-mediated Aggressive Models." *Journal of Abnormal and Social Psychology 66*, (1963):3–11.

BANDURA, A., and WALTERS, R. *Social Learning and Personality Development*. New York: Holt, Rinehart, & Winston, 1963.

BANKS, J., and GRAMBS, J. (eds.). *Black Self-concept: Implications for Education and Social Science*. New York: McGraw-Hill, 1972.

BARDWICK, J. *Psychology of Women: A Study of Bio-cultural Conflicts*. New York: Harper & Row, 1971.

BARDWICK, J. (ed.). *Readings on the Psychology of Women*. New York: Harper & Row, 1972.

_____"The Dynamics of Successful People." In D. G. McGuigan (ed.), *New*

Research on Women at the University of Michigan. Ann Arbor: Center for Continuing Education of Women, University of Michigan, 1974.

_____*In Transition: How the Feminist Movement, Sexual Liberation, and the Search for Fulfillment Have Altered Our Lives.* New York: Holt, Rinehart & Winston, 1979.

BARDWICK, J. DOUVAN, E., HORNER, M., GUTMAN, D. (eds.) *Feminine Personality and Conflict.* Belmont, Calif.: Brooks/Cole, 1970.

BARDWICK, J., and DOUVAN, E. "Ambivalence: The Socialization of Women." In J. Bardwick (ed.), *Readings on the Psychology of Women.* New York: Harper & Row, 1972.

BARNETT, R. "Sex Differences and Age Trends in Occupational Preference and Occupational Prestige." *Journal of Counseling Psychology 22*, 1 (1975):35–38.

BARNETT, R., and BARUCH, G. "Women in the Middle Years: Conceptions and Misconceptions." In J. Williams (ed.), *Psychology of Women: Behavior in a Biosocial Context.* New York: Norton, 1979.

BARRETT, N. S. "Women in the Job Market: Occupations, Earnings, and Career Opportunities." In R. Smith (ed.), *The Subtle Revolution: Women at Work.* Washington, D.C.: Urban Institute, 1979. (a)

_____"Women in the Job Market: Unemployment and Work Schedules." In R. Smith (ed.), *The Subtle Revolution: Women at Work.* Washington, D.C.: Urban Institute, 1979. (b)

BART, P. "Depression in Middle-aged Women." In V. Gornick and B. K. Moran (eds.), *Women in Sexist Society.* New York: Mentor New American Library, 1972.

_____"Emotional and Social Status of the Older Woman." In N. Trager (ed) *No Longer Young: The Older Woman in America,* Proceedings of the 26th Annual Conference on Aging. Institute of Gerontology, University of Michigan and Wayne State University, 1975.

BAR-TAL, D., and FRIEZE, I. "Achievement Motivation and Gender as Determinants of Attributions for Success and Failure." Manuscript, University of Pittsburgh, 1973.

_____"Achievement Motivation for Males and Females as a Determinant of Attributions for Success and Failure." *Sex Roles 3*, 3 (1977):301–313.

BARUCH, G. K. "The Achievement Motive in Women: Implications for Career Development." *Journal of Personality and Social Psychology 5*, 3 (1967):260–271.

_____"Maternal Influences upon College Women's Attitudes toward Women and Work." *Developmental Psychology 6*, 1 (1972):32–37.

_____"Maternal Career-Orientation as Related to Parental Identification in College Women." *Journal of Vocational Behavior 4*, 2 (1974):173–180.

_____"Sex Role Stereotyping, the Motive to Avoid Success, and Parental Identification: A Comparison of Preadolescent and Adolescent Girls." *Sex Roles 1*, 4 (1975):303–309.

BASS, B. M., KRUSELL, J., and ALEXANDER, R. H. "Male Manager's Attitudes toward Working Women." *American Behavioral Scientist 15*, 2 (1971):221–236.

BAXANDALL, R., GORDON, L., and REVERBY, S. *America's Working Women*. New York: Random House, Vintage, 1976.

BEARD, M. *Woman as a Force in History*. New York: Macmillan, 1946.

BECKER, G. S. *Human Capital: A Theoretical and Empirical Analysis with Special Reference to Education*. New York: Columbia University Press, 1964.

_____"A Theory of Marriage" (part I). *Journal of Political Economy 81* (July–August 1973):813–846.

BELL, M. "Pioneer." *New York Review of Books*, 27 April 1980, pp. 10–14

BELLE, D. (ed.). *Lives in Stress: A Context for Depression*. Report on the Stress and Families Project, to the National Institute of Mental Health. Bethesda; October, 1979.

BEM, S. L. "Psychology Looks at Sex Roles: Where Have All the Androgynous People Gone?" Paper presented to the U.C.L.A. Symposium on Women. Los Angeles, May 1972.

BEM, S. L., and BEM, D. J. "Training the Woman to Know Her Place." In D. J. Bem (ed.), *Beliefs, Attitudes, and Human Affairs*. Belmont: Brooks/Cole, 1970.

BENSTON, M. "The Political Economy of Women's Liberation." *Monthly Review 21*, 4 (1969):13–27.

BERNARD, J. *Academic Women*. University Park: Pennsylvania State University Press, 1964.

_____"The Paradox of a Happy Marriage." In V. Gornick and B. K. Moran (eds.), *Women in Sexist Society*. New York: Mentor New American Library, 1972.

_____*The Future of Marriage*. New York: Basic Books, 1973a.

_____"My Four Revolutions: An Autobiographical History of the ASA." *American Journal of Sociology 78*, 4 (1973):791b.

_____*The Future of Motherhood*. Baltimore: Penguin, 1975.

BEVIER, I. *Home Economics in Education*. Philadelphia: Lippincott, 1911.

_____*The Home Economics Movement*. Boston: Whitcomb & Barrows, 1918.

BIBB, R., and FORM, W. "The Effects of Industrial, Occupational, and Sex Stratification on Wages in Blue-collar Markets." *Social Forces 55*, 4 (1977):974–996.

BIRNBAUM, J. A. "Life Patterns and Self-esteem in Gifted Family-oriented and Career-committed Women." In M. Mednick, S. Tangri, and L. Hoffman (eds.), *Women and Achievement*. New York: Wiley, 1975.

BISCHOF, L. *Adult Psychology*. New York: Harper & Row, 1976.

BLAU, F. D. "The Data on Women Workers, Past, Present, and Future." In A. Stromberg and S. Harkess (eds.), *Women Working*. Palo Alto: Mayfield, 1978.

BLAU, Z. *Old Age in a Changing Society*. New York: Watts, New Viewpoints, 1973.

BOOCOCK, S. S. "Historical and Sociological Research on the Family and the Life Cycle: Methodological Alternatives." In J. Demos and S. Boocock (eds.), *Turning Points*. Chicago: University of Chicago Press, 1978.

BOSE, C. E. *Jobs and Gender: Sex and Occupational Prestige*. Baltimore: Johns Hopkins Press, 1973.

BOULDING, K. E. *Economics as a Science*. New York: McGraw-Hill, 1970.

BOWERMAN, C., and ELDER, G. "Variations in Adolescent Perception of Family Power Structure." *American Sociological Review, 29*, 4 (1964):551–567.

BOWMAN, G., WORTNEY, B. N., and GREYSER, S. H. "Are Women Executives People?" *Harvard Business Review 43*, 4 (1965):14–28, 164–178.

BRANCA, P. "A New Perspective on Women's Work: A Comparative Typology." *Journal of Social History 9*, 2 (1975):129–153.

BRIM, O. "Family Structures and Sex-Role Learning by Children." *Sociometry 21*, 1 (1958):1–16.

BRIM, O., "Male Mid-life Crisis: A Comparative Analysis." In B. Hess (ed.), *Growing Old in America.* New Brunswick: Transaction, 1976.

BRIM, O., and WHEELER, S. *Socialization after Childhood.* New York: Wiley, 1966.

BRONFENBRENNER, U. "Socialization and Social Class through Time and Space." In E. Maccoby, T. Newcomb, and E. Hartley (eds.), *Readings in Social Psychology.* New York: Holt, Rinehart, 1958.

_____"Freudian Theories of Identification and Their Derivatives." *Child Development 31*, 1 (1960):15–40.

_____"A Theoretical Perspective for Research on Human Development." In A. Skolnick (ed.), *Rethinking Childhood: Perspectives on Development and Society.* Boston: Little, Brown, 1976.

BROOKOVER, W. B., and ERIKSON, E. L. *Society, Schools, and Learning.* Boston: Allyn & Bacon, 1969.

BROVERMAN, I. K., BROVERMAN, D. M., CLARKSON, F. E., ROSENKRANTZ, P. S., and VOGEL, S. R. "Sex Role Stereotypes and Clinical Judgments of Mental Health." *Journal of Consulting and Clinical Psychology 34*, 1 (1970):1–7.

BROVERMAN, I. K., VOGEL, S. R., BROVERMAN, D. M., CLARKSON, F. E., and ROSENKRANTZ, P. S. "Sex-Role Stereotypes: A Current Appraisal." *Journal of Social Issues 28*, 3 (1972):59–78.

BROWN, D. G. "Sex Role Preference in Young Children." *Psychology Monographs 70*, 14 (1956):1–19.

BROWNLEE, W. E., and BROWNLEE, M. *Women in the American Economy: A Documentary History, 1675–1929.* New Haven: Yale University Press, 1976.

BUGENTAL D., LOVE, L., and GIANETTO, R. "Perfidious Feminine Faces." *Journal of Personality and Social Psychology 17*, 3 (1971):314–318.

BÜHLER, C. "The Curve of Life as Studied in Biographies." *Journal of Applied Psychology 19*, 4 (1935):405–409.

_____"Old Age and Fulfillment of Life with Consideration of the Use of Time in Old Age." *Vita Humana 4*, (1961):129–133.

BUTLER, R. "Age-ism: Another Form of Bigotry." In S. H. Zarit (ed.), *Readings in Aging and Death: Contemporary Perspectives.* New York: Harper & Row, 1977.

CAHN, A. *Women in the U. S. Labor Force.* Praeger: New York, 1979.

CAMPBELL, P. "Feminine Intellectual Decline during Adolescence." Ph.D. dissertation. Syracuse University, 1973.

CAPLOW, T. *The Sociology of Work.* Minneapolis: University of Minnesota Press, 1954.

_____*Two against One: Coalitions in Triads.* Englewood Cliffs: Prentice-Hall, 1968.

CARDEN, M. L. *The New Feminist Movement.* New York: Russell Sage, 1974.

CARROLL, B. (ed.). *Liberating Women's History.* Chicago: University of Illinois Press, 1976.

CHESLER, P. *Women, Money, and Power.* New York: Bantam, 1976.

CLARK, W. W. "Boys and Girls: Are There Significant Ability and Achievement Differences?" *Phi Delta Kappan 41*, 2 (1959):73–76.

CLARKE, A. M., and CLARKE, A. D. B. (eds.). *Early Experience: Myth and Evidence.* New York: Free Press, 1976.

CLAUSEN, J. A. (ed.). *Socialization and Society.* Boston: Little, Brown, 1968.

COLE, J. R. *Fair Science: Women in the Scientific Community.* New York: Free Press, 1979.

COLEMAN, J. "The Adolescent Subculture and Academic Achievement." *American Journal of Sociology 65*, 4 (1960):337–347.

_____*The Adolescent Society.* New York: Free Press, 1961.

_____(ed.). *Youth: Transition to Adulthood.* Washington, D. C.: Government Printing Office, 1973.

COLEMAN, J., CAMPBELL, E., HOBSON, C., McPARTLAND, J., MOOD, A., WEINFELD, F., and YORK, R. *Equality of Education and Opportunity.* Washington, D.C.: Government Printing Office, 1966.

COLES, R. *Children of Crisis.* Boston: Little, Brown, 1964.

COLLINS, R. "A Conflict Theory of Sexual Stratification." *Social Problems 19*, 1 (1971):3–21.

CONDRY, J., and DYER, S. "Fear of Success: Attribution of Cause to the Victim." *Journal of Social Issues, 32*, 3 (1976):63–83.

CONGER, J. J. "A World They Never Knew." *Daedalus 100*, 4 (1971):1105–1138.

CONSTANTINOPLE, A. "Masculinity-Femininity: An Exception to a Famous Dictum?" In A. Kaplan and J. Bean (eds.) *Beyond Sex-Role Stereotypes: Readings Toward a Psychology of Androgyny.* Boston: Little, Brown, 1976.

COOLEY, C. *Human Nature and the Social Order.* New York: Scribners, 1902. Rev. ed. 1909.

CORCORAN, M. "Economic and Legal Implications of Divorce." Paper presented to the Cornell Conference on Women in Mid-life Crises. Ithaca, New York, October 1976.

COSER, R., and ROKOFF, G. "Women in the Occupational World: Social Disruption and Conflict." *Social Problems 18*, 4 (1971):535–552.

CRANDALL, V. C. "Achievement Behavior in Young Children." *Young Children 20*, 2 (1964):70–75.

_____"Sex Differences in Expectancy of Intellectual and Academic Performance." In C. Smith (ed.) *Achievement Related Motives in Children.* New York: Russell Sage, 1969.

_____"Sex Differences in Expectancy of Intellectual and Academic Reinforcement." In R. K. Unger and F. Denmark (eds.) *Woman: Dependent or Independent Variable?* New York: Psychological Dimensions, 1975.

CRANDALL, V. C. and BATTLE, E. "The Antecedents and Adult Correlates of Academic and Intellectual Achievement Effort." In J. Hill (ed.), *Minnesota Symposium on Child Psychology, 4,* 1, Minneapolis: University of Minnesota Press, 1970.

CRANDALL, V. C., KATOVSKY, W. and CRANDALL, V. J. "Children's Belief in Their Own Control of Reinforcement in Intellectual-Academic Achievement Situations." *Child Development 36,* 1 (1965):91–109.

CRANDALL, V. J. "Achievement." In H. Stevenson (ed.), *Child Psychology Yearbook of the National Society for the Study of Education,* Part I. Chicago: University of Chicago Press. 1963.

CRANDALL, V. J., DEWEY, R., KATOVSKY, W., and PRESTON, A. "Parents' Attitudes and Behaviors and Grade School Children's Academic Achievement." *Journal of Genetic Psychology 104,* 1 (1964):53–66.

CRANDALL, V. J., KATOVSKY, W., and PRESTON, A. "A Conceptual Formulation for Some Research on Children's Achievement Development." *Child Development 31,* 4 (1960): 784–797.

CRANDALL, V. J., KATOVSKY W., and PRESTON, A. "Motivation and Ability Determinants of Young Children's Intellectual Achievement Behaviors." *Child Development 33,* 2 (1962):643–661.

CRANDALL, V. J., and RABSON, A. "Children's Repetition Choices in an Intellectual Achievement Situation following Success and Failure." *Journal of Genetic Psychology 97,* 1 (1960):161–168.

CROZIER, M. *The Bureaucratic Phenomenon.* Chicago: University of Chicago Press, 1964.

CUMMING, E., and HENRY, W. E. *Growing Old: The Process of Disengagement.* New York: Basic Books, 1961.

DAHRENDORF, R. *Class and Class Conflict in Industrial Society.* Stanford: Stanford University Press, 1972.

DALLA COSTA, M. and JAMES, S. *The Power of Women and the Subversion of the Community.* Bristol, England: Falling Wall Press, 1972.

DANIELS, A. "Development of Feminist Networks in the Professions." *Annals of the New York Academy of Sciences, 23,* 4 (1979):215–227.

DAVIES, M. "Woman's Place Is at the Typewriter: The Feminization of the Clerical Labor Force." *Radical America 8,* 4 (1974):1–28.

DEAUX, K. *The Behavior of Women and Men.* Monterey: Brooks Cole, 1976a.

_____ "Sex: A Perspective on the Attribution Process." In I. Harvey, N. Ickes and R. Kidd (eds.) *New Directions in Attribution Research.* Hillsdale: Erlbaum, 1976 b.

DEAUX, K., and EMSWILLER, T. "Explanations of Successful Performance on Sex-linked Tasks: What's Skill for the Male Is Luck for the Female." *Journal of Personality and Social Psychology 29,* 1 (1974):80–85.

DEAUX, K., and FARRIS, E. "Attributing Causes for One's Performance: The Effects of Sex, Norms, and Outcome" Manuscript, Purdue University, 1974.

DEAUX, K., and TAYNOR, J. "Evaluation of Male and Female Ability: Bias Works Two Ways." *Psychological Reports 32,* 1 (1973):261–262.

DEBEAUVOIR, S. *The Coming of Age.* New York: Putnam, 1972a.

_____"Joie de Vivre." *Harper's,* January (1972b) 33–40.

DECHARMS, R. *Personal Causation.* New York: Academic, 1968.

DECKARD, B. *The Women's Movement.* New York: Harper & Row, 1975.

DEITCH, C. "Unequal Work and Unequal Pay: Some Structural Explanations for the Earnings Gap between Men and Women." Paper presented to the Eastern Sociological Meetings. Boston, March 1980.

DENMARK, F., TANGRI, S., and McCANDLESS, S. "Affiliation, Achievement, and Power. In J. Sherman and F. Denmark (eds.) *The Psychology of Women.* New York: Psychological Dimensions, 1978.

DEPNER, C., and O'LEARY, V. "Understanding Female Careerism: Fear of Success and New Directions." *Sex Roles 2,* 3 (1976) 259–268.

DEWEY, J. *Human Nature and Conduct.* New York: Random House, 1957.

"Displaced Homemakers." *Ithaca New Times,* 5 May 1977.

DOHRENWEND, B. S., and DOHRENWEND, B. P. (eds.). *Stressful Life Events: Their Nature and Effects.* New York: Wiley, 1974.

DOLLARD, J., and MILLER, N. *Personality and Psychotherapy: An Analysis of Learning, Thinking, and Culture.* New York: McGraw-Hill, 1950.

DONLEY, P., and CONDRY, J. "Getting Out: A Study of Married Women Returning to School." Paper presented to the Eighty-fifth meeting of the Eastern Psychological Association. Boston, April 1977.

DOUVAN, E. "Sex Differences in Adolescent Character Processes." *Merrill Palmer Quarterly 6,* 4 (1960):203–211.

_____"Employment and the Adolescent." In I. Nye and L. Hoffman (eds.), *The Employed Mother in America.* Chicago: Rand McNally, 1963.

_____"Sex Differences in Adolescent Character Processes." In J. Bardwick, (ed.), *Readings on the Psychology of Women.* New York: Harper & Row, 1972.

_____"Family Roles in a Twenty Year Perspective." Paper presented to the Radcliffe Precentennial Conference. Cambridge, April 1978.

_____"Differing Views on Marriage, 1957–1976." *ISR Newsletter 12,* 1 (1979):1–2. Ann Arbor: Center for Continuing Education of Women, University of Michigan.

DOUVAN, E., and ADELSON, J. *The Adolescent Experience.* New York: Wiley, 1966.

DOUVAN, E., and KAYE, C. *Adolescent Girls.* Ann Arbor: Survey Research Center, 1956.

DUBERMAN, L. *Gender and Sex in Society.* New York: Praeger, 1975.

DUBOIS, E. "The Radicalism of the Woman Suffrage Movement: Notes toward the Reconstruction of Nineteenth-century Feminism." *Feminist Studies 3,* 1/2 (1975):63–71.

DUNCAN, O. D., FEATHERMAN, D. L., and DUNCAN, B. *Socioeconomic Background and Achievement.* New York: Seminar, 1972.

DUNKLE, M. "A Unification of Forces: Coalition Works for Sex Equity in Education." *Vocational Education* (April 1980): 43–54.

EHRENREICH, B., and ENGLISH, D. *Witches, Midwives, and Nurses: A History of Women Healers.* Old Westbury: Feminist Press, 1973.

ELDER G. H., Jr. "Achievement Motivation and Intelligence in Occupational Mobility: A Longitudinal Analysis." *Sociometry 31*, 4 (1968):327–354.

_____*Adolescent Socialization and Personality Development.* Chicago: Rand McNally, 1971.

_____"On Linking Social Structure and Personality." *American Behavioral Scientist 16*, 6 (1973):785–800.

_____*Children of the Great Depression.* Chicago: University of Chicago Press, 1974.

_____"Approaches to Social Change and the Family." In J. Demos and S. Boocock (eds.), *Turning Points.* Chicago: University of Chicago Press, 1978.

ELIASON, C. *Needs of Displaced Homemakers, Single Mothers, and Older Women.* Washington, D.C.: National Advisory Council on Women's Educational Programs, 1977.

ELLIS, E. "Social Psychological Correlates of Upward Social Mobility among Unmarried Career Women." *American Sociological Review 17*, 5 (1952):558–563.

ELSHTAIN, J. B. "Moral Woman and Immoral Man: A Consideration of the Public-Private Split and Its Political Ramifications." *Politics and Society 4*, 4 (1974):453–473.

EMMERICH, W. "Family Role Concepts of Children, Ages Six to Ten." *Child Development 32*, 4 (1961):609–624.

EMPEY, L. "Social Class and Occupational Aspiration: A Comparison of Absolute and Relative Measurement." *American Sociological Review 21*, 6 (1956):703–709.

ENTINE, A. A. (ed.). *Americans in Middle Years: Career Options and Educational Opportunities.*

ENTWISLE, D. R. "To Dispel Fantasies about Fantasy-based Measures of Achievement Motivation." *Psychological Bulletin 77*, 6 (1972):377–391.

EPSTEIN, C. "Encountering the Male Establishment: Sex-Status Limits on Women's Careers in the Professions." *American Journal of Sociology 75*, 6 (1970a):965–982.

_____*Woman's Place: Options and Limits in Professional Careers.* Berkeley: University of California Press, 1970b.

_____"Bringing Women In: Rewards, Punishments, and the Structure of Achievement." In R. Kundsin (ed.), *Women and Success: Anatomy of Achievement.* New York: Morrow, 1974.

_____"Institutional Barriers: What Keeps Women Out of the Executive Suite?" In F. Gordon and M. Straber (eds.), *Bringing Women into Management.* New York: McGraw-Hill, 1975.

ERIKSON, E. H. *Childhood and Society.* New York: Norton, 1950.

_____"Reflections on Dr. Borg's Life Cycle." *Daedalus 105*, 2 (1976):1–28.

ETZIONI, A. (ed.). *The Semi-professions and Their Organizations.* New York: Free Press, 1969.

FALK, W. and COSBY, A. "Women and the Status Attainment Process." *Social Science Quarterly 56* (September 1975):307–314.

FALK-DICKLER, F. "Federal Employment Programs for the Mature Woman." Paper presented to the Cornell Conference on Women in Mid-life Crises. Ithaca: October 1976.

FEATHER, N. T., and SIMON, J. G. "Reactions to Male and Female Success and Failure in Sex-linked Occupations: Impressions of Personality, Causal, Attribution, and Perceived Likelihood of Different Consequences." *Journal of Personality and Social Psychology 31*, 1 (1975):20–31.

FEATHERMAN, D. "Schooling and Occupational Careers: Constancy and Change in Worldly Success." Center for Demography and Ecology, University of Wisconsin, 1978.

FEE, T. "Domestic Labor: An Analysis of Housework and Its Relation to the Production Process. *The Review of Radical Political Economics 8*, 1 (1976):1–7.

FELD, S. C., and LEWIS, J. "The Assessment of Achievement Anxieties in Children." In C. Smith (ed.), *Achievement Related Motives in Childen*. New York: Russell Sage, 1969.

FELDMAN-SUMMERS, S., and KIESLER, S. B. "Those Who Are Number Two Try Harder: The Effects of Sex on Attributions of Causality." *Journal of Personality and Social Psychology 30*, 6 (1974):846–855.

FIELD, W. F. "The Effects of Thematic Apperception upon Certain Experimentally Aroused Needs." Ph.D. dissertation, University of Maryland, 1951.

FISHER, A. E. *Women's Worlds*. Rockville: Department of Health, Education, and Welfare, Mental Health Studies and Reports Branch, Publication no. 78–660, 1978.

FLEXNER, E. *Century of Struggle*. New York: Atheneum, 1968.

FLING, S., and MANOSEVITZ, M. "Sex Typing in Nursery School Children's Play Interests." *Developmental Psychology 7*, 2 (1972) 146–152.

FONER, A. (ed.) *Age in Society*. Beverly Hills: Sage Contemporary Social Science Series, no 30 (1976).

_____ "Age Stratification and the Changing Family." In J. Demos and S. Boocock (eds.), *Turning Points*. Chicago: University of Chicago Press, 1978.

FONER, P. S. *Women and the American Labor Movement*. New York: Free Press, 1979.

FRANKEL, E. "Characteristics of Working and Non-working Mothers among Intellectually Gifted High and Low Achievers." *Personnel and Guidance Journal 42*, 8 (1964):776–780.

FREUD, S. "Three Contributions to the Theory of Sex." In A. Brill (ed.) *The Basic Writings of Sigmund Freud*. New York: Modern Library, 1938.

FRIEDAN, B. *The Feminine Mystique*. New York: Norton, 1963.

FRIEDMAN, J., and SHADE, W. *Our American Sisters: Women in American Life and Thought*. Boston: Allyn & Bacon, 1976.

FRIEZE, I. H. "Women's Expectations for and Causal Attributions of Success and Failure." In M. Mednick, S. Tangri, and L. Hoffman (eds.), *Women and Achievement*. New York: Wiley, 1975.

FRIEZE, I. H., JOHNSON, P. B., PARSONS, J. E., RUBLE, D. N., and ZELLMAN, G. L. *Women and Sex Roles: A Social Psychological Perspective*. New York: Norton, 1978.

FRIEZE, I., and RAMSEY, S. J. "Nonverbal Aspects of Femininity and Masculinity Which Perpetuate Sex-Role Stereotypes." Paper presented to the Meeting of the Eastern Psychological Association. Philadelphia: April 1974.

GATES, M. "Occupational Segregation and the Law." In M. Blaxall and B. Reagan (eds.), *Women and the Workplace.* Chicago: University of Chicago Press, 1976.

GAUGHMAN, E. E., and DAHLSTROM, W. G. *Negro and White Children.* New York: Academic, 1968.

GAYLIN, J. "What Boys Look for in Girls: National Survey." *Seventeen,* March 1978, pp. 107–113.

GEWIRTZ, J. L. "Mechanisms of Social Learning: Some Roles of Stimulation and Behavior in Early Human Development." In D. A. Goslin (ed.), *Handbook of Socialization Theory and Research.* Chicago: Rand McNally, 1971.

GILLESPIE, D. "Who Has the Power? The Marital Struggle." In C. Greenblath, P. Stein, and N. Washburne (eds.), *The Marriage Game.* New York: Random House, 1975.

GILLIGAN, C. "In a Different Voice: Women's Conceptions of the Self and of Morality." Manuscript, Harvard Education School, 1976.

_____ "Woman's Place in Man's Life Cycle." *Harvard Educational Review* 49, 4 (1979) 431–446.

_____ "The Contribution of Women's Thought to Developmental Theory: The Elimination of Sex Bias in Moral Development Research and Education." Interim report to the National Institute of Education. Washington, D.C., 1980.

GILLIGAN, C., and MURPHY, M. J. "Development from Adolescence to Adulthood: The Philosopher and the Dilemma of the Fact." In D. Kuhn (ed.), *Intellectual Development beyond Childhood.* San Francisco: Jossey-Bass, 1980.

GILMAN, C. P. *The Home: Its Work and Influence.* New York: Charlton, 1910.

_____ "The Waste of Private Housekeeping." *Annals of the American Academy of Political and Social Science 48* (July 1913):91–95.

GILMER, B. *Industrial Psychology.* New York: McGraw-Hill, 1971.

GINZBURG, E., GINSBURG, S., AXELRAD, S. and HERMAN, J. *Occupational Choice: an Approach to a General Theory.* New York: Columbia University Press, 1951.

GLICK, P. C. "Marrying, Divorcing, and Living Together in the U. S. Today." *Population Bulletin 32,* 5 (1977a):3–39.

_____ "Updating the Life Cycle of the Family." *Journal of Marriage and the Family 39,* 1 (1977b):5–14.

GLICK, P. C., and CARTER, H. *Marriage and Divorce: A Social and Economic Study.* Cambridge: Harvard University Press, 1976.

GOFFMAN, E. *The Presentation of Self in Everyday Life.* New York: Doubleday Anchor, 1959.

_____ *Interaction Ritual: Essays on Face-to-Face Behavior.* New York: Doubleday Anchor, 1967.

_____ *Strategic Interaction.* Philadelphia: University of Pennsylvania Press, 1969.

GOLDBERG, P. "Are Women Prejudiced against Women?" *Transaction 5,* 5 (1968):28–30.

GOODMAN, E. *Washington Post*, 16 October 1978.

GORDON, A. D., and BUHLE, M. "Sex and Class in Colonial and Nineteenth Century America." In B. Carroll (ed.), *Liberating Women's History*. Chicago: University of Illinois Press, 1976.

GORDON, L. *Woman's Body, Woman's Right: A Social History of Birth Control in America*. Baltimore: Penguin, 1977.

GORDON, M. (ed.). *The Nuclear Family in Crisis: The Search for an Alternative*. New York: Harper & Row, 1972.

GORDON, M. *The American Family Past, Present, and Future*. New York: Random House, 1978.

GORDON, N. M. "Institutional Responses: The Federal Income Tax System." In R. Smith (ed.), *The Subtle Revolution: Women at Work*. Washington, D.C.: Urban Institute, 1979.

GOSLIN, D. A. (ed.). *Handbook of Socialization Theory and Research*. Chicago: Rand McNally, 1971.

GOULD, C. C. and WARTOFSKY, M. W. *Women and Philosophy: Toward a Theory of Liberation*. New York: Putnam, 1976.

GOULD, R. "The Phases of Adult Life: A Study in Developmental Psychology." *American Journal of Psychiatry 129*, 85 (1972):521-31.

_____*Transformations: Growth and Change in Adult Life*. New York: Simon & Schuster, 1978.

GOULET, L. R., and BALTES, P. B. *Life Span Development Psychology*. New York: Academic, 1970.

GOVE, W. R., and TUDOR, J. F. "Adult Sex Roles and Mental Illness." In J. Huber (ed.), *Changing Women in a Changing Society*. Chicago: University of Chicago Press, 1973.

GRIER, W. H., and COBBS, P. M. *Black Rage*. New York: Basic Books, 1968.

GRINDER, R. "Relations of Social Dating Attractions to Academic Orientations and Peer Relations." *Journal of Educatonal Psychology 57*, 1 (1966):27-34.

GROSS, E. "Plus Ça change . . .? The Sexual Structure of Occupations over Time." *Social Problems 16*, 2 (1968):198-208.

GROSZKO, M., and MORGENSTERN, R. "Institutional Discrimination: The Case of Achievement-oriented Women in Higher Education." Paper presented to the Eightieth American Psychological Association. Honolulu: September 1972.

GRUNE, J. (ed.). *Manual on Pay Equity: Raising Wages for Women's Work*. Report of the Women in The Economy Project. Washington, D.C.: Conference on Alternative State and Local Policies, Committee on Pay Equity, 1980.

GUSFIELD, J. P. "Social Structure and Moral Reform: A Study of the Woman's Christian Temperance Union." *American Journal of Sociology 61*, 3 (1955):221-232.

GUTTENTAG, M., and SALASIN, S. "Women, Men, and Mental Health." In L. Cater, A. Scott, and W. Martyna (eds.), *Women and Men: Changing Roles*. New York: Praeger, 1977.

HACKER, A. "Divorce à la Mode." *New York Review of Books*, 26 May 1979, pp. 23-27.

HACKER, H. "Women as a Minority Group." *Social Forces 30*, 1 (1951):60–69.

HAGGLUND, G. "Sex Discrimination: Job Evaluation and Wage Practices Which May Disadvantage Women." In J. Grune (ed.), *Manual on Pay Equity: Raising Wages for Women's Work.* Washington, D.C.: Conference on Alternative State and Local Policies, Committee on Pay Equity, 1980.

HALLER, A. O., and PORTES, A. "Status Attainment Processes." *Sociology of Education 46* (Winter 1973):51–91.

HAN, W. S. "Two Conflicting Themes: Common Values versus Class Differential Values." *American Sociological Review 34*, 5 (1969):679–690.

HAREVEN, T. K. "Family Time and Industrial Time: Family and Work in a Planned Corporation Town, 1900–1924." *Journal of Urban History 1* (May 1975):365–389.

_____"Family Time and Historical Time." In A. Rossi, J. Kagan, and T. K. Hareven (eds.), *The Family*. New York: Norton, 1978a.

_____"The Last Stage: Historical Adulthood and Old Age." In E. H. Erikson (ed.), *Adulthood*. New York: Norton, 1978. (b)

HARLAN, S. L. "Sex Differences in Access to Federal Employment and Training Resources." Manuscript. Center for Research on Women, Wellesley College, 1980.

HARMON, L. "The Childhood and Adolescent Career Plans of College Women." *Journal of Vocational Behavior 1*, 1 (1971):45–56.

HARRIS, D. *The Concept of Development: An Issue in the Study of Human Behavior*. Minneapolis: University of Minnesota Press, 1957.

HARRIS, J. *The Prime of Ms. America*. New York: New American Library, Signet, 1975

HARTLEY, R. "Children's Concepts of Male and Female Roles: Some Implications of Current Changes in Sex Role Patterns. *Merrill Palmer Quarterly 6*, 3 (1960):153–164.

_____"What Aspects of Child Behavior Should Be Studied in Relation to Maternal Employment?" In A. Siegal (ed.), *Research Issues Related to the Effects of Maternal Employment on Children*. University Park: Social Science Research Center, 1961.

_____"A Developmental View of Female Sex-Role Definition and Identification." *Merrill Palmer Quarterly 10*, 1 (1964):3–16.

HARTLEY, R., and HARDESTY, F. "Children's Perception and Expression of Sex Preferences." *Child Development 33*, 1 (1962):221–227.

HARTMAN, M., and BANNER, L. *Clio's Consciousness Raised*. New York: Harper & Row, 1974.

HARTUP, W. W., and ZOOK, E. A. "Sex-Role Preference in Three- and Four-year-old Children." *Journal of Consulting Psychology 24*, 5 (1960):420–426.

Hauser, R. *Socioeconomic Background and Educational Performance*. Washington, D.C.: American Sociological Association, 1971.

HAUSER, R., and FEATHERMAN, D. *The Process of Stratification*. New York: Academic, 1977.

HAVENS, E. M., and TULLY, J. C. "Female Intergenerational Occupational Mobility: Comparisons of Patterns." *American Sociological Review 37*, 6 (1972):774–777.

HECKHAUSEN, H. *The Anatomy of Achievement Motivation.* New York: Academic, 1967.

HENDERSON, L. F., and LYONS, D. J. "Sexual Differences in Human Crowd Motion." *Nature 240,* 5380 (1972):353-355.

HENLEY, N. M. "Status and Sex: Some Touching Considerations." *Bulletin of the Psychonomic Society 2,* 2 (1973):91-93.

HENNIG, M. M. "Career Development for Women Executives." Ph.D. dissertation, Harvard University, 1971.

HERMAN, A. "Progress and Problems for Working Women." *Labor Law Journal,* April 1979, 195-204.

HERZOG, R., BACHMAN, J., and JOHNSTON, L. "High School Seniors' Preference for Division of Labor in the Family." *ISR Newsletter 12,* 1 (1979a):9-10. Ann Arbor: Center for Continuing Education of Women, University of Michigan.

_____"Young People Look at Changing Sex Roles," *ISR Newsletter 12,* 1 (1979b):3-5. Center for Continuing Education of Women, University of Michigan.

HESS, B. (ed.). *Growing Old in America.* New Brunswick: Transaction, 1976.

HESS, R. D., and TORNEY, W. V. "Religion, Age, and Sex in Children's Perceptions of Family Authority." *Child Development 33,* 4 (1962):781-789.

HETHERINGTON, M. "A Developmental Study of the Effects of Sex of the Dominant Parent on Sex Role Preference: Identification and Imitation in Children." *Journal of Personality and Social Psychology 2,* 2 (1965):88-194.

HILL, U. *Charlotte Perkins Gilman: The Making of a Radical Feminist, 1860-1896.* Philadelphia: Temple University Press, 1979.

HOCHSCHILD, A. "The Role of the Ambassador's Wife: An Exploratory Study." *Journal of Marriage and the Family 31,* 1 (1969):73-87.

_____"A Review of Sex Role Research." In J. Huber (ed.), *Changing Women.* Chicago: University of Chicago Press, 1973a.

_____*The Unexpected Community.* Englewood Cliffs: Prentice-Hall, 1973b.

_____"The Sociology of Feeling and Emotion: Selected Possibilities." In M. Millman and R. Kanter (eds.), *Another Voice.* New York: Doubleday Anchor, 1975a.

_____Disengagement Theory: A Critique and Proposal. *American Sociological Review 40,* 5 (1975b) 553-569.

_____"Communal Life Styles for the Old." In B. Hess (ed.), *Growing Old in America.* New Brunswick: Transaction, 1976.

HOFFMAN, L. W. "Effects of Maternal Employment on Children: Summary and Discussion." In I. Nye and L. Hoffman (eds.), *The Employed Mother in America.* Chicago: Rand McNally, 1963a.

_____"Mother's Enjoyment of Work and Effects on the Child." In I. Nye and L. Hoffman (eds.), *The Employed Mother in America.* Chicago: Rand McNally, 1963b.

_____"Early Childhood Experiences and Women's Achievement Motives." *Journal of Social Issues 28,* 2 (1972):129-155.

_____"Effects of Maternal Employment on the Child: A Review of the Research." *Developmental Psychology 10,* 2 (1974a):204-228.

_____"Psychology Looks at the Female." In D. G. McGuigan (ed.) *New Research on Women at the University of Michigan*. Ann Arbor: University of Michigan, 1974b.

_____"A Re-examination of the Fear of Success." In D. C. McGuigan (ed.), *New Research on Women at the University of Michigan*. Ann Arbor: Center for Continuing Education of Women, University of Michigan, 1974c.

_____"Early Childhood Experiences and Women's Achievement Motives." In M. Mednick, S. Tangri, and L. Hoffman (eds.), *Women and Achievement*. New York: Wiley, 1975.

_____"Changes in Family Roles, Socialization, and Sex Differences." *American Psychologist 32*, 8 (1977):644–656.

_____"Maternal Employment." *American Psychologist 34*, 10 (1979): 859–865.

HOFFMAN, L. W., and NYE, I. *Working Mothers*. San Francisco: Jossey-Bass, 1975.

HOFFMAN, M. "Personality, Family Structure, and Social Class as Antecedents of Parental Power Assertion." *Child Development 34*, 4 (1963):869–884.

HOFFMAN, M. L., and HOFFMAN, L. W. (eds.). *Review of Child Development Research*, vol. 1. New York: Russell Sage, 1964.

HOGELAND, R. W. "The Female Appendage: Feminine Life-styles in America, 1820–1860," *Warner Modular Publication*, no. 36 (1973), pp. 1–14.

HOLSTEIN, C. "Irreversible, stepwise sequence in the development of moral judgment: A longitudinal study of males and females." *Child Development 47*, (1976):51–61.

HOMANS, G. *The Nature of Social Science*. New York: Harcourt, 1967.

HOOKS, J. *Women's Occupations through Seven Decades*. Washington D.C.: Department of Labor, 1947.

HORNER, M. "Sex Differences in Achievement Motivation and Performance in Competitive and Non-competitive Situations." Ph.D. dissertation, University of Michigan, 1968.

_____"Femininity and Successful Achievement: A Basic Inconsistency." In J. Bardwick, E. Douvan, M. Horner, and D. Gutman (eds.), *Feminine Personality and Conflict*. Belmont: Brooks/Cole, 1970a.

_____"The Motive to Avoid Success and Changing Aspirations of College Women." Manuscript, Harvard University, 1970b.

_____"Toward an Understanding of Achievement-Related Conflicts in Women." *Journal of Social Issues 28*, 2 (1972):157–175.

_____"Toward an Understanding of Achievement-related Conflicts in Women." In M. Mednick, S. Tangri, and L. Hoffman (eds.), *Women and Achievement*. New York: Wiley, 1975.

_____"The Measurement and Behavioral Implications of Fear of Success in Women." In J. W. Atkinson and J. O. Raynor (eds.), *Personality, Motivation, and Achievement*. New York: Wiley, 1978.

HORNEY, K. *The Neurotic Personality of Our Time*. New York: Norton, 1937.

_____*Neurosis and Human Growth*. New York: Norton, 1950.

_____*Feminine Psychology*. New York: Norton, 1973.

_____"The Problem of Feminine Masochism." In J. Williams (ed.). *Psychology of Women*, New York: W. W. Norton & Co., 1979.

HOUTS, P., and ENTWISLE, D. "Academic Achievement Effort among Females: Achievement Attitudes and Sex Role Orientation." *Journal of Counseling Psychology 15*, 3 (1968):284-286.

HOWE, F. "The Education of Women, 1970." In W. Martin (ed.), *The American Sisterhood*. New York: Harper & Row, 1972.

_____(ed.) *Women and the Power to Change*. New York: McGraw Hill, 1975.

HOWE, L. K. *Pink Collar Workers*. New York: Putnam, 1977.

HUBER, J. "Editor's Introduction." *American Journal of Sociology 78*, 4 (1973):763-766.

HUGHES, E. "Dilemmas and Contradictions of Status." *American Journal of Sociology 50*, 5 (1944):353-359.

_____"Social Change and Status Protest: An Essay on the Marginal Man." *Phylon 10*, 1 (1949):58-65.

_____"What Other." In A. Rose (ed.), *Behavior and Social Processes*. Boston: Houghton Mifflin, 1962.

HUGHES, H. *The Status of Women in Sociology, 1968-72*. Washington, D.C.: American Sociological Associaton, 1973.

HULICKA, I. *Psychology and Sociology of Aging*. New York: Crowell, 1977.

HULL, C. L. *Principles of Behavior*. New York: Appleton-Century, 1943.

_____*A Behavior System: An Introduction to Behavior Theory Covering the Individual Organism*. New Haven: Yale University Press, 1952.

HUNT, C. *The Life of Ellen H. Richards, 1842-1911*. Washington, D.C.: American Home Economics Associaton, 1942.

IGLEHART, A., *Married Women and Work*. Lexington: Heath, Lexington Books, 1979.

INKELES, A. "Industrial Man." *American Journal of Sociology 66*, 1 (1960):1-31.

ISR Newsletter 12, 1 (1979). Ann Arbor: Center for Continuing Education of Women, University of Michigan.

IRESON, C. "Girls' Socialization for Work." In A. Stromberg and S. Harkess (eds.), *Women Working*. Palo Alto: Mayfield, 1978.

JACKSON, J. J. "Older Black Women." In L. Troll, J. Israel, and K. Israel (eds.), *Looking Ahead: A Woman's Guide to the Problems and Joys of Growing Older*. Englewood Cliffs: Prentice-Hall, 1977.

JACOBSON, D. "Rejection of Retiree Role: A Study of Female Industrial Workers in Their 50's." *Human Relations 27*, 5 (1975):477-492.

JACQUES, E. "Death and the Mid-life Crisis." *International Journal of Psychoanalysis 4*, 4 (1965):502-514.

JANEWAY, E. *Man's World, Woman's Place*. New York: Morrow, 1971.

_____"Breaking the Age Barrier." *MS*, April 1973, 50-53, 109-111.

_____*Powers of the Weak*. New York: Knopf, 1980.

JAQUETTE, J. (ed.). *Women in Politics*. New York: Wiley, 1974.

Johnson, M. "Sex Role Learning in the Nuclear Family." *Child Development 34*, 2 (1963):319–335.

Johnson, P. "Women and Power: Toward a Theory of Effectiveness." *Journal of Social Issues 32*, 3 (1976):99–110.

Jones, J. B., Lundsteen, S. W. and Michael, W. B. "The Relationship of the Professional Employment Status of Mothers to Reading Achievement of Sixth Grade Children." *California Journal of Education Research 43*, 2 (1967):102–108.

Jourard, S. M., and Rubin, J. E. "Self-disclosure and Touching: A Study of Two Modes of Interpersonal Encounter and Their Interrelation." *Journal of Humanistic Psychology 8*, 1 (1968):39–48.

Jung, C. G. *Modern Man in Search of a Soul.* New York: Harcourt, 1933.

Kagan, J. "The Child's Perception of the Parent." *Journal of Abnormal and Social Psychology 53*, 2 (1956):257–260.

_____"The Acquisition and Significance of Sex Typing and Sex Role Identity." In M. L. Hoffman and L. W. Hoffman (eds.), *Review of Child Development Research*, vol. 1. New York: Russell Sage, 1964.

_____"Resilience and Continuity in Psychological Development." In A. M. Clarke and A. D. B. Clarke (eds.), *Early Experience: Myth and Evidence.* New York: Free Press, 1976.

Kagan, J., and Lemkin, J. "The Child's Differential Perception of Parental Attitudes." *Journal of Abnormal and Social Psychology 61*, 3 (1960):440–447.

Kagan, J., and Moss, H. A. *Birth to Maturity.* New York: Wiley, 1962.

Kanter, R. "Women and the Structure of Organizations: Explorations in Theory and Behavior." In M. Millman and R. Kanter (eds.), *Another Voice.* New York: Doubleday Anchor, 1975.

_____*Men and Women of the Corporation.* New York: Basic Books, 1977a.

_____"Some Effects of Proportions on Group Life: Skewed Sex Ratios and Responses to Token Women." *American Journal of Sociology 32*, 5 (1977b): 965–990.

_____"Families, Family Processes, and Economic Life: Toward Systematic Analysis of Social Historical Research." In J. Demos and S. Boocock (eds.), *Turning Points.* Chicago: University of Chicago Press, 1978a.

_____"Work in a New America." *Daedalus 107*, 1 (1978b):47–78.

Kaplan, A., and Bean, J. (eds.). *Beyond Sex-Role Stereotypes: Readings toward a Psychology of Androgyny.* Boston: Little, Brown, 1976.

Kaufman, D. "Women and the Professions: Can What's Preached Be Practiced?" *Soundings 60*, 4 (1977):410–427.

_____"Associational Ties in Academe: Some Male and Female Differences." *Sex Roles 4*, 1 (1978):9–21.

Kaufman, D., and Fetters, M. J. "The Executive Suite: Are Women Perceived as Ready for the Managerial Climb?" Paper presented to the Sixty-fifth Eastern Sociological Society Meetings. Boston: 1980.

Kaufman, M. "On Brecht." Lecture, Brandeis University, January, 1979.

KELLER, E. "Women in Science: An Analysis of a Social Problem." *Harvard Magazine*, October 1974, pp. 14–19.

KELLER, S., and ZAVAROLLI, M. "Ambition and Social Class: A Respecification." *Social Forces 43*, 1 (1964):58–70.

KESSLER-HARRIS, A. "Where Are the Organized Women Workers?" *Feminist Studies 3*, 1/2 (1975):92–110.

_____"Women, Work, and the Social Order." In B. Carroll (ed.), *Liberating Women's History*. Chicago: University of Illinois Press, 1976.

KOHLBERG, L. "Cognitive-Developmental Analysis of Children's Sex Role Concepts and Attitudes." In E. Maccoby (ed.), *The Development of Sex Differences*. Stanford: Stanford University Press, 1966.

_____"Stage and Sequences: The Cognitive Developmental Approach to Socialization." In D. A. Goslin (ed.), *Handbook of Socialization Theory and Research*. Chicago: Rand McNally, 1969.

_____"From Is to Ought: How to Commit the Naturalistic Fallacy and Get Away with It in the Study of Moral Development." In T. Mischel (ed.), *Cognitive Development and Epistemology*. New York: Academic, 1971.

_____"The Claim to Moral Adequacy of a Highest Stage of Moral Judgment." *Journal of Philosophy 70*, 18 (1978):630–646.

_____Foreword to P. Scharf (ed.), *Readings in Moral Education*. Minneapolis: Winston, 1978.

KOHLBERG, L., and ZIGLER, E. "The Impact of Cognitive Maturity on the Development of Sex-Role Attitudes in the Years 4 to 8." *Genetic Psychology Monographs 75*, 1 (1967):89–165.

KOMAROVSKY, M. "Cultural Contradictions and Sex Roles." *American Journal of Sociology 52*, 3 (1946):184–189.

_____"Functional Analysis of Sex Roles." *American Sociological Review 15*, 4 (1950):508–516.

_____*Dilemmas of Masculinity: A Study of College Youth*. New York: Norton, 1976.

KORMAN, A. K. *The Psychology of Motivation*. Englewood Cliffs: Prentice-Hall, 1974.

KRADITOR, A. S. *The Ideas of the Woman Suffrage Movement, 1880–1920*. New York: Doubleday Anchor, 1974.

KREPS, J. *Sex in the Marketplace: American Women at Work*. Baltimore: Johns Hopkins Press, 1971.

KUHLEN, R. "Developmental Changes in Motivation during the Adult Years." In J. E. Birren (ed.), *Relations of Development and Aging*. Springfield: Thomas, 1964.

_____"Age and Intelligence: The Significance of Cultural Change in Longitudinal versus Cross-sectional Findings." In B. Neugarten (ed.), *Middle Age and Aging*. Chicago: University of Chicago Press, 1968a.

_____"Developmental Changes in Motivation during the Adult Years." In B. Neugarten (ed.), *Middle Age and Aging*. Chicago: University of Chicago Press, 1968b.

KUHN, T. *The Structure of Scientific Revolutions*. Chicago: University of Chicago Press, 1962.

LADNER, J. A. *Tomorrow's Tomorrow*. New York: Anchor Books, 1972.

LANGER, J. *Theories of Development*. New York: Holt Rinehart, 1969.

LASLETT, B. "The Family As a Public and Private Institution: An Historical Perspective." *Journal of Marriage and the Family 35*, 3 (1973):480–494.

LAWS, J. L. "The Psychology of Tokenism: An Analysis." *Sex Roles 1*, 1 (1975): 51–67.

_____"Work Aspiration of Women: False Leads and New Starts." In M. Blaxall and B. Reagan (eds.), *Women and the Workplace*. Chicago: University of Chicago Press, 1976.

_____"Work Motivation and Work Behavior of Women: New Perspectives." In J. Sherman and F. Denmark (eds.) *The Psychology of Women: Future Directions in Research*. New York: Psychological Dimensions, 1978.

LEFFLER, D. and GILLESPIE, D. "Academic Feminists and The Women's Movement." *Ain't I A Women? 4*, 1, 1973.

LEIBMAN, M. "The Effects of Sex and Race Norms on Personal Space." *Environment and Behavior 4*, 2 (1970): 208–246.

LENHOFF, D. "Equal Pay for Work of Comparable Value as Strategy." In J. Grune (ed.) *Manual on Pay Equity*. Washington, D.C.: Conference on Alternative State and Local Policies, 1980.

LENSKI, G. *Power and Privilege*. New York: McGraw-Hill, 1966.

LERNER, G. "The Lady and the Mill Girl: Changes in the Status of Women in the Age of Jackson." *Warner Modular Publication*, no. 460 (1973), pp. 1–11.

_____"Placing Women in History: Definitions and Challenges." *Feminist Studies 3*, 1 (1975):5–15.

LERNER, R. *Concepts and Theories of Human Development*. Reading: Addison-Wesley, 1976.

LESSER, G. S. "Achievement Motivation in Women." In D. C. McClelland and R. Steele (eds.), *Human Motivation*. Morristown: General Learning Press, 1973.

LESSER, G. S., KRAVITZ, R. N., and PACKARD, R. "Experimental Arousal of Achievement Motivation in Adolescent Girls." *Journal of Abnormal and Social Psychology 66*, 1 (1963):59–66.

LEVINSON, D. J. *The Seasons of a Man's Life*. New York: Random House, 1978.

_____"Psychological Study of the Male Mid-life Decade." In D. Ricks, A. Thomas, M. Roff (eds.), *Life History Research in Psychopathology*, Vol. 3. Minneapolis: University of Minnesota Press, 1974.

LEWIN, K. *A Dynamic Theory of Personality*. New York: McGraw-Hill, 1935.

_____*Field Theory in Social Science*. New York: Harper, 1951.

LIPMAN-BLUMEN, J. "How Ideology Shapes Women's Lives." *Scientific American 226*, 1 (1972):34–42.

_____"Role De-differentiation as a System Response to Crises: Occupational and Political Roles of Women." *Sociological Inquiry 43*, 2 (1973):105–129.

_____"Toward a Homosocial Theory of Sex Roles." In M. Blaxall and B.

Reagan (eds.), *Women and the Workplace.* Chicago: Universtiy of Chicago Press, 1976.

LIPMAN-BLUMEN, J., and LEAVITT, H. J. "Vicarious and Direct Achievement Patterns in Adulthood." *Counseling Psychologist 6*, 1 (1976): 26–32.

_____ "Sexual Behavior, Achievement Patterns, and Sex Roles." Paper presented to the Conference on Sex and Its Psychosocial Derivatives. Stanford: January 1977.

LOBSENZ, J. *The Older Woman in Industry.* New York: Arno, 1974.

LOCKHEED, M. "Female Motive to Avoid Success: A Psychological Barrier or a Response to Deviancy?" *Sex Roles 1*, 1 (1975):41–50.

LOPATA, H. *Occupation: Housewife.* New York: Oxford University Press, 1971.

_____ "Social Relations of Widows in Urbanizing Societies." *Sociological Quarterly 13*, 2 (Spring 1972):259–271.

LOPATA, H., and STEINHART, F. "Work Histories of American Urban Women." *Gerontologist 2*, 4 (1971):27–28.

LORBER, J. "Women and Medical Sociology: Invisible Professionals and Ubiquitous Patients." In M. Millman and R. Kanter (eds.), *Another Voice.* New York: Doubleday Anchor, 1975.

LOWENTHAL, M., THURNHER, M., and CHIRIBOGA, D. *Four Stages of Life.* San Francisco: Jossey-Bass, 1976.

MACCOBY, E. (ed.). *The Development of Sex Differences.* Stanford: Stanford University Press, 1966.

MACCOBY, E., and JACKLIN, C. *The Psychology of Sex Differences.* Stanford: Stanford University Press, 1974.

MADDI, S. R. *Personality Theories: A Comparative Analysis.* Homewood: Dorsey, 1972.

MAEHR, M. "Culture and Achievement Motivation." *American Psychologist 29*, 12 (1974): 887–896.

MAKOSKY, V. "Sex Role Compatibility of Task and of Competitor, and Fear of Success as Variables Affecting Women's Performance." *Sex Roles 2*, 3 (1976):237–248.

MANDLER, G., and SARASON, S. B. "A Study of Anxiety and Learning." *Journal of Abnormal and Social Psychology 47*, 2 (1952):166–173.

MANIS, J. and MARKUS, H. "Combining Family and Careers: Views from Different Points in the Life Cycle." *ISR Newsletter 12*, 1 (1979):4–5. Ann Arbor: Center for Continuing Education of Women, University of Michigan.

MARINI, M., and GREENBERGER, E. "Sex Differences in Occupational Aspirations and Expectations." Paper presented to the Sixty-fourth American Sociological Association. New York City: August 1976.

MARTIN, W. (ed.) *The American Sisterhood.* New York: Harper & Row, 1972.

MASON, K. O. "Sex and Status in Science." *Science 208* (April 1980):277–278.

MATTHEWS, E., and TIEDEMAN, D. V. "Attitudes toward Career and Marriage and the Development of Life Style in Young Women." *Journal of Counseling Psychology 11*, 4 (1964):375–383.

McADOO, H. "Race and Sex-typing in Young Black Children." Paper presented to the Annual Meeting of the National Conference of Social Welfare. Cincinnati: May 1974.

McClelland, D. C. "Some Social Consequences of Achievement Motivation." In M. R. Jones (ed.), *Nebraska Symposium on Motivation.* Lincoln: University of Nebraska Press, 1955.

_____"Risk-taking in Children with High and Low Need for Achievement." In J. W. Atkinson (ed.), *Motives in Fantasy, Action, and Society.* Princeton: Van Nostrand, 1958a.

_____"The Use of Measures of Human Motivation in the Study of Society." In J. W. Atkinson (ed.), *Motives in Fantasy, Action, and Society.* Princeton: Van Nostrand, 1958b.

_____*The Achieving Society.* Princeton: Van Nostrand, 1961.

_____*Power: The Inner Experience.* New York: Irvington, 1975.

McClelland, D. C., Atkinson, J. W., Clark, R. A. and Lowell, E. I. *The Achievement Motive.* New York: Appleton-Century, 1953.

McClelland, D. C., Baldwin, A. L., Bronfenbrenner, U., and Strodtbeck, F. L. *Talent and Society.* Princeton: Van Nostrand, 1958.

McClelland, D. C., and Friedman, G. "A Cross-cultural Study of the Relationship between Child-training Practices and Achievement Motivation Appearing in Folk Tales." In G. Swanson and T. Newcomb (eds.), *Readings in Social Psychology.* New York: Holt, 1952.

McClelland, D. C., Rindlisbacher, A., and deCharms, R. C. "Religious and Other Sources of Parental Attitudes toward Independence Training." In D. C. McClelland (ed.), *Studies in Motivation.* New York: Appleton-Century, 1955.

McClelland, D. C., and Steele, R. *Human Motivation.* Morristown: General Learning Press, 1973.

McClelland, D. C., and Winter, D. G. *Motivating Economic Achievement.* New York: Free Press, 1969.

McClendon, M. J. "The Occupational Status Attainment Process of Males and Females." *American Sociological Review 41,* 1 (1976):52–64.

McCord, J., and McCord, W. "Effects of Maternal Employment on Lower-class Boys." *Journal of Abnormal and Social Psychology 67,* 2 (1963):177–182.

McCord, W., McCord, J., and Thurber, E. "Some Effects of Parental Absence on Male Children." *Journal of Abnormal and Social Psychology 64,* 5 (1962):361–369.

McCourt, K., Bycer, A., Currie, B., Greenstone, D. *Politics and Families: Changing Roles of Urban Women.* Chicago: National Opinion Research Center, 1979.

McGuigan, D. G. (ed.). *New Research on Women at the University of Michigan.* Ann Arbor: Center for Continuing Education of Women, University of Michigan, 1974.

Mead, M. *Sex and Temperament in Three Primitive Societies.* New York: Morrow, 1935.

Mead, M., and Kaplan, F. B. (eds.). *American Women.* New York: Scribner's, 1955.

Mednick, M., Tangri, S., and Hoffman, L. (eds.). *Women and Achievement.* New York: Wiley, 1975.

MEDVEC, E. "Quest Perspective on Money, Fame, and Power." *Quest 1*, 2 (1974):2–4.

MEIXEL, C. "Female Adolescents' Sex Role Stereotypes and Competence Motivation." Ph.D. dissertation, Cornell University, 1976.

MELVILLE, K. *Marriage and Family Today.* New York: Random House, 1980.

MILLER, J. B. *Toward a New Psychology of Women.* Boston: Beacon Press, 1976.

MILLER, N., and DOLLARD, J. *Social Learning and Imitation.* New Haven: Yale University Press, 1941.

MINCER, J. *Schooling, Experience, and Earnings.* New York: Columbia University Press, 1974.

MINCER, J., and POLACHECK, S. "Family Investments in Human Capital: Earnings of Women." *Journal of Political Economy 82* (March–April 1974):76–111.

MISCHEL, W. H. *Personality and Assesment.* New York: Wiley, 1968.

_____"Sex Typing and Socialization." In P. H. Mussen (ed.), *Carmichael's Manual of Child Psychology,* vol. 2. New York: Wiley, 1971.

MISCHEL, W. and LIEBERT, R. "The Role of Power in the Adoption of Self-reward Patterns." *Child Development 38,* 3 (1967):673–683.

MONAHAN, L., Kuhn, D., and SHAVER, Z. "Intra-psychic versus Cultural Explanations of the Fear of Success Motive." *Journal of Personality and Social Psychology 29,* 2 (1974):60–64.

MONTS, E., and BURGER, L. "The Status of Home Economics and The Status of Women." In J. Roberts (ed.), *Beyond Intellectual Sexism: A New Woman, A New Reality.* New York: David McKay Company, 1976.

MOORE, W. *Conduct of the Corporation.* New York: Random House, 1962.

MOOS, R. *Human Adaptations, Coping with Life Crises.* Lexington: DC Heath, 1976.

MORTIMER, J., HALL, R. and HILL, R. "Husbands' Occupational Attributes as Constraints on Wives' Employment." Paper presented to the Sixty-fourth American Sociological Association meetings. New York: August 1976.

MURPHY, J. and GILLIGAN, C. "Moral Development in Late Adolescence and Adulthood: A Critique and Reconstruction of Kohlberg's Theory." *Human Development 23,* 2 (1980):77–104.

MURSTEIN, B. I. *Theory and Research in Projective Techniques: Emphasizing the TAT.* New York: Wiley, 1963.

MYERS, L. "Black Women: Selectivity Among Roles and Reference Groups in the Maintenance of Self-esteem." *Journal of Social and Behavioral Sciences 21,* 2 (1975):39–47

MYRDAL, A. and KLEIN, V., *Women's Two Roles.* London: Routledge and Kegan Paul, 1968.

MYRDAL, G. *An American Dilemma,* New York: Harper, 1944.

National Commission on the Observance of International Women's Year. Report. Washington, D.C., 1976.

National Manpower Council. *Womanpower.* New York: Columbia University Press, 1957.

Neugarten, B. "Adult Personality: Toward a Psychology of the Life Cycle." In B. Neugarten (ed.). *Middle Age and Aging.* Chicago: University of Chicago Press, 1968a.

_____(ed.). *Middle Age and Aging.* Chicago: University of Chicago Press, 1968b.

Northby, A. "Sex Differences in High School Scholarship." *School and Society 86,* 2 (1958):63-64.

NYE, I., and HOFFMAN, L. *The Employed Mother in America.* Chicago: Rand McNally, 1963.

NYE, I., and BERARDO, F. M. *The Family: Its Structure and Interaction.* New York: Macmillan, 1973

OAKLEY, A. *Women's Work: The Housewife, Past and Present.* New York: Random House, Vintage, 1976.

ODENDAHL, T., PALMER, P., and RATNER, R. "The Pay Equity Research Conference: Comparable Worth Research Issues and Methods." In J. Grune (ed.), *Manual on Pay Equity: Raising Wages for Women's Work.* Washington, D.C.: Conference on Alternative State and Local Policies, Committee on Pay Equity, 1980.

O'LEARY, V. "Some Attitudinal Barriers to Occupational Aspirations in Women." *Psychology Bulletin 8,* 11 (1974):809-826.

_____*Toward Understanding Women.* Monterey: Brooks/Cole, 1977.

O'LEARY, V., and HAMMACK, B. "Sex Role Orientation and Achievement: Context as Determinants of the Motive to Avoid Success." *Sex Roles 1,* 3 (1975):225-234.

OPPENHEIMER, V. K. "The Sex-Labelling of Jobs." *Industrial Relations 7,* 3 (1968): 219-234.

_____"The Female Labor Force in the U.S.: Demographic and Economic Factors Governing Its Growth and Changing Composition." *University of California at Berkeley Population Monographs* , no. 5 (1970).

_____"The Sociology of Women's Economic Role in the Family." *American Sociological Review 42,* 3 (1977):387-406.

ORZACK, L. "Work as a Central Life Interest of Professionals." *Social Problems 7,* 2 (1959):125-132.

OSIPOW, S. (ed.). *Emerging Woman: Career Analysis and Outlooks.* Columbus: Merrill, 1975.

PALMER, P., and GRANT, S. *The Status of Clerical Workers: A Summary Analysis of Research Findings and Trends.* Washington, D.C.: George Washington University & BPW Foundation, 1979.

PALMORE, E. B. "Differences in the Retirement Patterns of Men and Women." *Gerontologist 5,* 1 (1965):4-8.

PAPACHRISTOU, J. *Women Together: A History in Documents of the Women's Movement in the U.S.* New York: Knopf, 1976.

PAPANEK, H. "Men, Women, and Work: Reflections on the Two-Person Career." *American Journal of Sociology 78,* 4 (1973):852-872.

PARKIN, F. *Class Inequality and Political Order.* New York: Praeger, 1971.

PARLEE, M. B. "The New Scholarship: Review Essays in the Social Sciences." *Signs 1,* 1 (1975):110-138.

PARSONS, J. E. "Cognitive-Developmental Theories of Sex-Role Socialization." In I. H. Frieze, P. B. Johnson, J. E. Parsons, D. N. Ruble, and G. L. Zellman (eds.), *Women and Sex Roles: A Social Psychological Perspective.* New York: Norton, 1978.

PARSONS, J., RUBLE, D., HODGES, K. and SMALL, A. "Cognitive Developmental Factors in Emerging Sex Differences in Achievement-Related Expectancies." *Journal of Social Issues 32*, 3 (1976):47-61.

PARSONS, T. *The Social System.* New York: Free Press, 1951.

_____*Social Structure and Personality.* New York: Free Press, 1964.

PARSONS, T., and BALES, R. *Family, Socialization, and Interaction Process.* New York: Free Press, 1955.

PASCAL, A., DURAN, B., DOUGHERTY, L., DUNN, W., THOMPSON, V. *An Evaluation of Policy Related Research on Programs for Mid-life Career Redirection*, vol. 2. Santa Monica: Rand Corporation, 1975.

PEPLAU, L. A. "The Impact of Fear of Success, Sex-Role Attitudes, and Opposite-Sex Relationships on Women's Intellectual Performance." Ph.D. dissertation, Harvard University, 1973.

_____"Fear of Success in Dating Couples." *Sex Roles 2*, 3 (1976):249-258.

PERRY, C., ANDERSON, B. E., ROWAN, R. L., and NORTHRUP, H. R. *The Impact of Government and Manpower Programs: In General and on Minorities and Women.* Philadelphia: University of Pennsylvania Press, 1975.

PERSELL, C. "Rewards and Research: A Comparison of Male and Female Researchers in Education." Report to the Department of Health, Education, and Welfare. Washington, D.C., 1978.

PETERSON, J. L. "An Agenda for Socioeconomic Life Cycle Research." *Journal of Economics and Business 32*, 2 (1980):95-110.

PETERSON, L., and ENARSON, E. "Blaming the Victim in the Sociology of Women: On the Misuse of the Concept of Socialization." Paper presented to the Sixtieth Pacific Sociological Association. San Jose: March 1974.

PETTIGREW, T. *A Profile of the Negro American.* Princeton: Van Nostrand 1964.

PHETERSON, G. I., KIESLER, S. B. and GOLDBERG, P. A. "Evaluation of the Performance of Women as a Function of Their Sex, Achievement, and Personal History." *Journal of Personality and Social Psychology 19*, 1 (1971):114-118.

PIAGET, J. "Intellectual Evolution from Adolescence to Adulthood." *Human Development 15*, 1 (1972):1-12.

PLECK, E. "Two Worlds in One: Work and Family." *Journal of Social History 10*, 2 (1976):178-195.

PLUMB, J. H. "The Great Change in Children." In A. Skolnick (ed.), *Rethinking Childhood.* Boston: Little, Brown, 1976.

POLOMA, M. M. "Role Conflict and the Married Professional Woman." In C. Safilios-Rothschild (ed.), *Toward a Sociology of Women.* Lexington: Xerox College Publishing, 1972.

POWELL, K. S. "Personalities of Children and Child Rearing Attitudes of Mothers." In I. Nye and L. Hoffman (eds.), *The Employed Mother in America.* Chicago: Rand McNally, 1963.

PRESTON, C. E. "An Old Bag: The Stereotype of the Older Woman." In N. Trager (ed.) *No Longer Young: The Older Woman in America.* Proceedings of the 26th Annual Conference on Aging. Institute of Gerontology, University of Michigan and Wayne State University, 1975.

PUTNAM, E. *The Lady: Studies of Certain Phases of Her History.* Chicago: University of Chicago Press, 1970.

RABBAN, M. "Sex-Role Identification in Young Children in Two Diverse Social Groups." *Genetic Psychology Monographs 42,* 1 (1950):81-150.

RAND, L. M. and MILLER, A. L. "A Developmental Cross-sectioning of Women's Careers and Marriage Attitudes and Life Plans." *Journal of Vocational Behavior 2,* 3 (1972):317-331.

RAYNOR, J. O. "Future Orientation and Motivation of Immediate Activity." *Psychological Review 76,* 10 (1969):606-610.

_____ "Relationships between Achievement-related Motives, Future Orientation, and Academic Performance." *Journal of Personality and Social Psychology 15,* 1 (1970):28-33.

_____ "Future Orientation in Achievement Motivation: A More General Theory of Achievement Motivation." In J. W. Atkinson and J. O. Raynor (eds.), *Personality, Motivation, and Achievement.* New York: Wiley, 1978a.

_____ "Motivation and Career Striving." In J. W. Atkinson and J. O. Raynor (eds.), *Personality, Motivation, and Achievement.* New York: Wiley, 1978b.

REBELSKY, F. *Life: The Continuous Process.* New York: Knopf, 1975.

REESE, M. F. "Family History: The Past in Relation to the Present." In D. Belle (ed.), *Lives in Stress: A Context for Depression.* Bethesda: National Institute of Mental Health, 1979.

RESKIN, B. "Sex Differences in Status Attainment in Science: The Case of the Postdoctoral Fellowship." *American Sociological Review 41,* 4 (1976):597-612.

RESKIN, B., and HARGENS, L. "Assessing Sex Discrimination in Science." Manuscript, Indiana University, 1977.

RICH, A. *Of Woman Born: Motherhood as Experience and Institution.* New York: Norton, 1976.

RICHARDS, E. H. *Euthenics.* Boston: Whitcomb & Barrows, 1910.

RICHARDSON, B. "Effects of Maternal Employment on Socialization for Achievement in New Zealand." Ph.D. dissertation, Cornell University, 1975a.

_____ "Perceptions of Maternal Power: Daughters of Working Mothers." Groves Conference on the Family. Dubrovnik: August 1975b.

RICHARDSON, B., and PERRET, Y. "Aging, Not a Bad Alternative: Analysis and Summary of the Cornell Conference on Women in Mid-life Crises." Manuscript. Washington, D.C., 1981.

ROBY, P. "Women and American Higher Education." *Annals of the American Academy of Political and Social Science 404,* 1 (1972):118-139.

ROETHEISBERGER, F. J., and DICKSON, W. J. *Management and the Worker.* Cambridge: Harvard University Press, 1930.

ROSEN, B. C. "The Achievement Syndrome and Economic Growth in Brazil." *Social Forces 42,* 3 (1964):341-354.

_____Introduction to B. C. Rosen, H. Crockett, and C. Nunn (eds.), *Achievement in American Society*. Cambridge: Schenkman, 1969.

ROSEN, B. C., CROCKETT, H., and NUNN, C. (eds.). *Achievement in American Society*. Cambridge: Schenkman, 1969.

ROSEN, B. C., and D'ANDRADE, R. "The Psychosocial Origins of Achievement Motivation." *Sociometry 22*, 3 (1959):185–218.

ROSEN, B., and JERDEE, T. H. "The Influence of Sex-Role Stereotypes on Evaluations of Male and Female Supervisory Behavior." *Journal of Applied Psychology 57*, 1 (1973):44–48.

ROSENKRANTZ, P. S., VOGEL, S. R., BEE, H., BROVERMAN, I. K., and BROVERMAN, D. M. "Sex-Role Stereotypes and Self-concepts in College Students." *Journal of Consulting and Clinical Psychology 32*, 3 (1968):287–295.

ROSSI, A. S. "Transition to Parenthood." *Journal of Marriage and the Family 30*, 1 (1968):26–39.

_____"Sexuality and Maternalism: A Feminist Perspective." Lecture, Cornell University, April 1973.

_____"A Biosocial Perspective on Parenting." *Daedalus 106*, 2 (1977):1–32.

RUBIN, J. Z., and BROWN, B. R. *The Social Psychology of Bargaining and Negotiation*. New York: Academic, 1975.

RUBIN, L. B. *Worlds of Pain: The Working Class Family*. New York: Basic Books, 1976.

RUBLE, D. N., FRIEZE, I. H., and PARSONS, J. E. (eds.). "Sex Roles: Persistence and Change." *Journal of Social Issues 32*, 3 (1976).

RUBLE, D. N., and HIGGINS, E. T. "Effects of Group Sex Composition on Self-Presentation and Sex Typing." *Journal of Social Issues 32*, 3 (1976):125–132.

RYAN, M. *Womanhood in America: From Colonial Times to the Present*. New York: Watts, 1979.

RYDER, N. B. "The Demography of Youth." In J. Coleman (ed.), *Youth: Transition to Adulthood*. Washington D.C.: Government Printing Office, 1973.

SAFILIOS-ROTHSCHILD, C. *Sex Role Socialization and Sex Discrimination: A Synthesis and Critique of the Literature*. Washington, D.C.: National Institute of Education, 1979.

SANDLER, B. "Sex Discrimination, Educational Institutions, and the Law: A New Issue on Campus." *Journal of Law and Education 2*, 4 (1973):613–635.

SARASON, S. B. *Work, Aging, and Social Change: Professionals and the One-Life Career Imperative*. New York: Free Press, 1977.

SAWHILL, I. "Discrimination and Poverty among Women Who Head Families." In M. Blaxall and B. Reagan (eds.), *Women and the Workplace*. Chicago: University of Chicago Press, 1976.

_____"Economic Perspectives on the Family." In A. Rossi, J. Kagan, and T. K. Hareven, (eds.), *The Family*. New York: Norton, 1978.

SCANZONI, J. H. *Sex Roles, Life Styles, and Childbearing*. New York: Free Press, 1975.

SCANZONI, L., and SCANZONI, J. *Men, Women, and Change*. New York: McGraw-Hill, 1976.

SCHARF, P. (ed.). *Readings in Moral Education.* Minneapolis: Winston, 1978.

SCHNEIDER, L. "Our Failures Only Marry: Bryn Mawr and the Failure of Feminism." In J. Stacey, S. Béreaud, and J. Daniels (eds.) *And Jill Came Tumbling After: Sexism in American Education.* New York: Dell, 1974.

SCHULTZ, T. W. (ed.). *Economics of the Family: Marriage, Children, and Human Capital.* Chicago: University of Chicago Press, 1974.

SCOTT, J. F. *Internalization of Norms: A Sociological Theory of Moral Commitment.* Englewood Cliffs: Prentice-Hall, 1971.

SEARS, P. S. "Correlates of Need Achievement and Need Affiliation and Classroom Movement, Self-concept, and Creativity." Laboratory of Human Development, Stanford University, Manuscript 1962.

SEARS, R. R., RAU, L., and ALPERT, R. *Identification and Childrearing.* Stanford: Stanford University Press, 1965.

SEARS, R. R., WHITING, J., NOWLIS, V., and SEARS, P. "Some Child-rearing Antecedents of Aggression and Dependency in Young Children." *Genetic Psychology Monographs 47,* 2 (1953): 135-236.

SEIDENBERG, R. *Corporate Wives—Corporate Casualties?* New York: Amacon, 1973.

SEWELL, W. H., HALLER, A. O. and OHLENDORF, G. W. "The Educational and Early Occupational Status Attainment Process: Replication and Revision." *American Sociological Review 35,* 6 (1970):1014-1027.

SEWELL, W. H., HALLER, A. O., and PORTES, A. "The Early Educational and Early Occupational Status Attainment Process." *American Sociological Review 34,* 1 (1969):82-92

SEWELL, W. H., and HAUSER, R. M. "Causes and Consequences of Higher Education: Models of the Status Attainment Process." *American Journal of Agricultural Economics 54* (December 1972):851-861.

_____*Education, Occupation, and Earnings.* New York: Academic, 1975.

SEWELL, W. H., and SHAH, V. "Socioeconomic Status, Intelligence, and the Attainment of Higher Education." *Sociology of Education 40* (Winter 1967):1-23.

_____ "Parents' Education and Children's Educational Aspirations and Achievements." *American Sociological Review 33,* 2 (1968):191-209.

SHAW, M., and McCUEN, C. "The Effects of Sex-Role Standards for Achievement and Sex-role Preference on Three Determinants of Achievement Motivation." *Developmental Psychology 4,* 2 (1971):219-231.

SHEEHY, G. *Passages: Predictable Crises of Adult Life.* New York: Dutton, 1974.

SHERMAN, J., and DENMARK, F. (eds.). *The Psychology of Women: Future Directions in Research.* New York: Psychological Dimensions, 1978.

SHIELDS, L. "Gaining New Rights, New Relationships." Paper presented to the Cornell Conference on Women in Mid-life Crises. Ithaca: October 1976.

SHIPLEY, T. E., and VEROFF, J. A. "A Projective Measure of Need for Affiliation." *Journal of Experimental Psychology 43,* 5 (1952):349-356.

SHORTER, E. *The Making of the Modern Family.* New York: Basic Books, 1975

SHORTRIDGE, K. "Working Poor Women." In J. Freeman (ed.), *Women: A Feminist Perspective.* Palo Alto: Mayfield, 1975.

SIEGEL, A., and HAAS, M. "The Working Mother: A Review of Research." *Child Development 34*, 3 (1963):513–542.

SKOLNICK, A. *The Intimate Environment.* Boston: Little, Brown, 1973.

_____(ed.). *Rethinking Childhood: Perspectives on Development and Society.* Boston: Little, Brown, 1976.

SMELSER, N., and HALPERN, S. "The Historical Triangulation of Family Economy and Education." In J. Demos and S. Boocock (eds.), *Turning Points.* Chicago: University of Chicago Press, 1978.

SMITH, M. B. "Competence and Socialization." In J. A. Clausen (ed.), *Socialization and Society.* Boston: Little, Brown, 1968.

SMITH, R. E. "The Movement of Women into the Labor Force." In R. Smith (ed.), *The Subtle Revolution: Women at Work.* Washington, D.C.: Urban Institute, 1979.

SMUTS, R. W. "The Female Labor Force: A Case Study in the Interpretation of Historical Statistics." *Journal of the American Statistical Association 60* (March 1960):71–79.

SOMMER, R. "Studies in Personal Space." *Sociometry 22*, 3 (1959):247–260.

SOMMERS, T. "Hope for Displaced Homemakers." *Primetime*, August–September 1976, 1–5.

SONTAG, S. "The Double Standard of Aging." *Saturday Review, 55*, September 1972, 29–38.

SOROKIN, P. *Social Mobility.* New York: Harper, 1927.

SPACKS, P. M. *The Female Imagination.* New York: Avon, 1975.

STEIN, A., and BAILEY, M. "The Socialization of Achievement Orientation in Females." In A. Kaplan and J. Bean (eds.), *Beyond Sex-Role Stereotypes: Readings toward a Psychology of Androgyny.* Boston: Little, Brown, 1976.

_____"The Socialization of Achievement Orientation in Females." *Psychological Bulletin 80*, 5 (1973):345–365.

STEIN, A., and SERBIN, L. "Masculinity-Femininity: An Exception to a Famous Dictum?" In A. Kaplan and J. Bean (eds.), *Beyond Sex-Role Stereotypes: Readings toward a Psychology of Androgyny.* Boston: Little, Brown, 1976.

STEIN, L. I. "Male and Female: The Doctor-Nurse Game." In J. P. Spradley and D. W. McCurdy (eds.), *Conformity and Conflict: Readings in Cultural Anthropology.* Boston: Little, Brown, 1971.

STELLMAN, J. M. *Women's Work, Women's Health: Myths and Realities.* New York: Pantheon, 1977.

STEWART, J. "Beyond Status Attainment: New Models of the American Occupational Structure." Manuscript, Cornell University, 1977a.

_____"Comparing Mobility Patterns: Nothing Else Being Equal." Paper presented to the fifth Temple University Conference on Culture and Communication. Philadelphia: March 1977b.

STOLZ, L. M. "Effects of Maternal Employment on Children: Evidence from Research." *Child Development 31*, 4 (1960):749–782.

STRAUS, M. "Power and Support Structure of the Family in Relation to Socialization." *Journal of Marriage and the Family 26*, 3 (1964):318–326.

STREIB, G. F., and SCHNEIDER, C. J. *Retirement in American Society.* Ithaca: Cornell University Press, 1971.

STRODTBECK, F. L. "The Family as a Three-Person Group." *American Sociological Review 19*, 1 (1954):23–29.

_____"Husband-Wife Interaction over Revealed Differences." In A. P. Hare, E. F. Borgatta, R. F. Bales (eds.), *Small Groups.* New York: Knopf, 1955.

_____"Family Interaction, Values, and Achievement." In D.C. McClelland, A.L. Baldwin, U. Bronfenbrenner, and F. L. Strodtbeck, *Talent and Society.* Princeton: Van Nostrand, 1958.

SUTER, L. E. "Income Differences between Men and Career Women." *American Journal of Sociology 78*, 4 (1973):962–974.

SYZMANSKI, A. "Race, Sex, and the U.S. Working Class." *Social Problems 21*, 5 (1974):706–725.

TANGRI, S. "Determinants of Occupational Role Innovation among College Women." *Journal of Social Issues 28*, 2 (1972):177–199.

_____"Implied Demand Character of the Wife's Future and Role Innovation: Patterns of Achievement Orientation among College Women." In M. Mednick, S. Tangri, and L. Hoffman (eds.), *Women and Achievement.* New York: Wiley, 1975.

TAYLOR, M., and HARTLEY, S. "The Two-Person Career: A Classic Example." *Sociology of Work and Occupations 2*, 4 (1975):354–372.

TEPPERMAN, J. *Not Servants, Not Machines: Office Workers Speak Out.* Boston: Beacon, 1976.

TERMAN, L. M., and TYLER, L. E. "Psychological Sex Differences." In L. Carmichael (ed.), *Manual of Child Psychology.* 2d ed. New York: Wiley, 1954.

THEODORE, A. *The Professional Woman.* Cambridge: Schenkman, 1971.

THORNE, B., and HENLEY, N. *Language and Sex: Difference and Dominance.* Rowley: Newbury House, 1975.

THORNTON, A., and FRIEDMAN, D. "Changes in the Sex Role Attitudes of Women, 1962–1977." *ISR Newsletter 12*, 1 (1979):3–4. Ann Arbor: Center for Continuing Education of Women, University of Michigan.

TIDBALL, M. E. "Perspectives on Academic Women and Affirmative Action." *Educational Record 54*, 2 (1973):130, 135.

TILLY, L. A., and SCOTT, J. W. *Women, Work, and Family.* New York: Holt, Rinehart & Winston, 1978.

TOBIAS, S. "Educating Women for Leadership: A Program for the Future." In D. G. McGuigan (ed.), *A Sampler of Women's Studies.* Ann Arbor: Center for Continuing Education of Women, University of Michigan, 1973.

TOLMAN, E. C. *Purposive Behavior in Animals and Men.* New York: Appleton-Century, 1932.

TOUHEY, J. C. "Effects of Additional Men on Prestige and Desirability of Occupations Typically Performed by Women." *Journal of Applied Social Psychology 4*, 4 (1974a):330–335.

_____"Effects of Additional Women Professionals on Ratings of Occupational Prestige and Desirability." *Journal of Personality and Social Psychology 29*, 1 (1974b):86–89.

TRAGER, N. (ed.) *No Longer Young: the Older Woman in America*, Proceedings of the 26th Annual Conference on Aging. Institute of Gerontology, University of Michigan and Wayne State University, 1975.

TREIMAN, J., and TERRELL, K. "Sex and the Process of Status Attainment: A Comparison of Working Women and Men." *American Sociological Review 40*, 2 (1975):174-200.

TRESEMER, D. W. "Assumptions Made about Gender Roles." In M. Millman and R. Kanter (eds.), *Another Voice*. New York: Doubleday Anchor, 1975.

_____"The Cumulative Record of Research on Fear of Success." *Sex Roles 2*, 3 (1976):217-236.

_____*Fear of Success*. New York: Plenum, 1977.

TROLL, L. *Early and Middle Adulthood*. Monterey: Brooks/Cole, 1975.

_____"Poor, Dumb, and Ugly." In L. Troll and J. Israel (eds.), *Looking Ahead: A Woman's Guide to the Problems and Joys of Growing Older*. Englewood Cliffs: Prentice-Hall, 1977.

TYREE, A., and TREAS, J. "The Occupational and Marital Mobility of Women." *American Sociological Review 39*, 3 (1974):293-302.

TURNER, J. "Entrepreneurial Environment and the Emergence of Achievement Motivation in Adolescent Males." *Sociometry 33*, 6 (1970):147-165.

TYLER, F. B., RAFFERTY, J., and TYLER, B. "Relationships among Motivations of Parents and Their Children." *Journal of Genetic Psychology 101*, 1 (1962):69-81.

TYLER, L. E. *The Psychology of Human Differences*. New York: Appleton-Century, 1965.

UNGER, R. K., and DENMARK, F. L. *Woman: Dependent or Independent Variable?* New York: Psychological Dimensions, 1975.

U.S. COMMISSION ON CIVIL RIGHTS. *Social Indicators of Equality for Minorities and Women*. Clearinghouse Publications. Washington, D.C.: Government Printing Office, 1978.

_____*Women Still in Poverty*. Clearinghouse Publications, no. 50. Washington, D.C.: Government Printing Office, 1979.

U.S. COMMISSION ON CIVIL SERVICE, OFFICE OF FEDERAL EQUAL EMPLOYMENT OPPORTUNITY. *Special Emphasis Program Developments*. Bulletin no. 713-749. Washington D.C.: Government Printing Office, 1968.

U.S. COMMISSION ON CIVIL SERVICE, OFFICE OF FEDERAL EQUAL EMPLOYMENT OPPORTUNITY. *Upward Mobility*. Bulletin no. 713-727. Washington, D.C.: Government Printing Office, 1974.

U.S. CONGRESS, HOUSE COMMITTEE ON EDUCATION AND LABOR, SUBCOMMITTEE ON SELECT EDUCATION. *Hearings on the Age Discrimination Act of 1975 and Extension of the Older Americans Act of 1965*. Ninety-fifth Congress, first session. Washington, D.C.: Government Printing Office, 1978.

U.S. CONGRESS, JOINT ECONOMIC COMMITTEE. *Compendium on American Women Workers in a Full Employment Economy*. Report to the Ninety-fifth Congress, first session. Washington, D.C.: Government Printing Office, September 15, 1977.

U.S. CONGRESS, SENATE COMMITTEE ON LABOR AND HUMAN RESOURCES, *Hearings on the Coming Decade: American Women and Human Resources Policies and Programs*.

Ninety-sixth Congress, first session. Washington, D.C.: Government Printing Office, 1979.

U.S. DEPARTMENT OF COMMERCE, BUREAU OF THE CENSUS. Marital Status and Living Arrangements, March 1976. *Current Population Reports*, series P-20, no. 306. Washington, D.C.: Government Printing Office, 1977.

U.S. DEPARTMENT OF LABOR, EMPLOYMENT STANDARDS ADMINISTRATION, WOMEN'S BUREAU. *National Educational Association Report on Annual Salaries of Faculty in Colleges and Universities by Sex 1973-1974*. Bulletin no. 297. Washington, D.C.: Government Printing Office, 1975a.

_____*Handbook of Women Workers*. Bulletin no. 297. Washington, D.C.: Government Printing Office, 1975b.

_____*Mature Women Workers: A Profile*. Washington, D.C.: Government Printing Office, 1976.

_____*Occupations Outlook Handbook 1976-1977*. Washington, D.C.: Government Printing Office, 1977a.

_____*Women and Work*. Manpower Research Monograph, no. 46. Washington, D.C.: Government Printing Office, 1977b.

_____*Employment and Earnings 1970-1977*. Bulletin no. 25. Washington, D.C.: Government Printing Office, January 1978.

U.S. DEPARTMENT OF LABOR AND U.S. DEPARTMENT OF HEALTH EDUCATION AND WELFARE. *The Work Incentive Program (WIN) 1968-1978: A Report of Ten Years*. Ninth Annual Report to the Ninety-sixth Congress, second session. Washington, D.C.: Government Printing Office, June 1979.

U.S. NATIONAL COMMISSION ON THE OBSERVANCE OF INTERNATIONAL WOMEN'S YEAR. *To Form a More Perfect Union*. Report to the President. Washington, D.C.: Government Printing Office, June 1976.

U.S. NATIONAL COMMISSION FOR MANPOWER POLICY. *Target Groups in Manpower Policy: CETA Issues*. Report no. 23. Washington, D.C.: Government Printing Office, 1978.

_____*The First Five Years: 1974-1979*. Report to the Ninety-sixth Congress, second session, no. 36. Washington, D.C.: U.S. Government Printing Office, September 1979.

VAUGHTER, R., GUBERNICK, D., MATASSIN, J., and HASLETT, B. "Sex Differences in Academic Expectations and Achievement." Paper presented to the Eighty-second meeting of the American Psychological Association. New Orleans: September 1974.

VEROFF, J. "Scoring Manual for the Power Motive." In J. W. Atkinson (ed.), *Motives in Fantasy, Action, and Society*, Princeton: Van Nostrand, 1958.

_____"Social Comparison and the Development of Achievement Motivation." In C. Smith (ed.), *Achievement Related Motives in Children*. New York: Russell Sage, 1969.

VEROFF, J., ATKINSON, J. W., FELD, S. C. and GURIN, G. "The Use of Thematic Apperception to Assess Motivation in a Nationwide Study." *Psychological Monographs 74*, 12, whole no. 499, 1960.

VEROFF, J., and FELD, S. C. *Marriage and Work in America*. New York: Van Nostrand Reinhold, 1970.

VEROFF, J., McCLELLAND, L., and RUHLAND, D. "Varieties of Achievement Motivation." In M. Mednick, S. Tangri and L. Hoffman (eds.), *Women and Achievement*. New York: Wiley & Sons, 1975.

VEROFF, J., and VEROFF, J. B. "Theoretical Notes on Power Motivation." *Merrill Palmer Quarterly 17*, 1 (1971):59–69.

VEROFF, J., WILCOX, S., & ATKINSON, J. W. "The Achievement Motive in High School and College Age Women." *Journal of Abnormal and Social Psychology 48*, 1 (1953):108–119.

WALKER, K., GAUGER, W. "Time and its Dollar Value in Household Work." *Family Economics Review, 62*, 5 (1973):8–13.

WALSH, A. Media Images of Female Achievement in Historical Perspective. Manuscript. Binghamton, N. Y., 1977.

WALUM, L. *The Dynamics of Sex & Gender: A Sociological Perspective*. Chicago: Rand McNally, 1977.

WEINER, B. *Theories of Motivation: From Mechanism to Cognition*. Chicago: Markham, 1972.

_____"Achievement Motivation as Conceptualized By an Attribution Theorist." In B. Weiner (ed.), *Achievement Motivation and Attribution Theory*. Morristown, N.J.: General Learning Press, 1974.

WEINER, B., FRIEZE, I., KUKLA, A., REED, L., REST, S., and ROSENBAUM, R. *Perceiving the Causes of Success and Failure*. Morristown, N.J.: General Learning Press, 1971.

WEINER, B. and KUKLA, A. "An Attributional Analysis of Achievement Motivation." *Journal of Personality and Social Psychology, 15*, 1 (1970): 1–20.

WEINSTEIN, E.A. The Development of Interpersonal Competence. In Goslin, D. A. (ed.), *Handbook of Socialization Theory and Research*. Chicago: Rand McNally, 1971.

WEISSMAN, M. "The Educated Housewife: Mild Depression and the Search for Work." *American Journal of Orthopsychiatry. 43*, (1973):565–573.

WEISSMAN, M., PAYKEL, E. *The Depressed Woman: A Study of Social Relationships*. Chicago: University of Chicago Press, 1974.

WELTER, B. "The Cult of True Womanhood 1820–1860." *American Quarterly 18*, 2 (1966):151–157.

WERTHEIMER, B.M. *We Were There: The Story of Working Women in America*. New York: Pantheon, 1977.

WHITE, M. "Psychological and Social Barriers to Women in Science." *Science 170* (October 1970):413–416.

WHITE, R. "Motivation Reconsidered: The Concept of Competence." *Psychological Review 66*, 5 (1959):297–333.

WHITING, J. "Resource Mediation and Learning by Identification." In I. Iscoe and H.W. Stevenson (eds.), *Personality Development in Children*. Austin: University of Texas Press, 1960.

WHYTE, W. *The Organization Man*. New York: Doubleday, 1956.

WILDER, D. "Issues in Education and Training for Working Women." Worker

Education and Training Policies Project, National Commission on Working Women. Washington, D.C.: 1980.

WILLIAMS, J. *Psychology of Women: Behavior in a Biosocial Context.* New York: Norton, 1977.

WILSON, C. "The IUE's Approach to Comparable Worth." In J. Grune (ed.), *Manual on Pay Equity: Raising Wages for Women's Work.* Washington, D.C.: Conference on Alternative State and Local Policies, Committee on Pay Equity, 1980.

WINTER, D. *The Power Motive.* New York: Free Press, 1973.

WINTERBOTTOM, M. R. "The Relation of Need for Achievement to Learning Experiences in Independence and Mastery." In J.W. Atkinson (ed.), *Motives in Fantasy, Action, and Society.* Princeton: Van Nostrand, 1958.

WOLF, W. C., and ROSENFELD, R. "Sex Structure of Occupations and Job Mobility." *Social Forces 56,* 3 (1978):823–844.

WOODRUFF, D. S., and BIRREN, J. E. (eds.). *Aging and Social Issues.* New York: Van Nostrand Reinhold, 1975.

WRIGHT, M. "Self-concept and the Coping Process of Black Undergraduate Women at a Predominantly White University." Ph.D. dissertation, University of Michigan, 1975.

WRONG, D. H. "The Oversocialized Conception of Man in Modern Sociology." *American Sociological Review 26,* 2 (1961):183–193.

YANKELOVICH, D. *The New Morality: A Profile of American Youth in the 70's.* New York: McGraw-Hill, 1974.

YARROW, M., SCOTT, P., DeLEEUW, L., and HEINIG, C. "Childrearing in Families of Working and Non-Working Mothers." *Sociometry 25,* 6 (1962):122–140.

YINGER, J. M. *Toward a Field Theory of Behavior.* New York: McGraw-Hill, 1965.

YOUNG, M., and WILLMOTT, P. *The Symmetrical Family.* New York: Pantheon, 1973.

ZARETSKY, E. "Capitalism, the Family, and Personal Life." *Socialist Revolution 3,* 13, 14, 15, (1973):69–125.

ZELDITCH, M. "Role Differentiation in the Nuclear Family: A Comparative Study." In T. Parsons, R. Bales (ed.), *Family, Socialization and Interaction Process,* New York: Free Press, 1955.

ZELLMAN, G. L., and CONNOR, C. "Increasing the Credibility of Women." Paper presented to the Eighty-first Meeting of the Western Psychological Association. Los Angeles: May 1973.

Index

Ability, 51
Academic performance, 7,10
Academic women, 101–103
Achievement motivation, 1–27, 91
  in adolescence: *see* Adolescence
  arousal cues and, 2–4
  asymmetry tradition, 5–7
  dependence and, 11–12
  gender identity, 3, 6, 14–17
  gender-role theory, 2–3
  independence and working moth-
    ers, 22–27
  intrinsic versus extrinsic, 8–9
  need-achievement theory, chal-
    lenges to, 7–12
  predictive value of need-achieve-
    ment model, 10–11
  socialization and, 12–17, 20–22
Acker, J., 85, 94, 97
Adelson, J., 32, 33, 54

Adolescence, 30–59
  anger, 37
  bargaining and negotiation,
    54–55
  dating relationship in, 34–35, 37
  expectations, 30–31, 48–50
  failure, fear of, 39–42
  internalization, 55–57
  interpersonal orientation, 53–55
  self-esteem, 30, 32, 38–42
  social sensitivity, 32–38
  success, fear of, 39, 40, 43–48, 50
Affiliation needs, 5–7, 141
Aging
  discrimination, 112
  mental health and, 119–21
  theories of, 113–118
Alexander, R. H., 105
Alimony, 126, 127
Allport, G., 8, 137
Almquist, E., 120

Alper, T. G., 45
Alpert, R., 14, 15
Altruistic achiever, 129, 130
American Home Economics Association, 71
American Telegraph & Telephone Company, 133
Anastasi, A., 10
Anderson, B.E., 132
Anger, 37
Angrist, S., 120
Anxiety, 12, 40–41
Appeasement, 36
Aries, P., 116–117
Aristophanes, 35
Arousal cues, 2–4
Ascription, 17
Aspiration, 90–93
Astin, H., 49
Asymmetry tradition, 5–7
Atkinson, J. W., xi, 1, 2, 4, 5, 9, 20, 31, 39–40, 47, 60
Attribution theory, 51–53
Autonomy, 20, 21
Axelrod, S., 48

Bachman, J., 62, 96
Bailey, M., 5–6, 10, 13, 39, 41, 42
Baird, 49
Baldwin, A. L., xi
Bales, R., 3
Baltes, P. B., 112, 113, 118
Banducci, R., 25
Bandura, A., 15, 22, 32
Banks, J., 38
Banner, L., xi
Bardwick, J., x, 5, 13, 24, 30–34, 37, 43, 44, 141
Bargaining, 20, 37, 54–55, 141
Barnes, 132
Barnes, R., 13
Barnett, N. S., 127, 130, 131, 132, 133
Barry, Leonara, 75

Bart, P., 73, 119, 116
Bar-Tal, D., 13, 51
Baruch, G. K., 13, 24, 26, 34
Bass, B. M., 105
Baxandall, R., 94
Bean, J., xi
Beard, M., 115
Beauty, 35
Becker, G. S., 128
Beecher, Catherine, xi, 72
Bell, M., 65–66
Belle, D., 120–121, 124
Bem, D. J., 39, 41–42
Bem, S. L., 39, 41–42
Berardo, F. M., 126, 127
Bernard, Jessie, 73, 87, 121, 139
Bevier, I., 71
Bibb, R., 98
Biological differentiation, 15
Birnbaum, J. A., 91
Birren, J. E., 116
Birth control, 70
Birth rate data, 62–63
Bischof, L., 113, 116
Blacks, 38–39, 56–57
Blau, F. D., 66, 86
Boocock, S. S., 117
Boring, 137
Boulding, K. E., 128, 129
Bowerman, C., 14
Bowman, G., 105
Branca, P., 94
Brecht, Bertolt, 140
Brim, O., 14, 114
Bronfenbrenner, U., xi, 21, 22
Brookover, W. B., 38
Broverman, D. M., 32, 38
Broverman, I. K., 32
Brown, D. G., 14, 54, 55
Brownlee, M., 66, 75, 78
Brownlee, W. E., 66, 75, 78
Bugental, D., 36
Buhle, M., 67, 73–74
Bühler, C., 116

Butler, R., 112

Cahn, A., 97
California Displaced Homemakers
    Act, 128
Campbell, P., 13
Caplow, T., 14, 102
Carden, M. L., 68
Chesler, P., 84, 126
Child support, 126
Childbearing, 62–63
Childhood developmental patterns,
    5–7, 12–27
Childlessness, 62
Chiriboga, D., 113, 121
Clark, R. A., xi, 1, 2, 7
Clarke, A. D. B., 112, 118
Clarke, A. M., 112, 118
Clarkson, F. E., 32, 38
Clausen, J. A., 22
Clerical work, 79
Cobbs, P. M., 56
Cole, J. R., 97, 100
Coleman, J., 7, 63
College aspirations, 25
Collins, R., 88
Competence, 31
Competitiveness, 12
Comprehensive Employment and
    Training Acts of 1973 (CETA),
    132, 134
Condry, J., 50, 73
Conformity, 18–19, 142
Conger, J. J., 116, 120
Connor, C., 35
Conscience, 137
Constantinople, A., 4, 39
Contraception, 70
Contributing vicarious achiever,
    129–130
Control of outcome, 51
Cooley, C., 27
Corcoran, M., 126
Cosby, A., 86, 87, 89, 92

Coser, R., 64
Crandall, V. C., 41, 53
Crandall, V. J., 5–6, 10, 41, 54
Cues, arousal, 2–4
Cultural ideals, 73–76
Cumming, E., 114

Dahlstrom, W. G., 56
Daniels, A., 103
Dating relationship, 34–35, 37, 54,
    141
Davis, Paulina Wright, 69–70, 80
De Beauvoir, S., 119
De Leeuw, L., 23, 24
Deaux, K., 13, 41, 51, 52, 55
deCharms, R., xi
Deckard, B., 68
Deitch, C., 97–99, 133
Delayed marriage, 62
Denmark, F., xi, 3, 55
Dependence, 11–12, 34–35, 72–73,
    119, 120
Depner, C., 47
Dewey, John, 114–115
Discouraged workers, 130–131
Discrimination, 100–106, 112,
    131–133
Disengagement, theory of, 114, 116
Displaced homemakers, current de-
    bate on, 125–129
Dispositional expectancy, 53–54
Divorce, 61, 62, 122, 126, 127
"Doctor-nurse game," 36
Dohrenwend, B. P., 114, 121
Dohrenwend, B. S., 114, 121
Dollard, J., 17
Domestic reform, strategies of,
    68–73
Domestic script, 61–63
    emergence of, 66–68
Donley, P., 73
Douvan, E., 24, 30–35, 37, 54,
    121–122, 141
Dual labor market model, 96–97

Duberman, L., xi, 19
DuBois, E., x, 67–71, 74
Duncan, B., 86, 89
Duncan, O. D., 86, 89
Dunkle, M., 133
Durant, Henry Fowle, 81
Dyer, S., 50

Economic life, 66–68
Education, 76, 80–81, 131
Effort, 51
Ehrenreich, B., 79
Elder, G. H., Jr., 14, 34, 116, 119
Eliason, C., 129, 130
Ellis, E., 87
Elshtain, J. B., 68–69, 115
Employed mothers, 22–27, 63, 123
Employment
   CETA, 132, 134
   discrimination, 100–106, 131–133
   factory labor, 74–77, 94
   household labor, 64–66, 72–73,
      84–85, 88, 123–124
   increased labor force participa-
      tion, 94–95
   occupational structure, 96–97,
      130, 133–134
   professions, barriers to entry in,
      100–106
   status attainment theory, 86–93
   tokenism, 101, 104
   wage inequities, 77–79, 97–100,
      130, 131, 133, 134
   Work Incentive Program,
      132–133
Emswiller, T., 13, 41, 51
Enarson, E., 19
English, D., 79
Entwisle, D. R., 10
Epstein, C., 87, 88, 100, 102, 103
Equal Pay Act, 133
Erikson, E. H., 30, 32, 35, 38, 116
Etzioni, A., 87

Evaluation, 14
   bias in, 51–52
Expectancy–value tradition, 9, 10,
   12, 20, 40, 42, 43, 76, 91
Expectations, 30–31, 48–50, 96
Extramarital sexuality, 70
Extrinsic motivation, 8–9
Extrinsic rewards, 6

Factory workers, 74–77, 94
Faculty, female, 101–103
Failure, fear of, 39–42
Falk, W., 86, 87, 89, 92
Falk-Dickler, F., 133
Farris, E., 13
Father's role, 14–17, 21–22
Fear, 12
   of failure, 39–42
   of success, 39, 43–48, 141
Feather, N. T., 9, 39
Featherman, D. L., 20, 86, 89, 93,
   138
Fee, T., 85
Feld, S. C., 6
Feldman-Summers, S., 51
Fels-Research Institute, 23
Female unemployment rate,
   130–131
Femininity, 3, 4, 38, 39
Fetters, M. J., 106
Field, W. F., 1, 2
Foner, A., 116, 119
Foner, P. S., 75, 77, 78, 79
Form, W., 98
Frankel, E., 25–26
Freud, S., 4, 14
Friedan, Betty, 72
Friedman, J., xi, 116
Frieze, I. H., 3, 13, 35, 36, 38, 39,
   41, 51, 52, 105

Gates, M., 101
Gaughman, E. E., 56
Gaylin, J., 35

Gender identity, 3, 5, 6, 14–17
  in adolescence: *see* Adolescence
Gender-role theory, 2–3
Gewirtz, J. L., 112
Gianetto, R., 36
Gillespie, D., 138
Gilligan, C., 114–115
Gilman, Charlotte Perkins, xi, 65, 71
Gilmer, B., 105
Ginsburg, E., 48
Ginsburg, S., 48
Glick, P. C., 62
Goffman, E., 36, 88
Goldberg, P., 51–52, 53
Goodman, E., 134
Gordon, A. D., 67, 73–74
Gordon, L., 67, 68, 69, 94
Gordon, M., 120
Goslin, D. A., 3, 14, 37, 54, 112
Gould, C. C., 68, 114, 115
Goulet, L. R., 112, 113, 118
Gove, W. R., 73
Grambs, J., 38
Gratification, delay of, 60
Greenberger, E., 96
Greyser, S. H., 105
Grier, W. H., 56
Gross, E., 87
Gross national product, 64
Groszko, M., 46
Gubernick, D., 52
Gusfield, J. P., 71
Gutman, D., 30
Guttentag, M., 120

Haas, M., 23, 24
Hacker, A., 95, 138, 139–140
Hacker, H., 87
Hagglund, G., 133–134
Haller, A. O., 89
Halpern, S., 117
Hardesty, F., 14
Hareven, T. K., 114, 116, 117

Hargens, L., 99–100
Harlan, S. L., 132, 133
Harmon, L., 91
Harris, D., 112
Hartley, R., 14, 24
Hartley, S., 95
Hartman, M., xi
Hartup, W. W., 3, 14
Haslett, B., 52
Hauser, R. M., 89, 93
Heckhausen, H., 12
Heinig, C., 23, 24
Henderson, L. F., 105
Henley, N. M., 105
Henry, W. E., 114
Herman, J., 48, 132
Herzog, R., 62, 96
Hess, B., 113
Hess, R. D., 14, 15
Hetherington, M., 14
Heyns, R. W., 5
Hill, U., 65
Hochschild, A., xi, 13, 18, 20, 35, 36, 37, 95, 114, 116
Hodges, K., 52
Hoffman, L. W., xi, 3, 4, 5, 11, 13, 14, 24–26, 44, 112, 141
Hoffman, M. L., 4, 14
Hogeland, R. W., 81
Homans, G., 22
Home economics movement, 71–73
  new, 128–129
Home study courses, 72
Horner, M., 1, 2, 30, 50, 141
Horney, K., 32
Housewifery, 64–66, 72–73, 84–85
  changing attitudes towards, 123–124
Howe, F., 80
Howe, L. K., 97
Huber, J., 88
Hughes, E., 87, 102, 103
Hulicka, I., 118
Human capital model, 98–99

Hunt, C., 71, 72
Huston, A., 15, 22

Identification: *see* Gender identity
Iglehart, A., 121, 123–124
Impulsiveness, 11
Independence, 13, 20, 21, 38–39
Independence training, 22–27
Individualism, x
Industrialization, 67
Institute of Life Insurance, 62
Institutional motherhood, 65
Instrumental vicarious achiever, 130
Intellectual performance, 7, 10
Internal Revenue Service, 129
Internalization, 6, 8, 18–20, 55–57
Interpersonal orientation in adoles-
    cence, 53–55
Intrinsic motivation, 8–9
Intrinsic rewards, 6
Ireson, C., 48–49

Jacklin, C., 2–4, 7, 12, 38, 41
Jackson, J. J., 116
Jacques, E., 114
Janeway, E., 116, 117
Jaquette, J., 68, 115
Jerdee, T. H., 105
Johnson, M., 17
Johnson, P., 35
Johnson, P. B., 3, 35, 38, 52
Johnston, L., 62, 96
Jones, J. B., 26, 75
Jones, Marry Harris, 75
Jung, C. G., 4, 113, 116

Kagan, J., 3, 17, 19, 112
Kanter, R., 100–101, 104, 116
Kaplan, A., xi
Katovsky, W., 5, 10, 41, 53
Kaufman, D., 101, 102, 103, 106
Kaufman, M., 140
Kaye, C., 32
Keller, S., 48, 90–91, 103

Kessler-Harris, A., 77, 78
Kiesler, S. B., 51–52
Kohlberg, L., 3, 14–17, 20, 115
Komarovsky, M., 138–139
Korman, A. K., 10, 40
Kraditor, A. S., 69
Kravitz, R. N., 4
Krussel, J., 105
Kuhlen, R., 113
Kuhn, D., 46, 50

Labor, Department of, 94, 111, 131,
    132
Labor, division of, 78–80
Labor movement, 75, 77–78
Labor Statistics, Bureau of, 94
Ladner, J. A., 38, 56–57
Lady, cult of the, 73–76
Laws, J. L., 48, 91, 101, 104
Learning theory, 14
Leavitt, H. J., 129–130
Legal profession, 101
Lemkin, J., 17
Lenhoff, D., 134
Lerner, G., 74, 75, 76, 80
Lerner, R., 76
Lesser, G. S., 4, 34, 86
Levinson, D. J., 114, 115
Liebert, R., 15
Life course, 118–125
Life expectancy, 120
Lipman-Blumen, J., 101–102,
    129–130
Lockheed, M., 45, 50
Loneliness, 64
Longevity, 62
"Looking-glass self," 27
Lopata, H., 95, 134
Lorber, J., 101
Love, L., 36
Lowell, E. I., xi, 1, 2
Lowell, Francis Cabot, 77
Lowenthal, M., 113, 116, 121
Luck, 51

Lundsteen, S. A., 26
Lyons, D. J., 105
Lysistrata (Aristophanes), 35

Maccoby, E., 2-4, 7, 10, 11-12, 38, 41
Maddi, S. R., 40-41
Makosky, V., 46
Mandler, G., 40
Mandler-Sarason Test Anxiety Questionnaire, 40
Manis, J., 122-123
Marini, M., 96
Markus, H., 122-123
Marriage, 49-50, 141-142
  changing attitudes towards, 121-122
  legal rights within, 69-70
  sociopolitical context of, 137-141
Masculinity, 3, 4, 38, 39
Mason, K. O., 100
Mastery training, 21
Matassin, J., 52
Maternal role loss, 119, 120
Mature women, 111-135
McAdoo, H., 38
McCandless, S., 55
McClelland, D. C., xi-xii, 1, 2, 6, 9, 20, 26, 40, 47, 86
McClendon, M. J., 93, 97
McCord, J., 14, 23
McCord, W., 14, 23
Mead, M., 42
Medical profession, 101
Mednick, M., xi, 3
Meixel, C., 90
Melville, K., 62
Menopausal women, 73, 114, 120
Mental health, 72-73, 119-121
Michael, W. B., 26
Middle-class role patterns, 13
Midlife crisis, 111, 114
Miller, 97
Miller, A. L., 49

Miller, J. B., 55
Miller, N., 17
Mincer, J., 131
Mischel, W. H., 3, 14, 15, 30
Monahan, L., 46, 50
Moore, W., 95
Moos, R., 112
Moral commitment, 136-138
Morgenstern, R., 46
Moss, H. A., 23
Mothers, as socializing agents, 21-22
Motivation, xi, 8-9, 90-93
Murstein, B. I., 10
Myers, L., 39
Myrdal, A., 87

National Advisory Council on Women, 125, 129, 130
National Conference of Commissioners on Uniform State Laws, 127
National Education Association, 101
National Longitudinal Surveys of Labor Force Participation (NLS), 119
National Trades' Union Committee on Female Labor, 78
Need-achievement theory, challenges to, 7-12
Need affiliation, 5-7
Neglected women, current debate on, 125-128
Negotiation, 14, 20, 37, 54-55, 141
Neugarten, B., 114, 116, 117
New home economics, 128-129
No-fault divorce, 127
Nonmarried older women, current debate on, 125-128
Northby, A., 7
Northrup, H. R., 132
Nowlis, V., 15, 17
Nuclear family, 15-16, 19, 65

Nursing, 79, 97
Nye, I., 24–26, 126, 127

Oakley, A., 64, 67
Occupational choice, 48–49
Occupational structure, female,
    96–97, 130, 133–134
O'Donnell, Edward, 78
Ohlendorf, G. W., 89
Old boy networks, 104
O'Leary, V., 38, 41, 42, 47, 51
Oppenheimer, V. K., 87, 95, 96
Orzack, L., 87
Osipow, S., 120, 123

Packard, R., 4
Papachristou, J., x
Papanek, H., 95
Parental independence training,
    22–27
Parlee, M. B., xi
Parsons, J. E., 3, 35, 38, 52
Parsons, T., 3, 15–17, 20, 32, 137
Passivity, 11–12
Patriarchy, 84
Pay: see Wage inequities
Peplau, L. A., 47
Perry, C., 132
Personality, 35
Peterson, J. L., 119
Peterson, L., 19
Pettigrew, T., 56
Pheterson, G. I., 51–52
Physical space, 105
Pietropinto, 138
Polacheck, S., 131
Portes, A., 89
Potential, loss of, 118
Power, 35–36, 87, 88
Pre-oedipal period, 15
Preston, A., 5
Preston, C. E., 119
Pride in accomplishments, 41–42

Professions, barriers to employment
    of women in, 100–106
Program for Better Jobs and In-
    come (PBJI), 132–133
Protégé system, 103
Putnam, E., 55

Rabban, M., 3, 14
Rabson, A., 5
Rafferty, J., 5, 13
Ramsey, S. J., 105
Rand, L. M., 49
Rape, 70
Rau, L., 14, 15
Raynor, J. O., 9, 31, 47, 60
Rebelsky, F., 113
Reformers, xi
Rejection, 21
Remarriage, 62, 139–140
Reskin, B., 99–100
Retirement plan, 127
Reverby, S., 94
Rich, A., 64, 65, 66, 120
Richards, E. H., 71
Richards, Ellen Swallow, 71–72
Rindlisbacher, A., xi
Risk-taking, 60
Roby, P., 80, 81
Rokoff, G., 64
Role theory, 14
Rosen, B., 105
Rosen, B. C., 20, 21, 88–89
Rosenfeld, R., 97
Rosenkrantz, P. S., 32, 38
Ross, D., 15
Ross, S., 15
Rossi, A. S., 64, 87, 116
Rowan, R. L., 132
Rubin, J. Z., 54, 55
Rubin, L. B., 49–50
Ruble, D. N., 3, 35, 38, 52
Ruhland, D., 6
Ryan, M., 79

Safilios-Rothschild, C., 38, 44
Salasin, S., 120
Sarason, S. B., 40
Sawhill, I., 117, 128, 129
Scanzoni, J., 62
Scanzoni, L., 62
Scharf, P., 115
Schonler, William, 75
Schneider, L., ix
Schultz, T. W., 128
Schwenn, 49
Scott, P., 23, 24, 137
Sears, P., 15, 17
Sears, P. S., 5
Sears, R. R., 14, 15, 17
Seidenberg, R., 95
Self, preoccupation with, 4
Self-concept and self-esteem, 30, 32, 38-42, 51, 56
Sewell, W. H., 89
Sex-linked personality traits, 12
Sex-typing of jobs, 13, 78-80, 132-134
Shade, W., 116
Shaver, Z., 46, 50
Sheehy, G., 114
Shields, L., 127
Shipley, T. E., 5, 11
Siegel, A., 23, 24
Simenauer, 138
Single mothers, current debate on, 125-129
Singleness, 62
Skolnick, A., 20, 112
Small, A., 52
Smelser, N., 117
Smith, R. E., 8-9, 76, 125
Smuts, R. W., 94
Social psychology, 47
Social Science Research Council, 119
Social security, 127
Social sensitivity, 32-38

Socialization, xi-xii, 3, 12-17, 20-22, 31, 52, 92, 117
Socioeconomic status, 20, 24-26, 49
Sommers, T., 127
Sommer, R., 105
Sontag, S., 119
Spacks, P. M., 137-138
Stanton, Elizabeth Cady, x, 68, 70
Status attainment theory, 86-93, 99
Status envy theory, 14
Stein, A., 5-6, 10, 13, 39, 41, 42
Stein, Gertrude, ix
Stein, L. I., 36
Steinhart, F., 134
Stellman, J. M., 63
Stereotypes, 3, 38, 52, 104
Stewart, J., 86
Stolz, L. M., 23
Straus, M., 14, 21
Stress, 120, 122, 124
Stress and Families project, 124
Strodtbeck, F. L., xi, 21
Strong Vocational Interest Blank, 91
Subordinate/superordinate relationships, 105-106
Suburban women, 64
Success, fear of, 5, 39, 40, 43-48, 50
Suffrage, 68-70, 74
Superiority-inferiority relationships, 15-17
Suter, L. E., 97

Tangri, S., xi, 3, 48, 55, 141-142
Task difficulty, 51
Tax, 129
Taylor, M., 95
Taynor, J., 52
Teaching, 79, 97
Temperance, 70-71
Terman, L. M., 7, 10
Terrell, K., 93, 97
Textile mills, 76-77

Thomas, M. Carey, ix
Thurber, E., 14
Thurnher, M., 113, 121
Timidity, 12
Tokenism, 101, 104
Torney, W. V., 14, 15
Touching, 105
Touhey, J. C., 51
Treiman, J., 93, 96
Tresemer, D. W., 3, 43, 45
Troll, L., 113, 117
Tudor, J. F., 73
Tyler, B., 5, 13
Tyler, F. B., 5, 13
Tyler, L. E., 7, 10

Unemployment, 130–131
Unger, R. K., xi, 3
Union of Electrical Workers, 133
U.S. Commission on Civil Rights, 131

Values, 91
Vaughter, R., 52
Verbal space, 105
Veroff, J., 1, 2, 4, 5, 6, 10
Veroff, J. A., 11
Veroff, J. B., 6
Vicarious achievement, 137–143
  costs of, 125–128
  retraining and, 129–134
Vogel, S. R., 32, 38

Wage inequities, 77–79, 97–100, 130, 131, 133, 134
Walters, R., 15, 32
Wartofsky, M. W., 68, 115
Weiner, B., 40, 51
Weinstein, E. A., 10, 54
Weissman, M., 73
Welfare, 126, 127

Welter, B., 74
Wertheimer, B. M., 74, 77
Wheeler, 50
White, M., 87, 102–103, 104
White, R., 20
Whiting, J., 14, 15, 17
Whyte, W., 95
Wilcox, S., 2, 4
Wilder, D., 133
Willard, Emma, 72
Williams, J., 42
Willmott, P., 95
Winter, D., xi
Wisconsin model, 88–93
Wolf, W. C., 97
Wollstonecraft, Mary, x
Women's Christian Temperance Union, 71
Women's Rights Convention, Seneca Falls, (1848), 74
Woodruff, D. S., 116
Work ethic, 89
Work Incentive Program (WIN), 132–133
Working mothers, 22–27, 63, 123
Wortney, B. N., 105
Wright, Larenia, 77
Wright, M., 39
Wrong, D. H., 22

Yankelovich, D., 72, 89
Yarrow, M., 23, 24
Yinger, J. M., 118
Young, M., 95

Zaretsky, E., x, xiii
Zavarolli, M., 48, 90–91
Zelditch, M., 15
Zellman, G. L., 3, 35, 36, 38, 52
Zigler, E., 3
Zook, E. A., 3, 14
Zuckerman, 50